C000183861

Carmyllie Its Land and F

1840 – 1975

Life in Carmyllie Parish through stories and pictures, 1840-1975

Carmyllie Heritage Society

Produced by the Carmyllie community
Editor: Anne Law
Graphic Designer: James Lindsay

Published by Carmyllie Heritage Society 2013

With a contribution from Angus Council

ISBN   978-0-9927128-0-8

Front cover image: *Bringing in the hay, Forehills, Carmyllie, 1920s (Gibb family)*

Back cover image: *Children at Slade quarries,Carmyllie, 1940s (Geddes family)*

Printed by Robertson Printers
7-9 Queen Street, Forfar, Angus, DD8 3AJ.
Tel: 01307 464078
Email: neil-robertson@btconnect.com

This book was published by Carmyllie Heritage Society in 2013.

For further information or to obtain copies, visit   **www.carmyllieheritage.co.uk**

Foreword

The Rt. Hon Lord Fraser of Carmyllie QC

When Peter became the MP for South Angus in 1979 and we moved to Carmyllie, we were not fully aware of the history of the parish and the community. Our three children attended Carmyllie Primary School, we became members of Carmyllie Church and always appreciated the way in which we were welcomed into the community.

In 1989, Prime Minister Margaret Thatcher recommended that Peter, on being appointed Lord Advocate, should become a Life Peer. It was to the local community in Carmyllie that he went to ask 'permission' to take the title of "Lord Fraser of Carmyllie". As he travelled the world as a politician he was very proud of that connection with the part of Angus he had chosen to make his home.

It was through living in the community and, more recently, through Carmyllie Heritage Society that the whole family became aware of the important role that the parish played in shaping history on a local, national and international level.

Lady Fraser

Lord Fraser of Carmyllie

(May 1945 - June 2013)

Preface

Carmyllie Its Land and People

A meeting of people interested in the heritage of Carmyllie was held in Carmyllie Primary School on the 29th of September 2009, and I was honoured to be asked along. Carmyllie Heritage Society was duly formed, and an interim committee appointed from those present.

Since then the society has held numerous meetings and outings, and I have been delighted to contribute on a few occasions. The society has gone from strength to strength, particularly under the leadership of Anne Law.

When I first heard of the plan to produce a history of the parish, I knew that the society would have its work cut out, and that it would involve its members in several years of research and the resultant writing up!

This they have done exceedingly well, however, and what we now have before us is an excellent account of the parish, which will be indispensable to all those who wish to learn of the Carmyllie story.

While the traditional Carmyllie industries of quarrying and farming are well covered, and the landed families of Panmure and the Guynd are dealt with, there is a great deal here about the ordinary folk who lived and worked in the parish and made it what it is today.

The fifteen chapters relate a fascinating story of Carmyllie over the years, interspersed with useful facts and figures, and fully illustrated with photographs and drawings.

I congratulate Carmyllie Heritage Society on the magnificent achievement of this splendid book, which I heartily commend to all who have an interest in Carmyllie.

Norman Atkinson

September 2013

Acknowledgements

Production Committee

Anne Law
Muriel Hume
Douglas Norrie
James Lindsay
Rae Smith

James Clark
Norma McDonald
Bill McDonald
Angela McGechaen

Those Interviewed

Arthur Jarret	Bothy Days	1980s
Rose Goetz	Greystone School/Soup Kitchen	2009
Nancy Whitton	(for Jack) Village Policeman	2009
Edith Garrow	East School/Carmyllie School Teacher	2009
Will & Mary Gardiner	Farmer, Tillyhoit	2009
Cathy Clark	Greystone Post Office/shop	2009
Jim Wallace	Traffic Rescue	2009
Andy Gibb	Farm worker	2010
Jimmy Gordon	Rural Auctioneer	2010
Anna Chalmers	Female farm worker	2010
Doreen Paul (nee Mudie)	Blacksmith's daughter	2010
Nita Smith (nee Gibb)	Farmer's daughter	2011
Minnie Souter (nee Clark)	House/Table Maid Guynd and Land Girl	2011
Dawn Robson (nee Gibb)	Farm Worker's daughter	2011
Jean Stewart (nee Law)	Cook at Guynd Mansion House	2011
Aggie Stott	Farm Worker	2012
David Young	Cononsyth Estate	2012
Muriel Hume	'Town Girl' to Farmer's Wife	2012
Rena Scott	Land Girl	2013
Carnie Fullerton	Combine Harvester	2013
John Kneen	Rural Vet	2013

In addition, our grateful thanks to all community groups who researched their old records to tell us about incidents especially for the 'After Work' chapter. Also Carmyllie Heritage is overwhelmed by the generosity of a large number of local people who have allowed us to copy their treasured photographs relating memories at the same time. It would not have been possible to publish this book without their help.

We are indebted for the professional advice received from Norman Atkinson, Angus Cultural Services, Graham McNicol, local historian, the National Library for Scotland (Maps), National Archives, Angus Libraries and Angus Archives. In addition, Adam McDonald's I.T. expertise was invaluable and Douglas Norrie was most beneficial in relieving the pressure of proof reading and publishing.

Finally, we appreciate the financial help we received from Angus Council Community Grant Scheme and the constant support and advice we received from Neil Paterson, Angus Council Community Learning and Development Service.

Contents

Carmyllie Parish Ordnance Survey, One inch (1:63,360) Sheet 49 (Arbroath) and Sheet 57, seamed, 1857-1863 (NLS, Ref 2622/13)

INTRODUCTION

As the title suggests, this book is about Carmyllie parish and its land which shaped the lives of the people through 120 years from c.1850 to c.1970; from the early reign of Queen Victoria to the early days of our Queen today. It has been necessary however to research into earlier years in order to form the background of the parish and roots. The year around 1975 was chosen as a closing date since parishes as administrative units were abolished, although agricultural parishes remained for the purpose of grant and subsidy payment to farmers.

Life in the parish would be similar to many parishes in Scotland, yet each had variations with for instance, location, land distribution, events and occupations that presented every parish with a separate history. In order to find this, a wide range of sources have been examined from Church, School and Estate records, Census, Agricultural returns, Personal Cash Books, Statistical Accounts and Valuation Rolls together with personal interviews, maps and family photographs.

Location

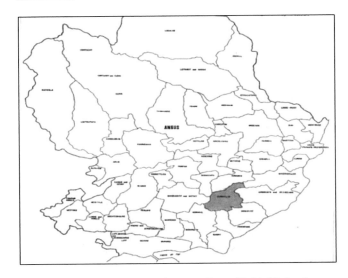

Parishes in the County of Angus, Carmyllie highlighted
(*Third Statistical Account*, (1977)

Carmyllie is one of 62 parishes within the county of Angus that borders the counties of Perthshire to the west, Aberdeenshire to the north and Kincardineshire towards the north-east. The parishes within the glens of north of Angus are larger and less populated, whereas south of the fault line in more fertile areas, the Angus parishes are smaller and more numerous.

The principal ancient burgh towns in Angus are Arbroath and Montrose on the coast and Forfar, Kirriemuir and Brechin inland. The more 'modern' towns of Carnoustie and Monifieth are situated on the River Tay, east of Dundee city.
Carmyllie to Arbroath or Carnoustie is six to eight miles, Forfar eight to eleven, Montrose and Brechin thirteen to sixteen, while Dundee is fifteen to seventeen; in fact, all towns are almost equi-distant to Carmyllie.

Landscape

Carmyllie is landlocked, without urban development and borders eight parishes, St Vigeans, Arbirlot, Panbride, Monikie,' Carbuddo' (Kirkbuddo, a detached part of Guthrie Parish[1]), Dunnichen, Kirkden and Inverkeilor. Carmyllie parish is about 12 square miles, approximately 4 miles in length by 3 miles wide. There is a gradual climb to reach the parish from sea level and starting at 400ft (121.92m) at the Guynd, it rises to 650ft (198.12m) at West Hills. There are no significant hills (although there is an incline in the East and West Hills area) lending itself to panoramic views. Yet generally, Carmyllie's

Part of Carmyllie Parish (Ainslie, 1794)

lands are at a high level resulting in exposure to all wind directions and the parish is often referred to as 'Cauld Carmyllie' which was probably derived from the 'Cauld Stane' (marked on OS maps), a round stone boulder, believed to have remained from the scourge of the Ice Age. The volcano that formed the Sidlaw hills continued its activity from a southeast to a northeast direction towards Redcastle on the coast, passing through Carmyllie and leaving a stratum 1½ miles long and approximately ½ mile in breadth of grey sandstone[2], suitable for pavement and slates for many centuries prior to a quarry industry in the nineteenth century.

There are two main 'burns' or streams in Carmyllie, one is the Elliot, the upper part of which is known locally as the 'Glester,' rising in Dilty Moss and joining another stream arising near Smallburn, running past the Milton which provided a working mill there until the end of nineteenth century. The 'Glester' continues through the Guynd and joins a second 'burn' known as the Black

---

[1] *New Statistical Account, (NSA)*Vol X1, Carmyllie (Wm Blackwood & Son, Edinburgh, 1843) p 351
[2] Ibid

Burn at the Black Den and the water, known as the Elliot Water, proceeds past Arbirlot on to the mouth of the River Tay. The Black Burn, its source being at Burnhead, Redford, passes the Milton of Conon and provided a second corn mill there.

The Parish

Before the parishes were formed, Carmyllie lands, c.1325, had been held by Maule of Panmure and were passed over to the Strachan family, through marriage (see Guynd Estate p.70). Carmyllie lands, however, included only part of the future parish. Other lands such as Conon are mentioned as early as 1180 in the *Aberbrothock Muniments* written by the monks of Arbroath Abbey. Later in 1189, Cononmoorchapel is referred to, but the locality is uncertain. Furthermore places such as Grundaly (maybe the Guynd), Tulloch (Tillyhoit), Cononsyth, Carmyly and Carnegy were mentioned in the *Muniments*, so it could be suggested that Conon proprietors were seeking to mark boundaries to their land at these particular areas[3]. The modern farm names give a clue to the extent of Conon lands; Grange of Conon, Highlands of Conon, Parkconon, West Grange of Conon, Cairnconon, Milton of Conon, Conon and Brae of Conon. It is thought that Cairnconon was central to the surrounding lands as there was a castle or tower house there. These lands were in the possession of Arbroath Abbey, since the *Muniments* state that the monks held a judiciary there where Charters were formed. Cairnconon had continued to be of importance as a Court after the collapse of Arbroath Abbey around 1550. At the beginning of the seventeenth century when the area was divided into parishes, the borders of St Vigeans and Carmyllie parishes cut through the lands of Conon with St Vigeans reaching out to its western extremities to include Cairnconon, Dummiesholes, leaving Cononsyth Estate, Milton of Conon and Conon in Carmyllie. Further studies suggest that Cononsyth Estate itself had no adherence to Arbroath Abbey[4] unlike most of the other landowners in the surrounding area who in time had sold their lands to the Roman Church Order so that their souls would be saved or there was a guaranteed place in heaven. Hence, it may be that as Cononsyth did not pay rent to the monks of Arbroath Abbey, this could be one of the reasons that the estate was not included in the surrounding parishes such as Inverkeilor or St Vigeans.

Tuttiesneuk, background, Greystone Village, 1985

Continuing on the possession of lands prior to the formation of Carmyllie parish, the history of Carnegie dates back to 1358 when John de Balinhard 'parted with the family estate' of Balinhard (Bonhard near Arbroath) to the family of Panmure. He exchanged for the lands and barony of Carnegie that included Carnegie, Dustydrum, Montquhir, Glaister, Mossholes, Drum and Greystone with the adjoining slate quarries, and Balinhard took the name 'Carnegie' when in possession of these lands[5]. After re-purchasing the forfeited estates in 1764, (see 'Panmure Estate' p.54) the lands of Carnegie were included in the Panmure estate in exchange for the lands of Southesk.

There was already a pre-reformation chapel on Strachan's Carmyllie lands when an act of Parliament was passed in 1609 to erect Carmyllie Kirk 'into a parochial charge'[6]; the whole parish was then named Carmyllie. The Guynd Estate, later acquired by the Ouchterlonys c.1615, was brought into the parish. The extremities of the Inverkeilor lands which included Cononsyth Estate and Backboath were brought within the Carmyllie boundaries together with Panbride's outlying lands round the Firth. All in all, the total acreage covering the parish amounted to approximately 6,382 acres (2,582 hectares)[7].

In 1621, Strachan of Carmyllie, thought to have been crippled by debt from the building of Carmyllie Church, saw his lands reverting to Maule of Panmure as feudal superior. Subsequently there were four

[3] Norman Atkinson, Head of Cultural Services, Angus Council, 2012
[4] Taylor, Simon, 'Place Names of Carmyllie', 2013 (unpublished) University of Glasgow
[5] Jervise, Andrew, *Land of the Lindsays* (Edinburgh: Sutherland & Knox, 1853) p194
[6] *NSA*, Carmyllie, Rev William Robertson, p356
[7] Agricultural Returns, AF39/14/2, 1910

proprietors in the parish until the end of the eighteenth century, Lord Panmure of Panmure estates, Carnegie of Southesk, John Ouchterlony of Guynd and Rait of Cononsyth.

Land

Up until the mid-eighteenth century, various pieces of more fertile land were cultivated around 'ferm toons' in a run-rig system, for instance at the Mains, the Newton and the Milton and it could be suggested that in the area of Milton of Conon there was similar activity. Yet a great deal of soil was shallow in a large part of Carmyllie with moss, whin and gorse encroaching on small 'biggins'(house with adjoining cowshed). But these small pendicles gave shelter to the small wage earners such as weavers, quarriers and farm day labourers. Commissary Maule noted in the *Registrum De Panmure* in 1611 'Carmyllie was ane pair place, fit only for bestial in summer' but Lord Panmure had a purpose when he went on to take over the lands of Carmyllie and finally Carnegie at the end of the eighteenth century. The land chiefly around the 'The Hilles' was of value where there was suitable stone for buildings, roofs, paving and 'dykes' throughout Panmure estate. Later in the nineteenth century the paving stone and slate industry at the Slade quarries was exceeding farming production by 20%[8].
Nonetheless in the nineteenth century, farmers endeavoured to improve the land by adding manure to the soil such as dissolved bones, blood manure and guano and particularly lime, sacrificing a sizeable part of their income[9]. Reclamation of land by draining, nurturing and feeding the soil was encouraged by the landlords.

Landowners

After Lord Panmure included Carnegie lands into his estate at the end of the eighteenth century, there were three landowners in Carmyllie until after World War 1.
These three landowners played a powerful role in the community, acting as heritors, that is, resembling a local government, looking after the welfare of the people, not only providing and maintaining the church, the manse and glebe and nominating a minister but also the upkeep of the school and assisting in the examination of the school master, over and above attending to their tenants' needs. In all they held an enormous influence, through church and school and tenantry, over the entire parish, Lord Panmure, being the largest landowner, had the biggest influence and the most responsibility. Although these powers were eroded gradually, for example, after compulsory education in 1872 when local School Boards were elected, the lairds still remained fatherly figures.

In Carmyllie this could be difficult to uphold, especially if the laird was not resident within the parish and official meetings were attended by representatives such as factors. The Panmure estate was very much larger than the Guynd, but the Ouchterlony family were the only all year round resident landowners in Carmyllie, opening their grounds for annual picnics, special celebrations and gatherings for the parishioners and neighbours. The family also took an interest in the church, school and local events. Cononsyth landowners on the other hand, apart from acting as a heritor, did not take a leading part in the community and took up residence only in the summer until the 1880s, thereafter a tenant occupied the mansion.

After 1922, the Panmure Estate, sold all its Carmyllie lands to private owners, leaving the Guynd Estate (except for the Conon which was sold c. 1928) intact until 1977 when Ouchterlony also sold the farms to private owners. The farms on Cononsyth Estate were gradually sold to their tenants starting after World War 11, the last being in 1989 when the Cononsyth mansion and home farm was sold to the tenant.

---

[8] *NSA*, Carmyllie, p371
[9] James Kydd, Farm Cashbook, 1832-1858

People

Throughout the nineteenth century Carmyllie people were self-contained, some would say isolated. But as a rule, they were robust, hardy people, supplementing a livelihood either within their home or within walking distance. The issue of travelling to town for daily work was burdensome and was overcome in many ways. Hand-loom weaving with the putting-out system, enabled the weaver to remain in his home while the manufacturer delivered the yarn and collected the web weekly. To rent a pendicle was beneficial for part-time workers such as the weaver, the quarrier and the farm day labourer as it gave scope to grow their own food and the ability to supplement their wage. The rise of the quarry industry meant that employment was obtainable within a short distance, while trades and shops were sprinkled over the parish to serve their needs. Certainly with large families, there was a likelihood that some members would branch out to reside elsewhere or take the offer of emigration tickets to settle in the British Empire countries such as Canada, Australia or New Zealand.

The schools were also self-contained within the Parish, first the heritors 'governing' the management followed by local elected School Boards until the end of World War1 when a School Management Committee met in Arbroath with two representatives from eight rural schools. Leaving school at 14 years old, it was not impossible for people to be born, live and work in Carmyllie all their lives until 1947 when universal secondary education began.

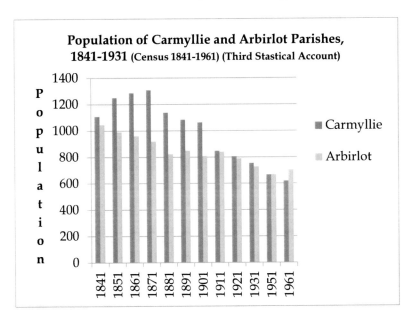

The chart shows that the Carmyllie population exceeded the Arbirlot population for the 60 year duration of the quarry industry, reaching 30% above Arbirlot in 1871, thereafter declining, especially after the beginning of twentieth century, until by 1961, when quarries and trades were closing, the population was less than Arbirlot. By 1951, modernised housing in urban areas was becoming attractive and with more automobile mobility, there was a wider range of suitable employment outwith the parish.

During the Victorian era, the population was large and employment high in Carmyllie, but there was little time for social events. In comparison, in the first half of the twentieth century, when employment was poor and the Depression years left a scar, the social clubs in the Parish gained impetus. There was time after work to meet, compete, act, sing, dance and generally socialise in the community. Certainly there was more mobility towards World War 2 with cars, buses and motor cycles offering a speedier alternative to cycling and walking. The telephone, particularly after the war, was a tremendous benefit for communication throughout the parish.

The end of World War 2 brought an end to Carmyllie parish attending to its own affairs, when governing became centralised and distant. There were definite new benefits however; the introduction of a health service for all, and the provision of utilities such as a common water supply and electricity, making the mundane tasks in households and farms less time consuming. Paradoxically as farms became more mechanised, less manual labour was required, local trades closed, while the parish became depopulated with less people to take the advantage of modern facilities. It was a national phenomenon where the 'draw' to towns and cities to find employment increased while rural population decreased.

Carmyllie Parish Church Picnic at Crombie, 1923

Chapter 1

CARMYLLIE CHURCHES
c.1843-1970

The first Parish Church was built on the site of St Mary's Chapel in 1609 and seems to have incorporated substantial elements from the old pre-reformation chapel. Recent study indicates that these elements survive in the present Church. Strachan the heritor built a substantial church that has stood the test of time. During the last quarter of the seventeenth century and the beginning of the eighteenth century there were troubled times at the Parish Church since four heritors[10] of the parish, with Jacobite leanings, wished an Episcopalian minister, but in 1709, the Presbytery demanded that their own minister should be appointed. Circumstances became more settled after Rev James Small became minister in 1720, although the manse fell into disrepair during the forfeiture of the Panmure Estate. After the estate was bought back from the Yorks Buildings Company, a new manse was built in 1772. The manse had a

Carmyllie Parish Church c. 1860

short life however, when it was vacated in 1820 for the new manse that stands today, with a garden and a glebe amounting to 17 acres.

The nineteenth century saw the rise of an organised labour movement which challenged the established social order. Within the General Assembly of the Church of Scotland, there were constant murmurings of complaint that the Heritors or Patrons of parishes, usually rich landowners, had too much control over the congregation, especially when choosing a minister. In 1834 objections were adhered to when the Evangelical Party, for the first time in a century, gained a majority at the General Assembly in Edinburgh stating ''if a majority of the male heads of the congregation objected to the Heritors' choice and were prepared to give reasons to the Presbytery, the Kirk Session had a right to reject the heritors' choice''. After the death in 1836 of Rev William Robertson (author of the New Statistical Account), the new rule was put to the test when Arbroath Presbytery supported Carmyllie congregation at the election of Rev William Wilson who was serving as a missionary in the Gorbals,

Glasgow[11]. He was also editor of the *Scottish Alliance*, a bi-weekly paper produced by the Evangelical Party in the Church of Scotland.[12] The result was, after he preached to the Carmyllie congregation, out of 170 male heads of families, 130 voted for Rev Wilson. The Home Secretary intervened and put forward four candidates as 'Rev Wilson, however qualified he may be, was not to be presented as minister of the Parish Church'.[13] Nonetheless, all four candidates only received 29 votes in total whereas William Wilson 'the Man of the People', in a second vote, gained 119.[14] During the six months' vacancy, there continued friction between Arbroath Presbytery and the Home Office until eventually the Presbytery forced the appointment of Rev Wilson due to delays from the Home Secretary[15]. However 'the man of the people', holding office as Parish minister for the next six years, was not accepted by the Carmyllie Heritors. In 1842 a meeting was held in the Church between the Carmyllie Heritors, Thomas Collier, factor for Rt. Hon Lord Panmure, James Barclay, writer, representing John

The Rev William Wilson

---

10 The four heritors for Carmyllie parish in 18th century were Lord Panmure, John Ouchterlony, Guynd, Earl Southesk, Carnegie of Carnegie and Ogilvie, Cononsyth

11 NAS. Parish Church Minutes, Carmyllie, CH2/558/5, 1837

12 *Third Statistical Account*, Carmyllie 1968

13 McBain, J.M., *Eminent Arbroathians*, 1179-1894, (Brodie & Salmon, Arbroath, 1897), p 348

14 Ibid, p 349

15 Personal Conversation with Graham McNicol, Local Historian, 2013

Ouchterlony and Alexander Smart, Cononsyth and the Kirk Session, including Rev Wilson and his elders, David Lindsay, William Scott, James Kydd and Robert Anderson. A protest 'was put on the table' by the Heritors against Rev Wilson 'pretended' minister, stating that he ''never received a legal presentation to the Charge, only from certain persons calling themselves the Arbroath Presbytery; all illegal and invalid''. The Heritors wished Rev Wilson and his elders to be excluded from voting at the meeting but Rev Wilson retaliated that it was illegal to 'levy any church seat rents for any purpose.'[16]

The six year tenure of Rev Wilson at the Parish Church, before he became minister of the Free Church was particularly unusual and the 'contest' in Carmyllie became a 'test case' and feelings ran high in Carmyllie because of this. William Maule of Panmure through his Factor, had induced Mr. Ireland, the farmer at the Firth, to return to the Established Church by renewing his lease on very advantageous terms, part of the conditions being that he should recommend a similar course to his fellow farmers who had gone to the Free Church. Some were initially tempted by this but Mr Ireland, having got his harvest safely gathered in, ironically died in the Parish Church during the Harvest Thanksgiving Service. The harvest for which he had forsaken the Free Church was still unsold in his stack-yard. This strengthened farmers' views that they should follow the Free Church, rather than be bribed by Maule, their Laird.[17]

In Carmyllie as elsewhere, a new spirit of independence was emerging amongst the people. Lord Panmure was the main heritor, yet a growing quarry labour employment that introduced various trades and commerce brought a new self-confidence, at least in Church matters and education.

FREE CHURCH

Carmyllie Free Church Manse, 1848

The following year, 1843, the Disruption of Churches took place at the General Assembly in Edinburgh when 200 ministers and elders signed a protest and walked out of the Assembly. They then went to Tanfield Hall where they joined other ministers and elders to form the Free Church and 474 ministers signed the Deed of Demission. With the Rev Wilson supporting the Free Church, he along with the other 473 ministers in Scotland, sacrificed their manse, the pulpit and an income.

In Carmyllie temporary measures were taken immediately and on Sunday 4 June the Rev Wilson conducted the church service in front of the Parish Church Manse to all his followers. Later that month; elders, David Lindsay, James Kydd, William Scott and John Gowans signed the Deed of Demission for elders separating them from the Established Church.[18]

Though initially, the majority of the congregation remained with the Established Church along with one member of the Kirk Session, the Free Church began the following week with a service in a barn at the Mains, tenanted by James Kydd[19].

An amusing story from these times is that one stormy Sabbath, members of the two congregations met and crossed each other on their way to worship at the Established Church and at Mr Kydd's Barn at the Mains. A member of the Established Church accosted an Elder of the Free Church '' Well John

---

[16] National Archives for Scotland (NAS) Heritors' Records, HR/573/1/1, August 1842
[17] Brown, The Rev Thos Brown, *Annals of the Disruption* (Edinburgh: McNiven & Wallace, 1893)p.266
[18] NAS, Free Church Records, CH/492/1, 18 June, 1843
[19] Ibid, 11 June, 1843

you are on the way to get a threshing',' alluding to the severity of the Rev Wilson's preaching. ''Na, Na'', said John, ''the threshing is ower and we are now on the dichting' (winnowing) D'ye no see the chaff blowing down yonder?'' pointing to the Established Church.[20]

Mr. Wilson resided in West Haven on the coast, travelling seven miles to and from his parish for the next two years while William Maule of Panmure's coercive methods caused a bitter struggle for the Free Church followers.[21] When permission to build a manse and a church on a plot of land at Wardneuk farm was refused (this could have been two years previous to the Disruption[22]) by Maule, a brave Mrs Gardyne, living at the Milton, offered part of her garden for Free Church services.[23] As the 1843-44 winter approached, a decision was taken to build a wooden church on the same site. After a great deal of expense (£18.2.4d to build) the building served its purpose, briefly accommodating over 300 of a congregation. The Free Church paid the expenses (£5.13/-) for an interdict action raised by Maule 'prohibiting the congregation from assembling in the wooden church' and further expenses of £5.13/- were paid to Maule as the Free Church lost the action. By Whitsunday 1844, worshipping was finally forbidden and Mrs Gardyne was evicted from her home and her interdict expenses (£3.14.10d) were met from a collection 'in Arbroath'.

Carmyllie Free Church, 1850

Graeme Gardyne visiting from New Zealand commented in 2013 that two members of a younger generation of Mrs Gardyne's family emigrated from Drummygar c.1858, to South Island, New Zealand and amongst their luggage were a musket and a bayonet. On arrival in N.Z., it was their priority to build a Free Church.

Once again services were conducted in the open air until the approaching winter of 1844-45, when a tent, ordered from Manchester and costing £20, was erected at the 'roadside'. Carmyllie Free Church still had to pay £26.3/- to Maule for rent 'in which the congregation assembled' and David Weir was paid £4.00 for 'forms for the tent'.[24] Mr John Anderson (stone mason) and his wife Margaret (nee Soutar), had lived in Carmyllie all their life and when celebrating their Golden wedding in 1894, John Anderson recalled that *they left the auld Kirk at the Disruption with Dr Wilson, and before a place of worship was erected, the Doctor preached on the green at the Milton. On this green they were 'kirked' and sometime later their first child was baptised in a tent at the same place.'*

In the spring of 1845, Maule was giving new leases to Free Church tenants including James Kydd, Mains, who allowed Mr Wilson to reside at the Mains and build another wooden church, but not without objection from Maule although this was eventually waivered in favour of the Free Church. That same year the Free Church was offered one Scotch acre on the same site that had been refused two years earlier. With circumstances more settled, this allowed the Free Church to plan building a manse, church and, in the foreseeable future, a school and a schoolhouse. There was an extraordinary effort to raise funds and in November 1845 'a collection for building' began and there were contributors from far and near such as Carmyllie £10, Inverkeilor £2.17.11, Montrose £12.10/-, Brechin £11, Ladyloan in Arbroath £6.3/-, Glasgow £4 and Dundee churches £35. By 1848 a substantial Free Church Manse was built, although it is questionable if the Rev William Wilson resided in the building as he was called to the Mariners' Church in Dundee that same year. The

[20] Ibid, p198
[21] *Third Statistical Account*, Carmyllie, ed. Illsley, William Rev James Thomson and Muriel Thomson, p 452
[22] Graham McNicol, 2013
[23] McBain, J.M. p 352
[24] NAS, Free Church Cash Book, CH3/492/1/18, Sept 1844

balance of the Local Manse Building (£12.14/-) was cleared by 1850 while contributions continued for a Local Church Building Fund. The new Free Church was opened in February 1850 when £31.19.5d was collected and the following year, to clear the cost of building the Church, the Bank loaned £174.10/-[25]. In Arbirlot parish, covering the expense was slightly alleviated since Maule's son, Fox Maule, gave generously towards Arbirlot Free Church and school.[26] Fox Maule, inheriting the Panmure estate in 1852, supported the Evangelical movement and thereafter gave generously to Carmyllie Free Church, initially donating £4,500 as a basis of an endowment fund for the stipend.[27] In the late 1850s, a school and a schoolhouse were built adjacent to the Free Church, and the school was opened in 1860 under the jurisdiction of the Presbytery until compulsory education in 1872, when it came under the wing of the Scottish Education Department.

Tenant farmers also contributed to the welfare of the community by paying annually to James Tailor, 'Road Money' as early as 1835, amounting to £2.1/-[28] and rising to £2.17.6 in 1876. Contributions to the Poor Assessment Fund commenced after the Disruption of Churches in 1843, when James Kydd paid £2.6.1d to James Tailor, rising to £5.2.8 in 1863. Later in 1874 when compulsory education began, the common fund rose to £6.4.7 which included the 'Poor Assessment and School'.[29]

The Rev John Gow replaced Mr Wilson in 1848 and was minister at the Free Church for seventeen years during which time the Established Parish Church was coming to terms with the loss of more than half of their congregation. However with Carmyllie population remaining high until end of nineteenth century, neither the Parish church nor the Free Church were bereft of members. In fact the Free Church had 245 communicants in 1846 and by 1872 this had fallen to 192[30], the funds kept buoyant by the congregation and Evangelical support. The Rev John Keith succeeded Mr Gow in 1865 and was minister of the 'Evangelical Union' at Carmyllie Free Church for thirty two years, during which time he had been aware of the rise of the quarry industry in the parish. He recalled that he held 'Sabbath' meetings in the Joiner's shop at the 'Benches' at the Slade.[31] As well acting as minister, he practiced other roles within the church such as Clerk to the Deacon's Court and Superintendent of 'Sabbath School'.[32] Although the Rev Keith retired in 1897, he continued to offer his services as a retired minister along with the Rev Stewart Crabbe, and for several years with the Rev John Thomson. After he died in Aberdeen in 1919, he left a legacy of £250 to the Carmyllie United Free Church.[33]

The Rev John Gow

The Rev Stewart Crabbe

A relatively younger minister, the Rev Stewart Crabbe followed Rev John Keith in 1897 with a congregation numbering 191. He remained with Carmyllie Free Church for seven years and during this time, a union was formed between the Free Church of Scotland and the United Presbyterian Church in 1900, thereafter called the United Free Church. The Rev John Thomson succeeded Mr Crabbe in 1904 and remained with the Carmyllie Churches until his retiral in 1948.

In 1907, among the Rev John Thomson's first communicants were Elsie McRobbie, Conon, Annie Milne, Smallburn and Hugh and George Black, Greystone, Peter Constable, Curleys and Andrew Duncan, Drummygar. In addition three new elders were elected; Charles McDonald, West Hills,

---

[25] ibid
[26] Conversation with Graham McNicol, Local Historian
[27] *Third Statistical Account*, p 452
[28] James Kydd, Cashbook, 1830-1865
[29] David Hume, Cashbook, 1871-1876
[30] NAS, Free Church Records,
[31] Carmyllie UF Church, Annual Reports, by Rev John Thomson, 1908
[32] Arbroath Year Book (Arbroath Herald) 1891
[33] Carmyllie UF Annual Reports, 1919

Robert Fyffe, the Birns and James Smith, Old Schoolhouse. Entertainment and talent were found within the members; for instance, a choir under the leadership of Mr Fyffe where there were soloists; Miss Hume, Miss McRobbie, Miss Susan Smith, Mr Davis and Mr Petrie, and duets were given by Miss Brown and Miss Mina Webster while Mrs Anderson, West Schoolhouse, played the organ.

The Rev John Thomson

In 1908, when there was a sudden stoppage of work at the quarries, the Rev Thomson remarked that 'few [his congregation] were connected with quarry employment',[34] suggesting that the UF church members consisted of artisans and farmers, who lived in the west of the parish and beyond into Kirkbuddo.

In 1911 the membership stood at 200 and there were continuous additional monthly services in the evening from April to October, though in winter this only took place on moonlight Sundays until the 1930s.[35] Usually Carmyllie United Free Church organised a summer picnic at different venues such as a field at Panmure policies, Fotheringham estate or Gardyne Castle, but in 1911, the year of George V's Cornation, a picnic was arranged by John Ouchterlony at the Guynd when congregations from the Established Church and the Free Church were invited. A remarkable 700 members enjoyed a day of celebrations.[36]

Part of the United Free Church's weekly collections was sent to Central Funds (usually considerably behind the minimum promised) while the remainder of the funds was spread over the functioning of church services and the maintenance of the Church and the manse. Unforeseen repairs were burdensome; for instance, in 1912 the water supply to the manse was inadequate, and to supply a new pump cost £180, paid partly through Sales of Work and a 'Penny' scheme (each member asked to give 1d extra to the weekly collection), yet this still left a debt of £90.[37]

The United Free Church had numerous loyal members including David Hume, Mains of Carmyllie, who was presented with an illuminated address in 1931 to commemorate sixty two years' service to the Church, first as a deacon in 1870, and then as an elder from 1875. The certificate was signed by the elders such as Chas McDonald, Thomas Johnston, Mr Shepherd and Hugh Black.

In 1929, Parliament conceded most of the principles that the Church of Scotland stood for at the 1843 Disruption such as patronage, leaving the way for the Established Church to merge with the United Free Church. This reunited much of Scottish Presbyterianism and placed the United Free Church at Greystone and the Established Church under one management. The two churches ran separately for another thirteen years and were renamed 'The West Church' and 'The East Church'.

Muriel, the Rev Thomson's daughter, recalled visiting with her father in the 1930s, a Church member's house on a rainy day, when they sat with their umbrellas up as the parishioner's roof was leaking. She also recalled that marriages either took place in the Manse or in the bride's house.

Those who attended the West Church in the 1930s, remember that the Rev John Thomson spread security and comfort by calling his congregation 'My People' and during this time there was contentment amongst the congregation.[38] Audrey Greig (nee Officer) as a child in the late 1930s lived in the schoolhouse and enjoyed the freedom of access from her house to the Manse garden, the Manse and the Church.

34 Ibid, 1908
35 Arbroath Year Book, 1911-1930
36 Carmyllie UF Annual Reports,
37 Ibid, 1912
38 Conversation with Mac Hume, 2013

By 1939, membership was falling in both churches (260 at East Church and 150 in West Church) and merging into one church became more possible as Rev Thomson and the Rev Robert McVicar shared churches and relieved each other of duty from time to time. When Rev McVicar died in 1943 it became natural and acceptable for the community that after after one hundred years of separation, they should appoint a single minister, the Rev John Thomson for both churches. Initially there were sermons on alternate Sundays at the West and East Church, but eventually it was uneconomical to persist with two churches. The East Church became the Parish Church and after the death of Rev John Thomson in 1948, the West Church and Manse were sold separately in 1952.

ESTABLISHED CHURCH

In 1843, the Rev Patrick Bell, well-known for his invention of the reaping machine at his father's farm at Auchterhouse, arrived as minister of the Established Parish Church after the Disruption and gradually inducted new elders to the Kirk Session, but the Church of Scotland never regained its powerful position after the schism. The Established Church was not free of patronage but the heritors no longer had the monopoly of power over schooling, poor relief and moral discipline. Parochial Boards were set up and paupers became registered through the Inspector of the Poor.

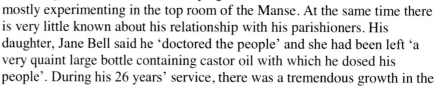

Apart from exhibiting his reaping machine at trials and agricultural shows, the Rev Patrick Bell became absorbed in other small inventions

such as a device to foretell the weather and the installation of gas lighting in the manse, as well as making modifications to the reaping machine; mostly experimenting in the top room of the Manse. At the same time there is very little known about his relationship with his parishioners. His daughter, Jane Bell said he 'doctored the people' and she had been left 'a very quaint large bottle containing castor oil with which he dosed his people'. During his 26 years' service, there was a tremendous growth in the quarry industry and the population rose by 300

The Rev Patrick Bell

The Rev George Anderson

from 1,107 to 1,309 while the membership and the contents of the Church collection box grew accordingly. After Patrick Bell's death in 1869 he was buried in Carmyllie churchyard.

The Rev George Anderson was ordained that same year and remained minister of the Established Church for 31 years until 1900. A bachelor, he employed two domestic servants and his sister was housekeeper and his brother was the farm manager of the Glebe. [39] With the increase in church members, the church was in need of extension and with healthy church funds, the project went ahead in 1874. The Church was practically gutted, the doors and porches on the east and west wings were

Church Choir c. 1890
Back Row: George Carrie, ?, David Buchan,?,
Mr Donald, ?, Wm Mudie
Mid Row: Mrs Anderson, Jas Fullerton,
Rev Geo Anderson, Mr Maxwell, ?, Betty Maxwell
Front Row: Mr Donald, Helen Carrie, Miss Low, ?, Carnegie Sim

removed and the doorways blocked up. In addition, the aisle leading to the north door was made more spacious and the seats were renewed and a heating system was installed. While the alterations were in progress the congregation shared the Free Church at Greystone. [40] No further major alterations have been carried out to the Parish Church to this day.

[39] Angus Census, Carmyllie, 1881, Arbroath Library
[40] NAS, Parish Church Minutes, CH2/558/4/110, 1874

By 1891 the Church membership reached 360 while the Free Church stood at 192. James Taylor, Old Schoolhouse was Session Clerk; the Superintendent of the Sabbath School was the Rev Anderson, Harmoniumist and Choirmaster was William Carr, Redford and the Church Officer was John Soutar, Berryhillock. [41]

John Lyon with his Sabbath School pupils

The two vertical stained glass windows by artist Stephen Adam, in memory of the Rev Patrick Bell, inventor of the reaper and minister of Carmyllie Parish Church

In 1900, a commemoration of 400 years of the Carmyllie Parish church was celebrated in the form of a congregational soiree in the church. The principal guests from Carmyllie were Rev Stewart Crabbe, James Wright and William Duncan, (quarry masters at Slade), Alexander Webster, Redford and David Hume, Mains of Carmyllie. The food was provided by Carnegie Soutar, Arbroath and David Buchan, Redford, sang the anthem.

Later that year the Rev George Anderson retired to Broughty Ferry and the Rev John Lyon, age 36, was ordained and remained with the Parish Church through World War 1 until 1926. Again he was a bachelor, farmed the glebe and mixed among his parishioners in an unconventional way. He was known to visit the farm labourers in their houses and bothies and enjoy jovial company of all classes, old and young. On occasions after a 'rollicking' evening out, his horse pulling the gig knew his way home to the manse without the Rev Lyon's guidance. Rev Lyon was the instigator in raising funds for the installation of the two stained glass windows in 1908, designed by the famous artist Stephen Adam, on either side of the pulpit in memory of Patrick Bell as the inventor of the reaper and as a minister of the Parish Church.

After World War 1, in 1922, the Rev Lyon, with 207 members, was bereft of office bearers, as he was acting as minister as well as Session Clerk and Superintendent of the Sabbath School, with only John Spink, Manse cottage, acting as Church Officer. [42] It begs the question why was this so? After the atrocities of World War 1, was the congregation disillusioned with religion or were they unwilling to support Mr Lyon's wayward habits? John Lyon was the last minister to farm the Glebe of seventeen acres and after he died in office in 1926, the farm implements were sold.

The Rev Robert McVicar was appointed in 1926 and arrived at the Manse with a wife and young family. He conducted himself amongst his parishioners in a quiet manner, quite the opposite of Rev Lyon. The Glebe was rented out and a few of the outbuildings were made obsolete. Mrs McVicar was popular in the community, helping with the Sunday school, presiding over the Women's Guild, [43] making costumes for plays and sewing clothes for deprived children in the area. [44]

---

[41] Arbroath Year Book, 1891
[42] ibid, 1922
[43] Arbroath Year Book, 1929
[44] Nita Smith (nee Gibb), 2012

The occasion is held at Carmyllie Manse in 1928 with the Rev McVicar as host. One of the twins in the pram is Mrs Lindsay (nee Brown) whose father, Charlie Brown, was the Carmyllie policeman.

Although Church membership was 260 in 1939, membership was falling, one of the reasons being the decline in quarry employment which consequently led to fewer tradespeople required.

UNION OF WEST AND EAST KIRKS

The Rev Robert McVicar

After the death of the Rev Robert McVicar in 1943, the two kirks united under the ministry of Rev John Thomson, his annual stipend amounting to £550[45] until he retired in 1948. Although he resided in the West Kirk manse until his death in 1951, the East Church, now to be known as Carmyllie Church, was now the regular place of worship.

The Rev James Thomson was ordained in 1948 and was for nineteen years the minister of the Parish Church, during which time the Parish population dropped by approximately 7% whereas from 1911 to 1948 there was drop of 15%.

In 1955, the Office bearers were Ronald Hume, Session Clerk and William Grant, East Schoolhouse who was Treasurer. They were also Joint Treasurers of the Maintenance of Ministry Fund and the Foreign Mission Fund. The Organist was Miss Muriel Thomson, Lavrockhall; Church Officer, Arch Paton, Glebe Cottage; Women's Guild, President Mrs Thomson and Secretary, Mrs W Grant, East Schoolhouse.[46]

In 1964, a small wooden hall, gifted by Mrs Ruth McDonald in memory of her husband, Charles McDonald, was built for the Sunday school beside the Manse buildings.

---

[45] Arbroath Herald, Dec 1943
[46] Arbroath Year Book, 1955

The Rev James Thomson

The Rev James Thomson died in office in 1967 by which time Carmyllie Church was labeled as having a small membership and consequently, the Church of Scotland stipulated that the next minister must be over 55 years old. When the Rev Alexander Spence was ordained in 1968, there were 216 on the Communion Roll. Mr Spence was minister for the next fifteen years and was the last resident minister in Carmyllie Manse; the first minister being the Rev William Robertson who entered the new building in 1820.

The Rev Alexander Spence

The small membership did not occur suddenly and there was as previously mentioned, a gradual decline since 1900. The Disruption began with an ideal plan that the minister was to be 'the Man of the People,' only to discover that there was a manse and a church to be maintained and those with capital; for instance, tenant farmers, successful tradesmen or those with a position, such as schoolmasters were, if willing, appointed to the Kirk Session who in turn 'ruled', at least in the nineteenth century, over the misdemeanours of some members. For the most part the next generations of these stigmatised church goers would shy away from membership.

There was a possibility of a stronger church unity in the Parish and elsewhere when in 1929, the Free Church gaining all that was fought for at the Disruption by joining with the Established Church. But rather than widening horizons, the church turned into itself to attend to the welfare of its own declining members.[47] Carmyllie in the 1930s, was losing employment and the numerous 'nomadic' farmworkers did not usually attach themselves to the Church. Furthermore, as described in the 'Farming' chapter, there was a marked change in the Parish during and after World War 2 due to mechanisation that required less employment and mobilisation allowed people to participate in a wider circle of activities and entertainment. Generally speaking, those whose parents attended church would continue to keep an interest. By 1970, only 17% of Scotland's population were traditional Church goers. It could be suggested that educational opportunities gave people the confidence to make individual decisions in religious beliefs.[48]

Parish Church Manse and Glebe, 1930s (Gibb family)

[47] Smout, T.C., *A Century of the Scottish People 1830-1950,* (Fontana Press. 1988) p 206
[48] Machin, Ian, 'British Churches and Moral Change in the 1960s'; Offprint from Crown and Mitre: *Religion and Society since the Reformation* (Woodridge, The Boydell Press, 1993)

Chapter 2

CARMYLLIE SCHOOLS

The Old Parochial School and Schoolhouse (now Viewfar) 1804

In the earliest known Kirk Session Records in 1689, the Kirk gave funds to Patt Sand and Robert Donaldson to build a school house[49] in the Milton of Carmyllie area and later the Kirk provided 'thack for the schoolmaster's house' and by 1705 workmen were paid for 'putting up a clay chimney in the school'.[50] Nevertheless it was not until the early 19th century, when enclosure of land took place, that Lord Panmure allocated a piece of ground to build the Public Parish School attached to a schoolhouse, constructed in 1804,[51] within the vicinity of the Church. The Schoolhouse and the school therefore, is possibly the oldest habitable building in Carmyllie today.

The parish heritors, being Lord Panmure (the principal), Ouchterlony of Guynd and the Laird of Cononsyth, were responsible for the provision and maintenance of the school and schoolhouse, made possible by levying a tax from themselves, the landowners, and the tenant farmers. The fees paid by the pupils contributed towards the headmaster's salary, but the Church of Scotland supervised all until 1839 when H.M. Inspectors were introduced, and grants were made available towards salaries, but the influence of the Kirk continued to remain strong.

Although the parish school was the principal school, it was not the only source of education in the area. Private schools developed where groups were within walking distance. For example, there was a side school on Cononsyth estate and

Remains of Podge School' 2012 (Paterson family)

another school at the Podge near Burnhead farm, close to the Slade quarries and schooling also took place in a barn near Dilty Moss on the west of the parish. Remains of the Podge school building still stand today. It is uncertain when the school was built, but it was in operation until the latter half of the nineteenth century, the roll increasing due to the growing employment at the quarries. These private schools were unpopular with the Heritors and the Kirk session because their system was unregulated and they charged lower fees in competition to 'public' education.

Another more permanent second school in the parish emerged after the Disruption of the Church in 1843, when a Free Church and Manse were built at Greystone. It would seem that in the Parish, boys were more encouraged to attend school than girls, since in 1852, the newly installed Free Church Kirk Session decided that as there was 'no female school in the Parish for many years and the female youth were sustaining great injury. Fox Maule, Lord Panmure should be approached for permission to use the cottage at the Milton [formerly occupied by Mrs Gardyne] as a girls' school''.[52] Lord Panmure

---

[49] NAS, Carmyllie Parish Kirk Session Records, 18 Mar, 1689
[50] ibid , 1704
[51] Historic Scotland, Listed Buildings, Category B (1971)
[52]NAS, Carmyllie Free Church Kirk Session, 24 June 1852

was more than helpful and gave permission to build a sustainable Free Church School within the vicinity of the new Free Church at Greystone and this opened as an education establishment in 1860.

Greystone School c. 1900

When the Education Act was passed in 1872 stipulating compulsory education, the system changed greatly. School provision was removed from the heritors and an elected School Board was formed, the first official elected body in the parish, and the State was responsible for the standards of teaching and the state of the buildings. Present at the first School Board meeting in April 1873 was David Guthrie commissioner acting for Lord Dalhousie (president), Rev John Keith, Minister of the Free Church, Rev George Anderson, Minister of Parish Church, David Falconer, Farmer & Quarrymaster, Milton of Conon, William Duncan, Farmer & Quarrymaster, Slade and James Taylor, Schoolmaster of the Parish of Carmyllie. Later in the year, the Carmyllie Free Church School, the School Master's house and ground were transferred to the Board of Education and were designated as Carmyllie West Public School and the Parish School was to be known as Carmyllie East Public School, both schools being guided by the local School Board.

Before compulsory education in 1872, written records were limited, but the first entry in the school Log Book in 1873 noted that James Taylor, headmaster, resigned after serving thirty years as headmaster to be replaced by James Mackay from Perceton school, Ayrshire.[53] Mr Mackay began with 55 pupils in attendance rising to 100 the following week, all under the control of one teacher. There was no limit on the number of pupils, since the fees contributed towards the teacher's salary. James Mackay's first comments were that 'the school buildings and furniture are quite unsuitable for proper methods of teaching', and furthermore, there was inadequate heating, ventilation and lighting and in December, Mr Mackay remarked that 'the school was dark and smokey'. Nevertheless, by the end of the year the headmaster received help when Miss Jane Fairweather commenced duties as a pupil teacher. Yet Mr Mackay remarked that 'we are still far from having an orderly school, nor can I

Extract fom the Parish School Minute Book, 1873

expect it to be much better in such a confined schoolroom.' The annual HM inspections tended to support the teacher regarding the state of the schoolroom and in the first report stated that 'it would not be at all desirable to continue the school in its present position so near to the other public school (Carmyllie West)......no grant next year if this school is still conducted in the same premises.' The following year in 1875, there was promise of a new school but HMI's patience was running thin mentioning that 'providing proper accommodation is long enough delayed.' The School Board, however, had collected costs for the erection of East Public school Buildings

Mason work, School and Residence	£775.03.0
Joiner	£416.15.0
Plumber	£53.00.0
Slater	£ 80.00.0
Plaster	£ 80.15.0
	£1,405.13.0

---

[53] School Log Book, East Public School, 24 Nov 1873

The Scottish Education Department provided £230.15/- towards the cost of the new building and the old East Public Schoolhouse, 'land and pertinents ' was sold to Lord Dalhousie to the value of £540.[54] The schoolroom, known as 'The Old Parochial School', remained available to the local community until the new community hall was built in 1960. Functions such as country dancing tuition, Ploughing Association

Carmyllie East Public School, built 1876 (2012)

meetings, Men's Club and Local and General Elections all took place there.

The new school opened at Redford in May 1876 and the headmaster 'found a very marked difference in the quietness and order of the school from the increased amount of accommodation'. Many new pupils enrolled from the neighbourhood and some transferred from the old school. With the roll at East and West reaching over 100 in each school, the School Board decided that a female teacher should be appointed to teach the First and Second Standard and the Infant classes in each school. The two male headmasters agreed to pay £30 per annum, half of the female teachers' salary, to the appointed teachers. The two headmasters however, resigned (or were dismissed) due to dismal teaching standards and a reduction in grants from HM Inspectors. Fortunately, expenses were allowable and Mr Gibson, headmaster at the West school, claimed:

Salary due to Martimas	£10.0.0
Proportion of the Government grant, say:	£20.0.0
Kitchen Grate (£1) Kitchen Mantle Piece (5/-)	£1.5.0
Pig Stye	£0.10.0
School Chair (10/-) School Clock (10/-)	£1.0.0
Picture and Reading Sheets	£0. 5.0
	£33.0.0

The expenses claim revealed that the classroom supply of books and furniture were meagre and mention of repairs to a pig 'stye' suggest that obtaining food from nurturing a pig helped to supplement and perhaps overcame the variable income from the teacher's salary.

The privately supported schools such as the Podge lost their momentum after 1872 and the East Public School was admitting pupils from the Podge in the next two years.[55] It is unclear when the Podge School closed although the School Board held their meetings there until the new school opened at Redford in 1876. Certainly by 1877, Podge School is paying no rent, only a Podge pendicle (James Findlay) was paying a rent of £10.10/- annually to the Earl of Dalhousie.[56]

HM Inspector's reports were discouraging. At the East school in 1878, the Inspector informed the headteacher and the School Board that 'There is nothing good in it. The children..... will not speak out, nor speak distinctly, nor give any sign of smartness.' Later the reports showed marked success in the Standard one and two and the infants, but there was little improvement with the older pupils.

---

[54] School Board Minutes, Carmyllie, Aug 1875
[55] School Log Books, East Public School 1874,1875
[56] Valuation Roll 1876/77

West School pupils, 1908

Poor attendance was a constant concern to the headmaster. From November to March, when fieldwork was at a minimum and quarry work was low, attendance could reach to 100, although illness and bad weather tended to restrict this. The high terrain in Carmyllie parish with various soils differed in farming practices from neighbouring parishes. The more fertile land was in the hollows near the streams and the poorer land on higher ground had pockets of soil as low as seven inches in depth[57]. During the agricultural improvements around the end of eighteenth century, the landowners and tenants enclosed the productive land into farms leaving aside less fertile areas. Here, the landowners saw an opportunity of fixing additional rent by letting out poorer land in the form of crofts or pendicles of approximately 4 acres, where families cultivated a field; tended a cow, pigs or hens for subsistence. These pendicles were scattered all over the parish. To pay the rent, adult males found work mostly in and around the quarries or farm labour, and so in the parent's eyes, tending to the necessities at home was above the importance of education. Some parents would 'cheat' their children's age in order to reduce their compulsory years at school. For example, the teacher was doubtful about the ages of James Ramsay's children on the school register and when approached, Ramsay replied that 'he did not know them' [the ages][58]. It is assumed that boys were required at home but the headmaster remarked in 1879 that 'the irregularity of attendance is chiefly amongst the girls'. It could be suggested that, if there was an advantage in schooling, then boys should have priority. Mr Taylor was one of the early School Board Attendance Officers (known locally as 'the Wheeper in') whose work entailed visiting the homes where there was regular truancy. However, the teacher complained that the Officer was lax in gathering names of the culprits from the school and remarked 'it might be better if our Board Officer were a strong and vigorous man'.[59] Child labour was required for herding, seed and potato planting, followed in the autumn by the harvest and 'tattie digging' which had various completion dates from October to the end of November. Also absence due to game shooting (beating) on the estates during winter months, was prevalent especially at the West school. 'Term time', which occurred every six months, caused another headache for the headmaster. It only needed two or three ploughmen with large families to move to another area to reduce the roll considerably, forcing the headmaster to mention that 'it is the cool way the majority of parents remove their children from school without notice'.

The graph shows the school roll at the East and West schools spanning over 100 years. The employment at the quarries had a marked influence on the school roll especially at the East school From the 1870s until around 1900, the East school roll rose over 100% and dropped rapidly by 120% before the First World War when work stopped at the quarries. After the War, when the quarries reopened on a smaller scale, the roll remained around 60 but dropped by 50% after the final closure of the quarries in 1950. The West school roll was built more around agriculture where there were many small farms and did not show a definite decline until after the First World War when many pendicles were merged into larger farms and sold to individual farmers. Before the West school closed in 1970,

57 NSA, Carmyllie, 1836
58 School Log Books, Carmyllie, 1878
59 ibid, May 1878

both school rolls were reduced to below thirty pupils but when the two schools amalgamated (together with a small number from the closure of Kirkden School) the roll rose briefly to over one hundred.

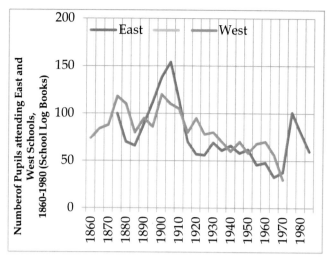

For the first two decades after compulsory education, the headmaster's income depended a great deal on the collection of school fees from the parents. In addition, parents were expected to share the coal bill for heating, but both payments proved to be irregular. Mr Whyte, the West schoolmaster, asked permission from the Board to prosecute for the recovery of outstanding fees. He was given permission but the Board was unprepared to pay 'expenses connected therewith'. However, by 1892, the headmaster's dependence on school fees became less crucial as Mr Whyte received an annual salary of £120 to be paid quarterly and in addition £5 per year for cleaning each of the schools. Consequently, charging school fees terminated and the School Board received £43 Sterling the following year from the Scottish Education Department as a balance from the relief of fees.[60] In 1885 the fees were: [61]

Infants	2/- per quarter
Standard I	2/6
Standard II	3/-
Standard III	3/6
Standard IV	4/-
Standard V	4/6
Standard VI	4/6

The members of a new School School Board formed in 1900 were; Lieutenant Colonel John Heathcote Ouchterlony, the Guynd, David Cargill, Farmer, Backboath, William Lindsay, Farmer, Chamberlain Knowe, William Duncan, Quarrymaster, Slade and James Wright, Quarrymaster, Slade. Later in the next decade, new members such as John L Soutar, Miltonhaugh and David Hume, Mains, called at the schools to check the registers but there was a gradual decline in School Board activity and eventually, during World War 1, action taken on truancy and older pupils leaving school before 14 years old was spasmodic.

Inevitably, big changes took place after the Education Act of 1918 when the Education Authority set up School Management Committees with a cluster of schools requesting representatives from each Parish to attend regular meetings. The aim was to ensure uniformity and connection with a wider number of schools. The committee had representatives from St Vigeans, Colliston, Auchmithie, Carmyllie East, Carmyllie West, Inverkeilor, Chapelton and Arbirlot and the meetings took place in Arbroath. This marked the end of Carmyllie School Board and Mr Macdonald, East school, 'bid goodbye [to the Board] without regret and welcomed the new'.[62] Yet it was also the end of the Parish having direct legal responsibility for their children's education. The Rev J. Lyon, Rev John Thomson and Mr G. Macdonald (Rev Lyon, the convener) were Carmyllie's representatives and the Management committee took control of all aspects of education such as care and repair of buildings and furniture, permission to let schools, purchase of fuel, light and cleaning materials, fixing school holidays, checking truancy and exemptions and school registers.

School holidays became more regular with a break at Easter, approximately five weeks in July and August and 'tattie' holidays beginning in October, although rural schools were often allowed to prolong the holidays until the potato harvest was complete, which could be up to five weeks. The Management Committee for a number of years was also lenient with the decision for the Christmas

[60] Ibid, 1894
[61] School Board Minutes, Carmyllie, Dec 1886
[62] East School Log Book, May 1919

break, giving the cluster of schools a choice of dates, either 24 December to 3 January or 30 December to 7-10 January. The two Carmyllie schools chose the latter remaining with the Yuletide celebrations rather than Christmas.

In addition, there were special school holidays. In the three decades up to 1900, the school closed for the day around May 1 for Carmyllie Market and Fair, and St Thomas Market falling on Monday and Tuesday in the last week in July was also celebrated. Usually there was a holiday to mark Royal occasions such as Queen Victoria's Jubilee in 1897 (one week). To celebrate Edward VIII's Coronation in 1902, Mr James Wright, chairman of the School Board, presented the pupils with a medal and a 'treat'. Nine years later, on the previous day to George V's Coronation, the East school pupils unfurled the flag and saluted. In Sept 8 1905, a school day was set aside from both schools when Col Ouchterlony entertained the children at the Guynd to celebrate the coming of age of his son. Empire Day was observed in May but was not ordered as a school holiday until the School Management Committee was formed in 1919. Sometimes a gramophone was brought into the classroom where the children listened to the King's speech. During the Second World War in 1944, it was agreed to name the holiday in May as Victoria Day.

The atrocities of the First World War were seldom mentioned in the headmasters' Log books although 'the children were eager to hear the latest news every morning'[63]. Most households were still without telephone, newspapers or radio and 'word of mouth' would be erratic. Nevertheless the community worked together and some sixty pairs of socks were knitted by the girls at the East School and sent to soldiers in France via Dundee and, at the West School, 37 dozen eggs were collected and sent to the wounded soldiers in Dundee in 1915. In addition, the senior pupils collected a large quantity of Sphagnum Moss, which was sent to War Dressing Depots at Montrose, Arbroath and Dundee. Both Mr Anderson and Mr Macdonald, on 16 August 1915, closed the schools in the afternoon to deliver Conscription Registration forms to all eligible men. Possibly the potential

Carmyllie West, Headmaster John Smith, 1920

conscripts required assistance to complete the registration forms as one whole day was required the following week to collect the completed documents. Ostensibly, the teachers display no sentiment in

---

[63] East School Log Book, 18 September, 1914

the Log Books though there is a sense that the headmasters would be 'dragging their heels' when collecting signed forms from young men who were possibly former pupils.

During World War 1, the headmaster's despondency was increased with low attendance, lack of stimulation from the pupils and older children ignoring the leaving age, together with coping with bad news, such as a visit from a former pupil, Leonard Bowden in December 1916, being discharged from the army as he had lost an arm at the Somme Battle. Rich food ingredients had become scarce during the war, as when closing the school on 5 Jan 1917, the usual treat of plum pudding from Mr James Falconer, Milton of Conon, was replaced by a meat bridie and cocoa. and the following year Mr Falconer provided a tea party.[64] On Armistice Day, the school Union Jack was raised and the school bell rang and Mr Macdonald remarked 'may future generations never experience the anxieties that have been ours during the last four years'[65]

Mr W F Anderson, 'closed his connections' with Carmyllie West School in November 1919 after acting as headmaster for 19 years while Mr George Macdonald, the longest serving headmaster, resigned in January 1924 after 32 years and 1 month service at the East School.

The two headmasters were expected to carry out responsible work in the community outwith school duties. George Macdonald was Inspector of the Poor, Collector of Rates and Clerk to the Parish Council for over twenty years while W.F. Anderson, West School was Registrar and Superintendant of the Free Church Sunday School for most of the years he was headmaster. John Smith continued as Registrar after Mr Anderson left and Ross McKay, East School, in the early 1930s was Inspector of the Poor while Harry Officer was Registrar. Later, only the office of Registrar remained and William Grant, East School held this position until he retired in 1958.[66]

Carmyllie East, Headmaster George Macdonald, 1921

The stipulated minimum school leaving age of 14 (earlier with exemption) remained in force until after the Second World War. Nonetheless, the Board and the headmasters sought to continue

---

[64] West School Log Book, Jan 1917
[65] East School Log Book, 11 November, 1918
[66] Arbroath Year Book

education beyond the minimum age. As early as 1893, the Board put forward a request for Secondary education, justifying that the population of the parish was 1100 and the school roll at East and West schools was 223.[67] It would seem that the East school was proposed for secondary education but in 1899 the Department of Education had refused to certify the school and the County Committee was

East School 'Soup Kitchen' donated by Duncan, Falconer, Whitton & Co. to mark Queen Victoria's Jubilee, 1887

unable to pay a grant for secondary education. Specialised teachers were not on offer for higher training in rural parishes, but an attempt was made by the two headmasters, Mr Macdonald and Mr Cox, to open an Evening Continuation School in the Old Parochial school in November, December and January and the subjects to be taught were Arithmetic, History, Writing, Composition and Agriculture. The teachers would take charge alternately and paid 7/- per night.[68] It is uncertain if these classes continued as financial assistance for higher training to outlying areas continued to be sparse. The Earl of Dalhousie offered bursaries of £5 for agricultural training and by 1912, cookery classes were in operation as Mrs John Ouchterlony and Miss Ouchterlony, the Guynd, called at the East school to observe 'the cookery class at work'.[69]

Monday was the chosen day for cookery classes so that the ingredients were as fresh as possible since Saturday was shopping day in Arbroath. Horticulture/gardening practice was of such high standard that the Rt Hon John Sinclair, Secretary of State of Scotland, and Lady Marjory Sinclair called at East School in 1907 and 'had explained the workings of the school gardens ..... very much interested in the work of the pupils'[70]. The following week Mr Michie, HM Inspector from Edinburgh and Mr Stacey, HM Inspector from Manchester, examined the pupils' work in the 'school farm'.

However, in the early 1930s, it still remained difficult for those with ability living in rural parishes, to gain a secondary education. Mrs Catherine Clark (nee Sturrock), Burnhead Farm, Redford, rec the problem:
I attended Carmyllie East School from 1923 and the headmaster was Donald Ross McKay who was a keen maths teacher. There were sometimes three teachers but mostly two and Miss Watson was the Infant teacher. I gained a bursary to attend Arbroath High School at the age of 12 together with Mary Garden of Backboath, travelling by bus. After two years, in 1932, the authorities changed the school bus service so those attending secondary education from Carmyllie were asked to travel to Forfar Academy (twice the distance) which upset the flow of education. Mary Garden left school at 14 although I continued for one year at Forfar but it was difficult to adjust so I left at 15.

Only a few received bursaries and for the remainder there was no alternative for further education. Will Gardiner, farmer, Tillyhoit remembers his school days:
I went to Carmyllie East School in 1927 where there were two teachers, Miss Peters and first, 'Domilie' McKay then 'Domilie' Dewar whom I remember as a 'good' teacher. I thought that most of the pupils' parents worked at the quarries and all the children walked to school. He recalls the Paton family (10 in total) walking along the Guynd/Conon road from Villa Bank in single file. I left the East School at 14 and went home to help my father.

[67] Carmyllie School Board, Feb, 1893
[68] ibid, 1897
[69] East School Log Book, Sept 1912
[70] ibid, Oct 1907

West School

Mrs Rose Goetz gives a vivid description of the West (Greystone) School, first as a pupil then, as an employee. She portrays the physical work entailed:-.

I attended Greystone School from 1934 to 1943 and was taught by two teachers, Miss Peters (infants) and Mr Harry Officer. During my school days there were fluctuations in the school roll, falling from 77 to 57 in 1936 to 51 in 1938, with the result that the school was down-graded to a two-teacher school.

Mrs Rose Goetz

There was not much provision for a playground but during my time, part of it was sprayed with tar.
Around 20 Evacuees arrived from Dundee in September 1939 although in a few weeks most had returned home.

At the East School, Mr Dewar reported that on 11th September 1939, 28 evacuated children arrived from Dundee and there were no desks, only forms to sit on. Desks, chairs and a blackboard arrived from Dundee but after the 'tattie' holidays only nine evacuees remained, the rest having returned to Dundee. The inside of the windows were covered in cellophane 'to render them splinter proof in the event of bomb explosions in the vicinity'. [71]

Rose Goetz continues with her memories at the West school:

In December 1939, it was a marked occasion when we were granted a holiday on Christmas day.
In January 1940, conditions were 'arctic' and only one class at a time was taught round the fire in the Infant room.
During the Second World War when food was rationed, the soup kitchen proved a great benefit and it was reported in 1941 that 'it was most appreciated since there was a scarcity of spread for 'pieces''
That same year Harry Officer attended a meeting in Arbroath High School concerning Emergency Feeding.
In 1942, school exemption for those over 12 years old was granted for a limited period to farmers who required assistance to herd cattle to market and any field work such as planting and harvesting or general farm labour. I left school in 1943 at 14.
I continued to live in Greystone after I married in 1949 and as well as attending to my young family, I helped Miss McKay clean Greystone school and cook the school dinners.

Soup Kitchen

Originally the building consisted of a soup kitchen with a cottage next door. In 1893 the building was made into one kitchen/dining room. Later in 1938, soup was served in a school classroom.

Derelect 'Soup Kitchen' West School, 1985

---

[71] ibid, Oct 1939

Soup Kitchen/Garden

The soup was made in a cast iron boiler, which was set on big stones with a coal fire underneath. There was also a deep earthenware sink nearby. The soup kitchen was open from December to March and the school relied on the generosity of the local farmers to provide potatoes, 'neeps' and the odd rabbit. The preparation of the soup entailed peeling the potatoes into large buckets then plunging them into the boiler with the stock. I recall the butcher delivering huge bones twice per week for the stock and at the 'dinners', the children were partial to the taste of marrow. When the soup kitchen closed in March, the headmaster Harry Officer would boil a kettle and provide mugs of cocoa if required.

Periodically Whist Drives and other fundraisers were held in the evening in the school and some of the money would benefit the Soup Kitchen Fund.

I remember that part of the soup kitchen was used as a storage room where stage apparatus for concerts was kept.

Miss McKay and I washed the towels and cloths in our own homes.

After World War2, soup ceased to be made on the premises and school dinners were delivered from Forfar. In 1950 the pupils paid 5d each for a school meal.

West School Picnic, Carnoustie, 1955 (Brown family)

25

Heating and fuel

At 7.45am the fires were lit in the three classrooms. On extra cold days (32°F and as low as 27°F indoors) all pupils would assemble in one room with additional heat from a paraffin cooker.

The attendance officer (the 'wheeper-in'), Mr Esplin, carted the coal from the coal merchant at Redford.

Hot water was obtained from the boiler in the soup kitchen and carried down in buckets to the school in order to scrub the flagstone floors and for general classroom cleaning.

In 1950, two stoves were installed in the school and in 1951, the kitchen boiler was replaced by a 'better' heating system.

An electricity supply was installed and the power was switched on in November 1954, a few months after Ronald Brown became headmaster.

There was a new heating system in operation with electric storage heaters in 1968. In that same year frequent power cuts occurred, so stronger fuses were inserted.

Drainage and Toilets

The drainage proved to be a continual problem.

The cleaner and Mr Esplin were responsible for clearing the drains manually.

'Dry' toilets were outside and the refuse was periodically removed by Mr Esplin and discarded into a lidded pit between the girls and boys toilets, then later removed by horse and cart.

In 1938, a 'modern' water supply was installed which provided sinks and running water in the school.

Flush toilets were installed in the outside toilets in the early

Miss Beattie's class with outside sheds and toilets in background (1950s)

1940s but caused problems in the winter months when the water froze. To help solve the difficulty, candles burned in the building overnight.

In the early fifties, water was supplied from a small reservoir in one of Lochlair's fields and was proving to be inadequate as there was an increase in the installation of bathrooms in the surrounding dwelling houses. This led to a crisis in 1956 when there was no water for six months which hastened a more efficient connection to the Crombie Water Supply.

School Closure, 1970.
Margaret Sturrock, Mrs Goetz,
Mr C Macdonald, Miss I Beattie
and Morag Findlay

In 1957, the inside coal room was replaced by a staffroom and toilet and a new coal shed was built in the playground. Pupils had access to the staffroom when outside toilets were frozen.

Inside pupil toilets were built in 1964 and by the end of 1968 the water consumption had quadrupled, so water was switched off in the boys' urinal when not in use.

Miss McKay retired in 1966 at the age of 80, and I continued to hold the post of cleaner and dinner attendant until the school closed in 1970.[72]

Before Harry Officer became headmaster in 1924 at the West, Mr John Smith filled the post from 1919 for five years. In order to retain assistant teachers longer and to overcome the problem of

---

[72] Testimony, Mrs Rose Goetz

weather conditions, a house was made available behind the school to board the teachers. Miss Gray who taught in the 1930s remembers:

I had an older sister Grace, who came as a third teacher to Greystone in 1922. She stayed in the teacher's cottage with Miss Meg Imrie, her sister Aggie as housekeeper, plus her aged father. All three teachers, Mr Smith, Miss Imrie and Miss Gray were musical and Mr Smith was the organist at the West Church.

Fred Smith, Carmyllie football team, 1953

Harry Officer arrived as headmaster at West School in 1924 from a post as assistant at Parkhouse School, Arbroath and was the longest serving headmaster at the West School, a total of 22 years. He contributed a great deal to the social life in the area when modes of transport were limited. He introduced a weekly social club, concerts and drama groups and organised football teams. He had a thorough understanding of the land and country people. His daughter, Audrey, remembers:

He spent his holidays in the farmers' fields – ploughing, planting, harvesting, 'gaffering' in the rasp field or the 'tattie' field. He had many good friends and if he was not out socialising he invited friends into our house to play cards.

Miss Betty Gray taught for three years from 1934 to 1937 and remembers:

These were very happy years of my life. The roll fluctuated a great deal as the cottar moved at the 'term' and Harry O encouraged the farmers to 'fee' ploughmen with big families to keep up the roll. I stayed with the two sisters, Joan and Janet Hume at the Mains through the week because Miss Peters occupied the teacher's cottage. At the weekend, I travelled home to Careston, catching the bus for Forfar at the War Memorial, and then waiting for a connection to Careston. The reverse was carried out on Sunday evening. Later I caught the train at 7am at Brechin to Dundee, stopping off at Kirkbuddo and walking to Greystone in time for 9a.m

Fred Smith with his class, 1953

By 1937 Senior Secondary education was free, so no bursaries were required and if pupils passed the Qualifying Test (11+) in rural areas then the bus fare was clear of payment. For those who did not qualify, secondary education eluded them for another ten years. Education Authorities varied with decisions, as Perthshire Authority made allowances for secondary education in 1936[73]. All was settled in Angus, however by 1945, when secondary education was made free for all and the minimum leaving age of 15 was compulsory. Yet the qualifying classes in rural parish schools continued to be separated, those

---

[73] Young, Mary, *Abernyte The Quiet Revolution'* (Perth & Kinross Libraries), 2008

qualified travelled to Forfar Academy while remaining pupils were destined to Junior Secondary at Letham with the belief that they would excel in practical subjects rather than academia. In Carmyllie, August 1947, this proved to be a daunting task for those moving to junior secondary since they were the first pupils compelled to finish their education outwith the parish. Mr Fred Smith, headmaster at the West from 1946 to 1954 remembers:

When I took over in the aftermath of the War, a large section of the school playground was under 'The Dig for Victory' scheme.

At the end of the session in 1947, there were 17 pupils scheduled to start the Junior Secondary at Letham. To my surprise when I returned to start the new session in August, all 17 pupils were sitting in the classroom refusing to face the new challenge. After a great deal of persuasion, the pupils were safely installed at Letham the following day.

Yet with all good intentions, there was a sense of failure amongst some who attended the Junior Secondary. In the Angus rural parishes, pupils attended Junior Secondaries such as Letham, Tannadice or Murroes; whereas pupils in the burgh schools all attended the same secondary school regardless of qualifying results, albeit placed in separate grades. Some parents in rural schools took advantage and sent their children to the last year of burgh primary schools (paying for transport) so they automatically entered the senior secondary school. Others from rural primary schools who did not reach the grade could enter the Senior Secondary provided their parents paid transport.

Mr Fred Smith left Carmyllie West in 1954 as he was appointed headmaster at Friockheim. He was replaced by Mr Ronald Brown who remained headmaster for nine

West School, Ronald Brown and Miss Beattie, teachers, 1956

years during which time electricity was installed in both the school and schoolhouse in 1954 and later a more efficient water supply improved the facilities enormously. Mr Brown was the main instigator in setting in motion a building programme for the new community hall which opened in 1960. After Mr Brown moved in 1963 to be headmaster at Reform Street, Kirriemuir, there were two headmasters for short periods, Mr Dow for three years and by Mr MacDonald for four years before the school closed in 1970.

West Schaill, Carmyllie (anonymous but last 2 verses by Alex Whitton)

I bide in Carmyllie, my name it is Jack
I gang every day wi' a bag on my back
Tae the West Schaill, Carmyllie, that stands in Greysteen
And I'm telt I maun bide there until I'm fourteen

Chorus: *'Singing Tooler a' ooler a' ooler a' ay*
If Joe Esplin speers whaur I've been a' the day
Just say I'm awa' on cook's tooler a' ooler a' ooler a' ay'

Wi' accounts an' dictation I'm nae guid ava'
I'm en' different writer, and nae hand tae dra
Wi' pen or wi' pencil I'm no very smart
I'm a far better hand wi' a stick at the Mart

The West Schaill is closed noo, it's used as a hoose
For learning o' bairns it's nae further use
The reading and writing's now done in the East
In the East schaill Carmyllie, whaur the Heritage meet

A'thing aye changes wi' the passing o' time
Nae mair is the Mert or the railway line
The quarries lie silent, unlike days o' before
Locked in the memories o' Carmyllie's folk lore

Miss Cowie, Curleys at West School

East School

By the mid-1960s the 11+ test was abolished in Scotland and a comprehensive education was introduced whereby all children beyond primary school age attended the same secondary school. Pupils from the East and West schools travelled by bus, with a personal bus pass to Arbroath High School but could choose a High School such as Brechin or Carnoustie, providing their own transport. Miss Edith Garrow taught at Carmyllie East School for twenty years and after the two schools amalgamated in 1970, she taught for a further nineteen years. She relates a lively account of her experiences:

In 1950, I accepted a temporary post at Carmyllie East until I found a vacancy nearer home. I was advised by the headmaster, Mr William Grant, to find lodgings in Arbroath to prevent familiarisation with the local community.

My first day at Carmyllie was memorable. Two taxis pulled up at my lodgings in Arbroath and, after choosing one taxi, I was driven out to Carmyllie East where the children were lined up against the wall in the playground with a welcome 'Here's her noo!' I was the

Miss Betty Watt's Class, 1948

third teacher at the 'East' together with Miss Watt and Mr Grant. I would have preferred to teach the older pupils but Miss Watt refrained from teaching infants so I had no alternative but to settle with the youngest pupils. There I remained in the Infant department for 39 years. The school roll stood at

Infant Class, Miss Garrow, 1952

80 pupils in 1950 and the majority travelled from the Slade Quarry cottages and the newly built Burnhead Terrace houses, Redford. In the very first week, Mr Grant requested that for one day I deputise for Mr Fred Smith, Greystone. Mr Grant assured me that if I 'walked straight up the road and turn right at the Monument I would soon be there.' I, not having time to be orientated, was completely lost and continued to ask directions all the way, eventually arriving mid-morning!

The following year Miss Watt left to be married and the school was reduced to two teachers. Because I enjoyed teaching at the school tremendously, I asked the Education Officer at Forfar County Buildings, for a permanent post at Carmyllie East and was duly accepted.

In my early teaching days, the first two years of school were referred to as the Infants, then Primary 1 began in the third year making Primary Five the top class. There were sufficient books in the infant department but more sparse in the senior class.

The pupils used slates as well as paper and pencil although the Inspectors wished the slates to be made obsolete because the pupils' work was not recorded. Nevertheless, the slate practice continued for some time and when Mr Grant spied the Inspector approaching, the slates were disposed of quickly. I used the belt very rarely although I always hung it on an obvious spot, usually at the edge of the blackboard. When Mr Grant wished to administer the 'tawse', he sent a pupil through to my room requesting my belt as it had a better 'sting'.

Mr William and Mrs Lily Grant, 1950s

Classrooms were heated by a small stove, later replaced by an anthracite pot-bellied stove brought from Perth Prison and on wet days, coats, hats and gloves were hung around the fire causing steam to rise. The heating system changed when electricity was installed.

Mr Grant retired in 1958 and took up residence in Arbroath. He was replaced by a very much younger, Mr Dick Manders who brought his own talents and conveyed them to the pupils. He was interested in drama and held various school concerts and competitions with other schools. A two-teacher school continued but there were visits from gym, art and music teachers, although in the early days their attendance was erratic. Mr Manders left in 1968 and was posted to a Montrose primary school.

Teachers, Miss Garrow, Mr Manders, cleaner/dinner lady, Mrs Spence, 1960s

A very young Mr Graeme Murray arrived in 1968 as the new headmaster. He also brought along new disciplines and talents, especially music. The school roll was gradually declining due to such reasons as the closure of the quarries in the 1950s, reduction of farm labour and a tendency for smaller families. However, Mr Murray's term saw a 'new' Carmyllie School since in 1970, Kirkden School closed, adding to the school roll as well as the closure of Carmyllie West/ Greystone School a few months later, increasing the roll to over 60. Miss Isobel Beattie from 'the West' joined the staff making a total of three teachers. The school's new name was Carmyllie Primary School. In the past

Carmyllie School, full school roll, teachers:- Graeme Murray, Miss Edith Garrow, Miss Isobel Beattie: presentation to Mrs Spence, cleaner/ dinner lady, 1971

Miss Beattie and I were transported from Arbroath to the East and West school by taxi (except in the most severe weather conditions) sometimes collecting a few children en route.

However, after the schools amalgamated in 1970, a more complex bus system was required and Miss Beattie and I shared a private car. If snowstorms prevented us from reaching Carmyllie we were instructed to attend the nearest school in Arbroath Mr Murray left in 1972 to a deputy-headmaster post in Peebles.

Mr Ian Hendry arrived as the new headmaster, once again with, fresh ideas and a community spirit. With the rising school roll, there arose a need for more accommodation, so a plan for an extension was organised by the Council with Mr Hendry as an advisor.

School is out, 1978

By 1974, Mrs Anne Law was appointed as an additional teacher making four full-time teaching staff, but as there was no classroom for a fourth teacher, my P1 class took up a temporary room in the Carmyllie Hall for ten months during 1974/75. A mini-bus transported me and my class (the only year I taught one single class) to and from the hall four times per day as dinners were served at the school. I thought it was the best year in my teaching life as I was dealing with only one age group and no interference from older pupils.

The following year four classrooms were available since port-a-cabins were installed, providing improved staff toilet facilities and staffroom accommodation, while the old building underwent alterations. As the 'new' school was taking shape, the Carmyllie East School's centenary celebrations took place in 1976. Mr Hendry organised a community gathering when badges were presented in the

31

midst of speeches and music. Each class provided poems, stories and art, which were placed in a casket, which during a small ceremony, was placed with the help of me and one of my pupils, in a hole in the school grounds with the message 'to be opened up in 100 years'. A plaque was made with these instructions, which I hope is placed on the wall in the vicinity.

Unfortunately, Mr Hendry experienced little of the altered school as he was promoted to headmaster

Teachers, Miss Beattie, Mr Ian Hendry, Miss Garrow, 1975   Teachers, Miss Beattie, Miss Garrow, Mr Crawford Taylor, 2 dinner ladies/cleaners, Mrs Ella Martin, Mrs Lena Clark and Secretary, Mrs Doreen Brown, 1981

at Torphins School, Aberdeenshire in 1976.

Mr Crawford Taylor arrived as the new headmaster at the end of 1976. The renovated school was a vast improvement. In addition to four classrooms, there is a nursery, library, office, dining/gym hall, kitchens, toilets for staffroom and children and underfloor heating, while retaining the old stone school building.

The school dinners were served in the stone building at right angles to the road (donated by Duncan, Falconer & Whitton, Quarrymasters, Carmyllie in 1887) until the school was altered in 1976. The meals wre delivered from a central school kitchen at Berryfauld by Arbroath. Children had to 'take it or leave it' as there was no choice or packed lunches. This gradually changed when dinners were served in the 'new' building and the meals were sent from Timmergreens School.

The style of school desks and chairs changed throughout my time. In the early days, there were long seats which caused imbalance if children stood up at one end. It was the teacher's dread on a Friday afternoon when they were notified that there would be a social function such as a Whist Drive and dance in the evening in the school as this entailed removing the partition and lifting all the desks from the classrooms. However, on Monday morning, usually all was restored to normal. Later Mr Manders changed to individual desks with a lid to store the books until a member of the Educational Council attended a meeting in the school classroom and wished to see a more modern approach. The result was that tables were introduced where children sat in groups.

Needlework and knitting was my 'extra-curricular'. One afternoon per week, the older girls settled in my room with their activities and relaxed in a convivial manner. Hats and mitts were produced along with lapbags and, with the sewing machine, the girls advanced on to making skirts and tops.

The school roll reached a peak in the second half of the 1970s, then dipped to a level that only three teachers were required. In 1981, Anne Law moved on to teach at Ladyloan, Arbroath and Miss Beattie and I remained with Crawford Taylor. By 1989, I felt it was time to retire after 39 years service (only one day off work) and I was satisfied that I had taught my pupils well. Miss Beattie who had a similar length of service, retired shortly afterwards.[1]

---

[1] Testimony, Edith Garrow, 2009

Up until 1946 most pupils left school in Carmyllie at 12-14 years old. It was assumed that 6-8 years school education was sufficient for their needs. For over one hundred years, the education was self-contained in the parish, first under control of the heritors then the Local School Board followed by a district School Management and finally all schools were under Angus Council. But self-containment and self-reliance had highlighted how both Angus Council and Carmyllie were unprepared for the wider Council authority when pupils required higher education. It could be suggested, not until the mid-1960s, after the abolition of the '11+', when all children were transported to burgh secondary education, that Carmyllie children were all integrating with both rural and burgh pupils.

Chapter 3

CARMYLLIE QUARRIES and RAILWAY

About 4000 million years ago, our planet formed, though in geological terms, it was only very recently; about 10 thousand years ago that modern man began to populate the Earth. Long before man's arrival, the weather conditions on the planet were very different. It was extremely hot, so hot that desert conditions prevailed over much of the Earth. Some parts were covered in desert sand, whereas other parts like Carmyllie had wide expanses of lakes and lagoons. The grey sandstone found in Carmyllie was formed in these lagoons and is referred to as mudstone. We know this from the many fossils found in the Carmyllie quarries, in particular from the shellfish. An example is a fossilised hard-backed shell-fish called *Pterygotus Anglicus* found in Carmyllie Quarry, an example of which can be seen in Montrose Museum today. This desert landscape was in existence for fifty million years and is known as the Red Sandstone Era, developing a maximum thickness of twenty thousand feet, and some of these fossils have been found in this grey sandstone about one thousand feet deep.

Many millions of years later, volcanic activity resulted in the formation of the Sidlaw hills. In the area which is now Carmyllie, pressure and heat underground metamorphosed the grey sandstone and formed new minerals that stratified the rocks, thus allowing layers to split easily. A bed of this grey sandstone runs from the Montrose area, south-west towards the Sidlaw Hills and there is an area in Carmyllie, 1½ miles in length and ½ mile wide, where this metamorphosed rock outcrops through the Old Red Sandstone that overlies most of Angus. In Carmyllie, this stratified rock is in abundance and has produced high quality Carmyllie Pavement of varying thicknesses.

The geological sketch map shows the different rock structures and the principal quarries in Angus. The nearby

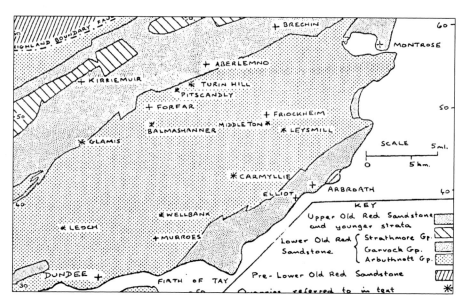

Geology Sketch of principal quarries and towns in Angus (*Geology after Armstrong and Paterson, 1970*)

quarries, similar to Carmyllie are Middleton at Friockheim, Leysmill and Wellbank, but the best quality and most extensive deposits of 'pavement' were at Carmyllie. There were many other old quarries in Angus including those worked for whinstone and although whinstone never gained the importance of the sandstone quarries in the 18th and 19th centuries, there are whinstone quarries active today utilising the crushed rock to build roads. Denfind Quarry at Monikie produced very similar pavement to Carmyllie and was operated by the Nairn Brothers who also latterly operated the Slade Quarries. This quarry has recently been re-opened and produces stone for house facings, dyking and garden ornament.

Stone was quarried in Carmyllie and used locally for centuries. In early times, all quarrying would seem to be carried out near the surface, as stronger implements were unavailable to obtain stone from lower strata. Quarrying slate and pavement in Carmyllie in fact was practiced for centuries as

Carmyllie stone is found in the soutterains, which date to the time of the Roman occupation. Commissary Maule, the historian of the Maule family, writing in 1611(*Registrum de Panmure*), said Carmyllie was 'the four part of the baronie of Panmor' and 'for the maist part it is al heighe'. There were fourteen main settlements in 'Carmyly' *viz.* Mains, Auchlair, Quhythil, Westhilles, Midhilles, Backhilles, Paupertland, Newtowne, Miltone, Crospos Hil, Goit, Murheads, Newlandis and Corsden. Most of the settlements, especially Quhyhil, Westhilles, Midhilles and Backhilles had been important to the Panmure Estate, providing quarried stone for such things as buildings, walls and millstones and he refers to 'the bak hilles of Carmyly' as the furthest north of the 'four part of the baronie of Panmor'.[i]

In 1682, John Ouchterlony (*Account of the Shire of Forfar*) noted that 'the country abounded in quarries of freestone excellent for hewing and cutting.' At the end of seventeenth century, there was no mention of the Carmyllie quarries in the Panmure Estate Rental books but by the beginning of the eighteenth century, Lord Panmure managed the Slade quarry as a separate business. In 1739, during the forfeiture of Panmure Estate, the Yorks Buildings Company sub-leased the quarries to Mr Gorden Troup.

With the aid of lime and marl(*e*), farmland was much improved and from 1770 onwards, the run-rig system changed to farm enclosures that would have required large quantities of stone for buildings and dykes. Carmyllie has lost a great many of its dykes but those at Glentyrie, in particular, represent good examples of vernacular dyking. By 1790, Carmyllie slate and pavement was transported to Fife, Perthshire, and the Mearns. In the early days of quarrying in Carmyllie, the local

Road leading to Carmyllie (Slade) quarries, 1880

farmers seem to quarry stone as a sideline. In 1810, it was reported that the farmer at East Hills employed eight quarrymen who reported to their master there was no stone left. Suitable stone close to the surface was probably becoming scarce, requiring stronger implements to quarry at deeper levels. Several small quarries round the Slade belonging to the Panmure Estate, were let to a single tenant around this time. In 1809 and 1810, Carmyllie roof slate of 1 inch to 1 ¼ inches and pavement from 1 inch to 14 inches thick was advertised in the press and a substantial industry was now developing.

The quarries began to work more intensively, excavating and obtaining larger slabs of stone using such tools as picks and crowbars. This brought its own problems with floodwater and moveable framed windmills were introduced to pump the water but these were only successful when there was a drive of wind. Around 1820, Panmure concluded that it was necessary to prevent flooding. He funded, at the cost of £3000, the building of a drain through hard sandstone, part of it through a cut of forty feet depth, to drain the main quarry between East Hills and Slade farm. The tunnel was 180 yards long, 3 feet deep and 3½ feet high. It was reported that they employed a small crane fit to lift a ton in weight, the strongest piece of machinery available at that time.

The pavement stone (becoming known as 'Arbroath Pavement') was squared in the quarry and up to 30 cartloads were transported to Arbroath where it was shipped to Leith, London, Glasgow and Aberdeen. Shipping to Aberdeen became more feasible after the removal of the coastal duty beyond Redhead near Montrose. In 1837, J.Carmichael stated 'that flagstones, some 60 feet long, were raised by crowbars and mattocks [a type of pick]'. Sixty men were now employed, some earned 10/- to 12/- per week or £4 - £6 for 1000 feet of pavement. All stones were squared into uniform sizes and were sold as common pavement, stair steps or roof slates

Remains of engine shed, Slade quarrires (2010)

and sent to London, France and America. In addition, urbanisation was increasing in Scotland requiring pavements for new streets as well as flagstones for housing, hence pavement stone was more in demand than slate. The New Statistical Accounts indicate in 1836, that income from paving stone (£2579) and slates (£172), far exceeded that of barley (£1768).

Stone quarrying was about to be revolutionised. In 1833, James Hunter, Leysmill, was inventing a stone planing machine encouraged by the local Laird, Lindsay-Carnegie of Boysack and by the 1840s, it was ready to be manufactured in Arbroath. His son George, continued in his father's footsteps and invented a stone cutting, cast iron circular saw and together with the planing machine, quarrying changed into a manufacturing industry. There were 30 machines distributed to quarries in Angus, 10 of which were required at Carmyllie and with the addition of the 'new age' of steam, a quarry 'factory' developed.

The new cutting machinery allowed a great increase in the production of pavement stone and to allow the ever-increasing orders to be fulfilled with this heavy product, Lord Panmure instigated the building of a branch railway line from the Dundee-Arbroath line at Elliot to Redford and this was completed in 1855. On the way up from Elliot to collect paving stone, the railway wagons often carried coal and delivered to small stations en route to Redford. Gradually the railway developed to carry other products such as sugar beet, potatoes and cattle and for a time, there was also a passenger service.

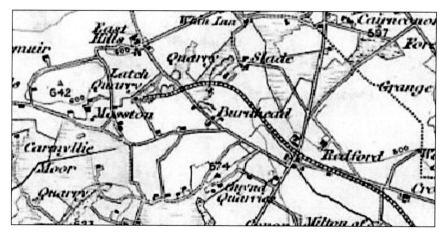
The railway line extended beyond Redford, past the Slade to Latch Quarry
(NLS, O.S.1"1.63,360 1st edition, 1857-63)

36

With the invention of the new machines, the 'Benches' at the Slade became the factory where the stone was cut, planed and shaped. As well as the machines increasing productivity, they also allowed the production of a variety of specialised stone items such as cisterns, parts for chemical works, paper works and bleach fields, columns, balustrades and other architectural ornaments. All the machines were set in line and a belt, powered from the steam engine room, drove the machinery. One of the quarry workers, Chae Fairweather, who was a quarry labourer from 1925 to 1927, recalls that each worker carried a spanner and if for any reason a machine was faulty or someone was in danger, the spanner would throw the belt on to a smaller wheel, thus stopping the machinery.

Railway track from Guynd quarry joining the Slade track towards the 'Benches'. (NAS, RHP 2600, 1880)

In addition to the Slade Quarries, often referred to as the Carmyllie Quarries and part of Panmure Estate, there was also the Guynd Quarry that was run on a smaller scale and under separate management.

The Guynd quarry was owned by James Pierson, then proprietor of the Guynd and brother-in-law of the Ouchterlony family. It was leased to a firm run by David Barry and George and William Galloway paying an annual rent of £120. The Quarry also benefited from the Elliot to Redford railway line. A junction from a railway track leading to the Slade quarries connected to the Guynd quarry and the direction of the track from the Guynd veers towards the Slade quarry, as shown on the map. This suggests that there was co-operation between the quarrymaster of the Guynd quarry and the Slade quarrymasters, since trucks would load on or off at the 'Benches'. Perhaps some stone was dressed there, but all would be loaded on railway wagons en route to Redford then onwards to Elliot.

Nonetheless, there was less production from the Guynd quarry and the duration of trade was shorter although the quality of stone was in demand and in 1872, the quarry was denoted on the map as 'Pavement Quarry, Quarryhead and Cottage'. There had however been a sizeable number of men employed as the Arbroath Guide newspaper reports in 1876 that there was an annual outing to the 'pond' at the Guynd mansion house, permission given by Mrs Pierson. Messrs Barry and Galloway, Guynd quarry masters, entertained the quarriers accompanied by wives and sweethearts:-

Remains of shop, Slade quarries (2012)

.....'A party of 140 left the quarries at 1pm with flags flying and pipers playing. They marched down in front of the mansion house to the pond. Luncheon was served followed by sports and dancing. Messrs Barry & Galloway supplied tea. It started to rain so the party proceeded to a barn where dancing resumed until 9pm.'

Messrs Barry and Galloway continued trading after 1876 at the Guynd Quarry and Quarryhead but trading ceased in the early 1880s. As the quarry was at the extremities of the Guynd Estate, the quarriers were limited when following a seam of pavement stone as work would stop before encroaching on the land at

Drummygar, which was owned by Panmure Estates. Therefore the land suitable for quarrying at the Guynd quarry had its limitations and they simply ran out of workable stone.

By 1870 pavement production at the Slade was at its peak when 300-500 men were employed.

The quarrymaster's names varied although the Duncan family were known as quarrymasters for generations. In 1871, the firm Duncan, Falconer, Whitton & Co had two quarrymasters residing at the Slade, William Duncan and David Whitton while Donald Falconer lived at Milton of Conon.

Almost twenty years later in 1890, the quarrymaster William Duncan had 'the representatives' of Whitton and Falconer in the firm, but by 1891 there remained only William Duncan but now joined by his son, William Duncan, jnr.

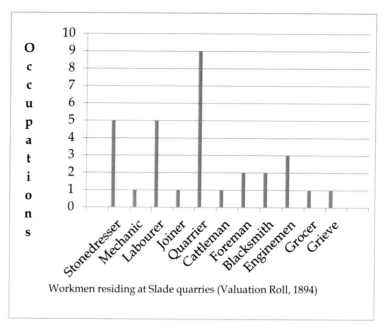

Workmen residing at Slade quarries (Valuation Roll, 1894)

By 1894, William Duncan jnr. and his brother-in-law, James Wright were the two partners in the firm, Duncan, Falconer &Co which leased both the Slade Farm and the Quarries from Panmure Estate.

The adjacent graph shows that there were 31 people employed and living in the Slade quarry environs in 1894. There were twice as many quarriers as there were stonedressers and labourers because excavating the stone was more labour intensive. Yet the stonedressing employment was relatively high and there was a demand for stonedressing skills to make columns, steps and ornamental objects. The engine room was the 'hub' of the industry requiring three men to operate the steam power. Two blacksmiths were engaged in making and repairing metalwork. The grieve, cattleman and perhaps one foreman would be attached to the Slade farm which was leased to neighbouring farms. There was also a grocer's shop run by Miss Isa Duncan to serve the various trades and labourers residing at the Slade.

Stained glass window in Carmyllie Parish Church, donated by William Duncan in memory of his father, c.1900 (artist unknown)

James Wright had an impact in the area. He came to the Parish in 1892 as a mature man (age 53) and took a wide interest in the community. When he joined the Church in1892, he was very shortly found 'fit to be made an elder' and was soon a member of the Kirk Session, donating various gifts to the Church in the last decade of the century. He was appointed Chairman of the School Board. In 1898, David Duncan occupied the Slade House, which was built for him as quarrymaster around that time while James Wright lived in the Slade farmhouse.

Joe Fairweather of Redford Post Office was interviewed in the mid 1960s when he was over 80 years old and he had lived and worked in the Carmyllie quarries at the beginning of the 20th century. He remembers......

The quarries were owned by Duncan, Galloway & Co. The quarrymasters must have rented the Slade farmhouse and the other house was at the quarry. They did not work the farm however, and it was probably leased to someone else.
The quarries could be seen from far around because of the large hill of waste.
Unlike earlier times, the men were employed all the year but if the weather was frosty, they were paid off. Last century {19th century} the men employed at the quarries would come from Letham, Friockheim, Arbroath and the entire district around. They had to walk to work or lodge in the area during the week. They worked a 12 hour day:

6.a.m.- 9a.m.	- work
9am – 9.30am.	- breakfast
1.30pm – 2.30pm	- lunch
6 pm	- home

At the turn of 20th century, the pay was about 12/- to15/- per week, generally paid in gold and silver. The workers included a foreman, men and boys, the latter starting as soon as they left school at 14 or, in earlier years, at 11.

Latterly there were two blacksmiths employed to renew the blades of cutting and planing machinery and a mechanic for repairs. A mason was also employed to do the final finishing or to carry out any fancy work for special orders. His work was all done by hand.

Conditions were very dusty and dirty – many of the older people suffered from dust in the lungs (silicosis). Even so, many lived to a ripe old age. A doctor came to check the men

Slade Quarries, c. 1900

and conditions, but this examination was not always thorough.

When a good seam of pavement stone was found, the men just followed it, and the working of the quarries was not systematic. As the quarries worked further into the ground, water had to be pumped away. Today as this is not done, the quarries have a considerable depth of water in them.

The amount of slate or pavement produced each year ran into many thousands of tons. It varied however, with the thickness of the pavement. Once ready it was sent by rail to Elliot and then on to Glasgow. There was a little donkey engine on the premises for the purpose of shunting"

James Geddes at the 'bottling machine, early 1940s (Geddes family)

Joe remarked that when he worked at the quarry at the end of the 19th century, the quarriers were employed all year round but in earlier years work was on-going only if the weather was favourable. It is thought that in the last quarter of the century, a light timber and corrugated iron roof was built over the Benches to protect men and machinery from bad weather.

By 1900, there was a fall in demand for pavement stone due to competition from other materials such as brick, concrete and cement and perhaps this prompted quarrymasters, Duncan and Wright, to form a limited Company. In 1901 James Wright registered as a director along with four other directors in Duncan, Galloway & Co. Ltd.

Being a director, James Wright was now salaried, enabling him to dispose of his own income without inconveniencing the Company. His generosity extended to commissioning the renowned stained glass designer, Stephen Adam from Glasgow, to place the 'rose' window in Carmyllie Parish Church in 1903. James Wright probably developed an interest in the arts while the Company was trading in Glasgow as

Joe Fairweather remarked that much of the Carmyllie stone was then transported from Elliot to Glasgow. This window is an example of the genius of Stephen Adam's work and influenced the parishioners, as in 1908, subscribers throughout the country commissioned a further two long windows by the same artist in memory of Patrick Bell, the inventor of the reaper.

The old Quarry lease from Panmure Estate expired in 1908 and the Slade farm and Carmyllie Quarries were let separately. Charles McDonald leased the Slade farm and farmhouse. A further fall in production was caused by a building trade slump and that coupled with increasing transport costs, started to make the quarries unprofitable. James Wright moved into Arbroath in 1909 but remained quarrymaster and a director until 1914. Duncan, Galloway & Co Ltd fell into liquidation in 1918.

Panmure Estate sold all of its property in Carmyllie around 1922 and the quarries, quarry master's

At work in Slade quarries, Jim Murray, Jim Geddes with Davie Nairn (quarrymaster), early 1940s (Geddes family)

house and cottages were bought by two brothers, Alexander and David Nairn who had leased the quarry after the War. They took up residence in the Slade house. Slade farm and cottages were bought by their tenant, Charles McDonald.

George Robertson and Jim Geddes at the 'Benches', early 1940s

Chae Fairweather was interviewed in the 1980s. He was a labourer at the quarries between 1925 and 1927 and remembers.....

I was paid 35/- per week or 10d. per hour. The workers' hours were from 6am to 6pm with a half day on Saturday and a full day off on Sunday. If bad weather occurred, the quarrying stopped and the men were paid by the hour."

There were around 30-50 men employed, among them being a stone mason, a blacksmith and a 'gaffer' at the Benches and another 'gaffer' and sawman at the quarry face.

At the Benches there were two blades used for cutting the stone; each blade was five feet in diameter, and these could be set to the width required. The planing machine smoothed down the stone and the bottling machine formed

shapes. The 'breakers' broke the rejected stone into uniform sizes to be used for road works but this was not too successful. The hammer mill crushed the stone into powder, which was used for surfacing asphalt roofing. A crane driven by steam power from the engine, lifted the rough stone on to the benches and also lifted the dressed stone on to train wagons.

The water for the steam power was pumped from a deep hole nearby into a large boiler which was heated by a big furnace stoked with cheap coal. On the first day of the annual holiday (one week), three men were employed to clean out the 'fur' inside the boiler and also the flues leading to the furnace.

The 'donkey' engines brought the stone from the quarry face and the rail track was extended so that it would always be near the actual quarrying. The stone was dug out manually as explosives would shatter it, especially if a big slab was required and further care was needed to ensure that each stone was free of cracks, as it would split in the cutting machine. Paving stones were made but demand was falling. Repairs to worn-down stone steps were common. Specifications were sent so that a piece of stone would fit the curve to level the step. At this time, one train load of stone was transported to Arbroath daily.

Ernie McKay worked in the Slade quarries from 1938-1940. In 1938, Ernie left Kirkden School at 14 and followed his father to work in the Slade quarries as 'the loon'. He remembers....

"I was employed by the Nairn brothers (Dave & Eck) who lived in the Slade house where their mother kept house. There were at least 16 men working in the quarries at that time, another boy was the same age as me but the remainder were middle aged and older. We worked five and a half days per week, 7.45am to 5pm on weekdays with one hour for our lunch and 7.45 – 12noon on Saturday. I cannot remember having any holidays. I was paid 10/- per week which went directly towards my mother's housekeeping. When I received a rise of 2/6, I kept that for myself

My job was mostly helping around the 'Benches', although I went to the Post Office at Redford every day to

The 'Benches' after the closure of the quarries, early 1950s

Derelict quarry buildings after closure, early 1950s.George Robertson with grandchild (Geddes family)

collect the mail. If the train was collecting stone I would get a lift to the Redford station near to the P.O. My favourite job was collecting all the rubble from the dressed stone with a barrow, and this was loaded on to a trailer, which was pulled up by a wire rope to the top of the 'bing'. I watched through the high window at the Benches, noting the bogie rising and when it reached the top there was a man ready to tip the load after which the emptied trailer returned to be filled again. Lorries came constantly to collect the rubble to be delivered to HMS Condor at Arbroath to form a base for the air runway. Sometimes I would accompany the lorry driver on a return trip down to Condor.

There were many window and door lintels made at the quarries but there was also a high standard of shaped columns from the bottling machine. The men working close to these machines were usually surrounded by dust. (My father suffered from silicosis in later life). The high-pitched screeching noise from the cutting machine was excruciating.'The Benches' was a long line of equipment enclosed by a roof starting at the west end with the coal fired *engine room which drove the long shaft connecting to the bottling machine, followed by the planer then the saw.*

There was a gaffer at the Benches (George Petrie) and a gaffer at the quarries (George Robertson). Every year (spring/summer), the Benches stopped say, for about two weeks, and all the men (except me) worked in the quarries removing slabs of stone.My duty was watchman in the engine room but I was a bit apprehensive being alone with this massive, spitting, hissing engine.

The railway was the only means of transporting the stone. One of my jobs was to go out searching for squares of turf used for placing in between the layers of stones for protection when loading on to the train. I think the trains were irregular when picking up a load, not every week.

I do not remember much about the quarry office being used by Dave and Eck Nairn although Dave was often overseeing the benches whereas Eck would be at the quarry face.

I left the quarries to become a farmworker in early 1940 where the pay was slightly better although the insecurity of the Second World War made me look for fresh pastures. The older men continued to work at the quarries, including my father.

Collapsed 'Benches' after windstorm, 1953

The Nairn Brothers closed the quarries after the Second World War and in 1953, after a violent windstorm, the buildings at the Benches collapsed. The picture shows the extent of the tin and slate roof on a wooden frame. Later in 1953, the quarries closed and the property and land were sold to the McDonalds of Slade farm.

Tractor Rescue

After the Guynd quarries closed c.1880, the area was neglected and the quarry holes filled with dangerously deep water. Jim Wallace relates why a tractor, rescued from the water in 1976, came to be there under tragic circumstances.

I was told that there was an iron-wheeled 1919 Fordson tractor lying at the bottom of a water hole in the Guynd quarry. Having a tremendous interest in old tractors and puzzled as to why the tractor landed there, I furthered my enquiries to discover that in 1941, the Drummygar farmer was harrowing a field bordering the quarry when, as he was turning at the end, he ventured too near the edge of the quarry drop. Perhaps he panicked since, if he had removed his foot from the clutch the tractor would have stalled. Instead, the tractor lost grip and tractor, harrows and tractorman fell

Tractor rescued after 35 years under water, 1976
(Jim Wallace)

into the twenty feet hole with the harrows on top of the tractor. (After the tractor was rescued, it was discovered that a tooth had broken in the steering box so the tractor driver had lost the power of steering). Miraculously the man broke free and swam to the edge where field workers looked down at the predicament. It was reported that ropes were thrown to the casualty. However, more recent reports highlight that horse harness reins were used, being what was at hand. (Horses had not been completely replaced by the tractor as yet and together they worked the machinery). He grasped the reins and, while being pulled up the steep edge of the quarry face, the excessive strain caused the reins to snap and the man fell back into the deep water. The rescue was in vain.

Guynd Quarry, 1976 (Jim Wallace)

Carmyllie Railway

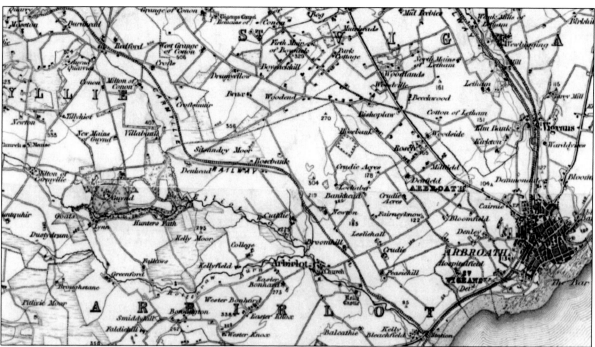

The Carmyllie railway line running from Elliot junction on the Dundee/Arbroath line to Redford (NLS, Ref: 2622/13, 1856-63)

The construction of the single-track mineral line began in March 1854 and was completed in April 1855. The need for a railway line was accelerated by the invention of the stone-cutting machine that increased the output of Carmyllie paving stone.

The building plan for the railway had few complications since the five-mile stretch of line was within Lord Panmure's land and it was in his interest to encourage the quarry industry growth, receiving a substantial rent from the quarrymasters (rateable value, £519.00 in 1876).[2]

The Arbroath Guide reported in 1854 that:-

> 'The whole of the line is now marked out, with the exception of a portion of the
> east side of Kelly Den on which there will be considerable labour. A good deal
> of trees will have to be cut down some hundred yards before the descent into the
> Dell called Teuchat, below the Bank of Arbirlot, and other patches further north.'[3]

Ticket Office, Redford Station (Arbroath Guide) 1904

On the 7 April 1855, the railway was formally opened by the Directors of the Dundee and Arbroath line who proceeded in a first class carriage from Elliot to Redford to inspect it. There were halts on the picturesque line at Bank of Arbirlot, Cuthlie and Denhead, rising from sea level to almost 600 feet with sharp curves and steep gradients, the most severe being 1 in 36 at Kelly Den. There was a 'staff'(key) held at Elliot to be given to the engine driver. This ensured that two trains could not be on the single line at the same time.

---

[2] Valuation Roll, 1876
[3] Files of Arbroath Guide, 1854

Goods train at Redford crossing

(Arbroath Herald)1950s

By 1860, the railway was working to full capacity bringing coal, fertiliser, cattle feed and livestock on the upward journey but always returning with paving stone. Wagon loads of coal from Elliot was a beneficial fuel power for Carmyllie parish as previously, either coal was hauled from Easthaven on the Tay estuary by horse and cart, or peat was collected locally from Dilty Moss for domestic heating. From Redford, the empty wagons were shunted to the 'benches' at the Slade quarries and loaded with paving stone. There was also a track to the Guynd quarries that used 'donkey' engines to drive stone to 'the benches' sharing the wagons with the Slade quarries.

Passenger Line

Carmyllie Passenger line is noteworthy as it was the first light railway to allow passengers after the Light Railway Act in 1898. The line was reconstructed and opened to passengers in February 1900. Initially there were three coaches and a few goods wagons with a second engine. Passengers all travelled 3rd Class and the coaches were four wheeled with no dividing partitions and the interior had plain chocolate-coloured wooden seats. The first engines had stove-pipe chimneys but the wheel arrangement was unsuitable for the sharp curves on the line. Later, alternative engines were provided but because of the steep gradient, there were many jibes about the 'Carmyllie Express'. One Carmyllie lady, Mrs Law, remembers travelling to school by train to Arbroath from Arbirlot. On the return journey, while climbing Kelly Den, the children leapt off the train, ran back to shout at the guardsman, then jumped on again before the train gained speed. The train timetable had been lax as the train driver was able to stop at convenient spots to set his rabbit snares and on his return journey, he would collect his spoil.

Nevertheless, the farmers' wives used the train on Saturdays when they travelled to Arbroath market with their baskets full of eggs and butter. It was a common sight to see the farmers with their horse and gig lined up at Redford in the late afternoon, waiting for their wives to return from the town.

At first three passenger trains ran per day except Sunday but throughout the twenty-nine years of service, passengers were meagre and later only two trains ran per day. The waiting room and ticket office at Redford were small and rarely busy. William Walker was stationmaster for a number of years and Sandy Duncan was porter.

Alastair Garden, Backboath remembers travelling by train to and from Arbroath to attend the High School (now Arbroath Library):
I cycled from Backboath farm to Redford, leaving my bicycle at Alex Webster, shoemaker and coal merchant. I travelled by train from 1926 to 1929, accompanied by Rev McVicar's family, two of the boys

Approaching Redford Station with ticket office and waiting shelter on left

and I attended the High School while Dorothy was employed in the town. I bought a weekly ticket at Redford station and this was not checked, as the stationmaster (Mr Duncan) knew everyone who was travelling. The train was invariably late in the morning, especially in winter months – October to March- due to leaves and debris on the line and the engine's wheels struggled to take grip. Delays

45

could be also due to the irregular delivery of parcels at the small stations en route to Redford. We were often late for school. Very few passengers disembarked on the journey down but some pupils would embark, especially at Bank of Arbirlot. When the train arrived at Elliot junction, the train stopped in order to change the points before moving into Arbroath at Keptie. On the return journey,

we joined the Arbroath/Dundee train, which stopped at Elliot where we got out and joined the Redford train that was waiting for us.

The passenger train stopped in 1929, as there were not many customers. Duncan, the stationmaster, repaired clocks in his spare time. I continued to travel by bus for the last two years of my schooling. The bus driver had extra duties,

Railway Enthusiasts Special heading for Carmyllie with Locomotives 46464 (The Carmyllie Pilot) and 46463. 1959

for example, he picked up a can of milk from Melville, Dummiesholes, to be delivered in Arbroath. One morning, the driver, driving recklessly, braked heavily at the Den of Arbirlot. The can of milk shot down the passageway of the bus, tilted against the bus doors, which flew open, and the passengers heard the milk can contents gurgling on to the road.

Jack Clark was a porter on duty at Redford Station between 1951 and 1956, since Carnie Fullerton remembers visiting and chatting with Jack in the station master's house after Carnie came off the school bus around 4.30 pm.

The goods service continued until the early sixties although latterly carrying only wagon loads of potatoes. Finally the railway line closed in 1965 and the rail tracks were lifted shortly afterwards.

Alexander 'Podge' Duncan, last Stationmaster at Carmyllie (photo gifted by Mrs Pearl Duncan Arbroath)

After the demise of the Carmyllie quarries at the outbreak of World War 2, there was still a certain amount of activity with the railway serving agricultural needs as related in the following poem:

The Carmyllie Express (Anonymous)

(Donated by Iain Bell, Arbroath whose father, Thos. W.L. Bell, was a railway enthusiast and a retired coal merchant at Forfar Station, which closed due to the 'Beeching Cuts' in 1967)

About Arbroath and its Abbey O
We often read with pleasure
Its model railway, its famous
Smokies
Have both received full measure
But in our midst runs a train
With fame you may not guess
And known to railmen, old and
young
As the Arbroath and Carmyllie
Express

Each morning in the yard
Be it sunshine, snow or rain
The Guard goes off to sort his
van
And prepare this famous train
We shunt off first the 'Caley
Goods'
And the 'Kirrie' too no less
Then comes our most essential
task
To run the Carmyllie Express

One trip per day is all we run
For the farmers and their need
Some coal and goods and odd
livestock
With potatoes for England as
seed
The engine power, old 5622
Without disgrace I confess
No modern stream-lined
locomotive
But affectionately called 'Old
Jess'.

It's really most important of
course
That we should run to time
Six days a week in winter
And three in summertime
No matter if the yard is full
Or otherwise in a mess
Or Muir and Hood want wagons
placed
Can't stop the Carmyllie Express

So off we go to Elliot Junction
Where the Driver gets the staff
Crossing the road to Kelly Den
And the Fireman starts to graft
Then up the braes we begin to
climb
Giving Old Jess all she's got
While gauges show a full head of
steam
As we pass through Arbirlot

No thriving towns with busy works
Or tunnels to thunder through
With shrieking whistles that
Drivers jerk
Like a boy with a toy that's new
But woods and fields are our
daily scene
Perhaps a wave from the kiddies
on foot
And we bring the cottars to their
doors
At the crossing with a 'toot'.

But higher still we climb to
Cuthlie
With a stop for Ganger Wyllie
And if no traffic for Denhead
The next stop is Carmyllie
And so we reach our destination
Once again we do it on time
All the way from Elliot junction
Five miles of single line.

We see a spot of wild life here

Which makes our trips quite
pleasant
With rabbits, hares and pitraiks
too
And sometimes a pair of
pheasants
Of course, it's true, we have our
trials
It's certainly not all fun
With greasy rails, bad steaming
coal
And sands that will not run

The Appendix says our railway's
light
Tho' sometimes our traffic is
But when we load the potatoes
and beet
It's then we see some 'biz'
Ten, twelve, or even fourteen
wagons
They hang on old 'Tess's' tail
And tho' she groans an squeaks
and squeals
You never see her fail

About the staff, there're nine in
all
First Charlie the Porter, that's ane
A Driver, Fireman and a Guard
And of course Inspector McKae
With his two men that repair the
line
Along with Ganger Wyllie
And lastly we have the Agent on
From Elliot to Carmyllie

You may have heard of other
famous trains
All over the railway system
'The Royal Scotsman', 'The
Aberdonian'
But do we need to list them
For no matter where you travel
From Carlisle to Inverness
There's not a train I will maintain
Like the Arbroath and Carmyllie
Express.

Sources for Chapter 3

Primary Sources
Angus Census 1871, 1881, 1891
NAS, Kirk Session Minutes, CH2/558/5, 1890-1910
Old Statistical Account (OSA) Carmyllie, Rev Patrick Bryce, 1790
New Statistical Account (NSA), Carmyllie 1843
National Archives for Scotland (NAS) Company Papers, Duncan, Galloway & Co Ltd, 1901-1918, West Register House, Edinburgh
Angus Valuation Rolls 1890- 1952

Published Primary Sources
Ouchterlony, John, *Account of the Shire of Forfar* (The Forfar and District Historical Society, Nov 1969)
Registrum De Panmure by John Stuart, (Editor). Privately Printed, Edinburgh 1874

Maps
County of Forfar, by John Ainslie, 1794, 1801
National Archives for Scotland, RHP 2600 (1880)
Ordanance Survey, Sheet XLV – 6 inch to 1 mile, 1859, 1926

Personal Interviews
        Alastair Garden, 2012
        Chae Fairweather, 1985
        Ernie McKay, 2009
        Joe Fairweather, 1960s

Newspapers
Arbroath Guide 1876, 1902 and1908
Arbroath Herald, cuttings miscellaneous, Vol. 3 Nov 1908

Other Sources
Bremner, D., 'The Industries of Scotland, 1869

Carmichael, J., 'An Account of the Principal Marble, Slate, Sandstone, and Greenstone Quarries in Scotland', Prize Essays and Transactions of the Highland and Agricultural Society of Scotland, new series, v.5, p409. 1837.

Hay, George, *Around About the Round 'O'*, (Arbroath: Thomas Buncle & Co, 1883)

Hay, George, *History of Arbroath*, (Arbroath: Thomas Buncle & Co., 1899)

Hickling, George, 'The Old Sandstone Rocks near Arbroath', Part lll, Proceedings of the Geologist Association Vol 23, Issue 5, pp 299-301 (Elsevier Ltd, 1912)

Mackie, Alexander, 'Sandstone Quarrying in Angus – some thoughts of an old craft', (Reprinted from 'The Edinburgh Geologist' Autumn 1980, no. 8)

McBain, J.M., *Arbroath Past & Present*, 1887

Chapter 4

HANDLOOM WEAVERS AND QUARRIERS

In 1836, there were remarkable numbers of handloom linen weavers in the parish. The Rev William Robertson wrote that 'the pavement quarries are not worked in winter' and 'several of the quarriers having been bred to the loom, resume that employment [weaving] during that season.' However he further explains that 'spinning flax by machinery has increased in neighbouring towns and many young women have betaken themselves to weaving....and in the event of their becoming wives, forms no good training for their management of household affairs'[1]

Handloom Weaving

Keeping to our study period, this chapter will explain the demise of the handloom weavers in the parish and the rise of quarriers, which accounted for the higher population in Carmyllie when most Angus rural populations were in decline. (See graph p.5)

In the second half of the eighteenth century and the first few decades of the nineteenth, manufacturers built up a large coarse linen industry within Dundee's hinterland, using the 'putting out' system. That is, spun yarn delivered by horse and cart, to weavers in their own homes where they had a static loom that required room space.This proved to be more economical than employing weavers in town factories, where there were larger overheads. Also weavers, sustaining themselves on pendicles or crofts, were advantageous to the manufacturer as there was no real hardship if wages were kept to a minimum during slumps in the trade.

During the last decade of the eighteenth century, the hand spinner was replaced by successful factory spinning mills and by the early 1800s there was an increased demand for handloom weavers to weave the increased supplies of yarn although rates of pay remained low.

Mossend, Carmyllie (2013)

By 1820, the steam power loom factories in towns were producing regular supplies of coarse linen that should have replaced rural and inland town handloom weavers, but factory employment was set at a higher rate of pay. Just as modern day textiles are made in parts of the world where labour is cheaper, coarse linen manufacturers from the Angus seaports, Dundee, Arbroath and Montrose, still found it profitable to deliver yarn to weavers and collect webs from inland towns and rural pendicles in Angus some forty years after power looms became operational.[2]

NLS, O.S. 1 inch 1st edition, 1857-1863

Carmyllie's many pendicles spread over the parish allowed a way of life where there was suitable weaving employment for part-time quarriers and

---

[1] *NSA,* Carmyllie Parish
[2] Law, p 132

an opportunity for manufacturers to 'put out' yarn on weekly carriers, returning with webs of coarse linen to Dundee, Arbroath and perhaps Montrose. Probably Dundee carriers attended to weavers on the west of the parish while carriers from Arbroath or Montrose served the east.

Handloom weavers in Carmyllie tended to live in clusters, usually accessible to main thoroughfares. For example, in 1841, there were 10 at Cononsyth and 8 at Drummygar serving Arbroath while there were 16 at Greystone, 5 at Currend, 10 within the vicinity of Cotton of Carnegie and 14 around Diltymoss, all within easy access to the Carmyllie-Dundee road.[3]

By 1851, although there were fewer weavers, the clusters remained, 16 at Drummygar, 8 around

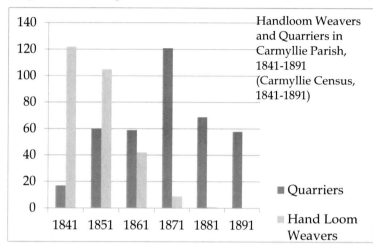

Handloom Weavers and Quarriers in Carmyllie Parish, 1841-1891 (Carmyllie Census, 1841-1891)

Cononsythh, 17 at Greystone, 12 on the fringes of Dilty Moss and 13 at Cotton and Muir of Carnegie. By 1861, handloom weavers had halved in number and were grouped in smaller numbers, 3 at Greystone, 3 at Smallburn and 7 from East Skechen to Dilty Moss for Dundee collections and approximately 5 in the Redford area and 6 at Cononsyth.

The graph shows the declining number of handloom weavers over thirty years from 120 to fewer than 10 while there was an extraordinary increase in quarriers from 1861 to 1871, over 100%, falling back to under 50% in the next ten years. Yet the drop of quarriers in ten years from 1871 to 1881 was partly due to the closure of the Guynd quarry in the 1870s.[4] From the first graph showing the decrease of weavers and the rise of quarriers, it could be assumed that weavers moved to quarrying as less weaving was required. However, the second graph reveals male weavers' employment was reduced by half by 1851 while there was an increase in women weavers, possibly receiving wages cut to the bone. It also illustrates that more quarry labour was available at more attractive wages than say, farm labourers.

At this stage of the weavers' decline, to keep work sustainable, households were maximising the output from one loom. For example, David Muggins' family consisting of himself, his wife and three daughters were handloom weavers plus an elderly female relative who was a yarn winder, all occupying a croft of ten acres at Greystone.[5]

Ten years later, female weavers' work was supplementing the household income as sole operators but this eventually became unsustainable. Weavers' wages were squeezed even further with the downturn of the linen industry, gradually replaced by jute manufacturing after 1841 and in full production by 1871. Some still struggled on and at Berryhillock, a pendicle near West Hills, there were three weavers, one male and two females as well as a female (age 40)' formerly a weaver but now a pauper'.

[3] Census, Carmyllie, 1841
[4] Ibid, 1871, 1881
[5] Census, Carmyllie, 1851

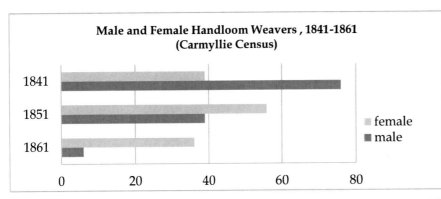

Male quarriers tended to occupy homes around Redford and the Slade although in 1861 there were 7 in Greystone and one or two in the vicinity of Mossend, but a noticeable reduction in small pendicles. With the build up of the Guynd quarry, 6 lived in cottages at Glentyrie while there were three at the Slade and 5 at East Hills. Around 1871, the most productive years of stone quarrying in the parish, there was a heavy concentration of quarriers at the Slade, 37 in total, although there were 10 in Greystone, 3 at North Mains, 5 at Milton and Muirhead, 5 at Drummygar with 4 at the Podge and 13 at Mosston. This does not mean that all quarriers employed at the quarries lived in the parish since the Galloway brothers employed 40 men at the Guynd quarries and William Duncan employed 173 men and 7 boys, therefore approximately 140, that is, two thirds of the quarriers travelled from outwith Carmyllie for employment.[6] From 1881 to 1901, quarriers settling in the parish numbered around 55 to 60 and interestingly by 1901, quarriers were identified with different skills, such as pavement dresser, pavement quarrier, stone dresser and stone quarry labourer and one instance of a freestone quarrier.

In conclusion, in the nineteenth century, Carmyllie had a high number of male handloom weavers 'born to the loom,' but following the downturn, many found employment as quarriers, keeping the population higher than average parishes. Latterly female weavers were supplementing the household income but eventually found weaving rates of pay too low to continue. The quarrier employment was at its peak in 1871, gradually decreasing towards the end of the century.

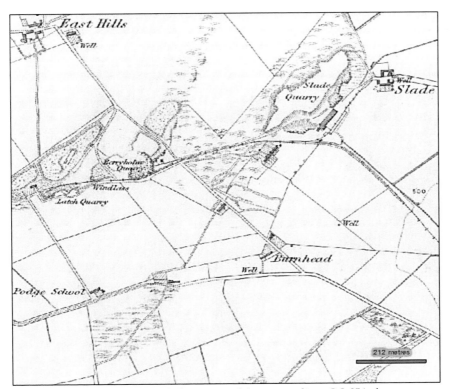

The location of the Slade quarry and the surroundings, O.S. 25 inch

---

[6] Carmyllie Census, 1871

Chapter 5

PANMURE ESTATE AND ITS LAIRDS

The Maule years

In 1124, David, Earl of Huntingdon became King David I of Scotland and he swept away the Scottish tenure system of landholding and with it most of the old aristocracy, most of whom were of Gaelic or Irish descent. He and his successors brought in Anglo-Norman and Norman Knights to administer the Kingdom and Norman clerics to administer the Church. A feudal system of land holding on the European model was established, land was granted to favoured knights and a new Norman aristocracy was established.

Panmure House c.1800

One of these favoured knights was Philip de Valoniis who was an 'attendant' of William the Lion and was awarded a charter of the Baronies of Panmure and Benvie and appointed High Chamberlain of Scotland about 1180. His son William de Valoniis inherited the Baronies of Panmure and Benvie. He left one daughter, Christina de Valoniis, who married Sir Peter Maule from another family of Norman descent.

Peter de Maule had come over with William the Conqueror and was awarded lands in Yorkshire for his services, His son Robert de Maule came to Scotland with David, Earl of Huntingdon and was granted 'several lands in the Lothians'. Robert's oldest son, William de Maule was awarded 'lands of

Earl James Maule of Balumbie (1658-1723)

Fowlis in Gowry' by David, Earl of Huntingdon. William de Maule had no sons and it was to be his brother, Roger de Maule's grandson, Sir Peter Maule who was the heir and married Christina de Valoniis, thus uniting the two families and estates. The Maule dynasty was thereby established and endured until 1782 when the male line failed and the Ramsays, also of Norman descent, had married into the Maule family in 1726. The village of Maule from where the family originated is about 35 km. due west of Paris.

There was a difficult time for the Maules in 1716 when Panmure was one of a number of estates seized by the Crown because of their proprietor's support for the Jacobite Rebellion. James Maule of Ballumbie was a staunch Royalist and a Privy Councillor to King James VII and II. He became the Fourth Earl of Panmure on the death of his elder brother George. Earl James and his brother Harry Maule of Kelly were great adherents to the cause of the Stuarts, despite the family having embraced the Reformed Religion as far back as the time of their grandfather, Sir Robert Maule in the Reign of James VI and I.

Earl James and his brother Harry Maule of Kelly were involved in the Jacobite Army at the Battle of Sherriffmuir on the 15th November 1715. Earl James was wounded and taken prisoner. He was being held in a cottar house guarded by six government dragoons when he was heroically rescued by his brother Harry Maule and they escaped to Ardoch where Earl James recovered sufficiently to return to Dundee to recover from his wounds. Robert Burns was to celebrate this story in verse some 70 years later.

Sherriffmuir was fought to an inconclusive end and so James Stuart, known to some as Chevalier de St George and to those on the Hanoverian side as the 'Old Pretender', continued with his plan to land in Scotland. He landed at Peterhead in the dying days of 1715 and was entertained by Earl James at Brechin Castle on the 2nd January 1716 and subsequently at Panmure. It was said that the bell of Carmyllie Kirk was 'rent' at the rejoicings of the Chevalier's visit to Panmure.

Harry Maule of Kelly (d.1734)

The rebellion failed because of a lack of popular support in Scotland and because the promised support from France did not materialise. James Stuart and his entourage embarked at Montrose to escape to France and shortly thereafter, he was followed by Earl James and his nephew, the treacherous Earl of Mar. His brother Harry Maule of Kelly fled to Holland.

There is a tradition at Panmure that the 'Old West Gates' at Panmure were closed after Earl James and the 'Pretender' rode through them. Earl James left strict instructions that they were not to be opened again after he left Scotland, until a Stuart was back on the throne.

There was a local legend (most recently committed to print by the late Colin Gibson), that Earl James did in fact return to Panmure to visit his Estate and his wife Lady Margaret, who was herself the youngest daughter of the powerful Duke of Hamilton. It was said that he returned disguised as a beggar. The truth of that legend will never be known, but from his letters, we know he retained his interest in Panmure. In fact, despite the difficulties, Earl James and Lady Margaret did correspond and they met regularly in France. In the Registrum de Panmure, some of these letters are reproduced. In one, Lady Margaret tells of being robbed by two highwaymen between London and Dover and in another, Lady Margaret advises Earl James on how to address his letters to her to avoid them being intercepted.

Earl James was attainted for high treason and his Estates were forfeited to the Crown. He was however; twice afforded the opportunity to have his Estates returned and to allow his return to Scotland provided he would take the oath of alliegance to the House of Hanover. This he refused to do despite Lady Margaret protesting that refusal was ''done out of a very ill designe'' and he died in Paris in April 1723.

The Panmure Estate at a rental of £3,456 was the largest of the confiscated properties but other estates forfeited included Marischal, Southesk, Linlithgow, Fingask, Pitcairn, Winton, Kilsyth and Widdrington in Northumberland. A further tranche of estates were confiscated after the 1745 rebellion.

The Yorks Buildings Company Years

The acquisition, management and disposal of the forfeited estates caused the Government no end of trouble and Commissioners were appointed to act for the Government. Right from the start, the body of the Scottish people was greatly prejudiced against the Commissioners and their management was thwarted at every opportunity. The creditors of the forfeited proprietors reasonably raised actions against the estates for payments of debts. This however turned into a farce with all sorts of spurious claims being made by friends and relatives of the dispossessed lairds to the Court of Session, which were readily granted. Another device that was used to thwart the Commissioners efforts to obtain possession was to dispute the ownership of the forfeited estates. The Court of Session seems to have been happy to go along with this and claimants for ownership of the estates sprang up from all quarters.

Yorks Buildings Water Supply London c.1700 (Thames Embankment)

The tenants of the forfeited estates also refused to recognise the factors appointed by the Commissioners and continued to pay their rent to the previous owners. The tenants on Panmure were induced to pay their rent to Lady Panmure. All this chaos must have created happy times indeed for the legal profession in Scotland.

Eventually however, the forfeited estates including Panmure, were prepared for sale in 1719 and 1720, but it was impossible to find buyers for such a large amount of landed property in Scotland. Very few Scots were prepared to bid against the rightful owners of these estates. Also Scotland was still rather impoverished due to the rebellion and the Darien Scheme debacle of 1698-1701.

As there were no Scottish buyers for these estates, the 'Company of Undertakers for raising the Thames Water, in York Buildings, London, in England' came to the aid of the government.

York House was at one time the London residence of the Archbishops of York and stood between the Strand and the Thames, just a little to the north - east of what is now Charing Cross Railway Station. In 1665, Charles II gave 'letters-patent' to Ralph Bucknall and Ralph Wayne empowering them to erect buildings in the grounds of York house for the purpose of supplying the inhabitants of the City with water. The Company was incorporated in 1691 and traded respectably and very profitably for the next 20 years. This was clearly a highly innovative concern as they had a very early steam pump to raise the water. The first decade of the 18th century was a period of wild speculation of which the 'South Sea Bubble' was one example and the Yorks Buildings Company became another.

A solicitor called Mr. Case Billingsley with five associates bought the whole stock of the 'Yorks Buildings Company' for £7,000 and in October 1719, the Company floated a joint stock fund of £1,200,000 for purchasing the forfeited estates. The money was at once forthcoming and by the end of the year, the fund stood at £1,259,575 and the £10 shares stood at £305.

A Mr. John Wicker and a Mr. Robert Hackett attended the auctions in London of the forfeited estates on behalf of the Yorks Buildings Company. Despite protests by Lady Panmure, the Panmure Estate was exposed for sale on the 9th October 1719 at an upset price of £57,032. Agents on behalf of Harry Maule of Kelly bid to £60,300 which must have been their financial limit. The auctioneers offered to stop the auction till more security could be found, but two or three days would have been required to raise more money. An altercation ensued but the Estate was knocked down to Mr. Hackett of the Yorks Buildings Company for £60,400 after much protest.

Lady Panmure, Lady Margaret Hamilton seems to have been a woman of great intelligence, energy and strength of character and she travelled to London where she managed to obtain from the Yorks Buildings Company, long leases on the two principle mansions. She settled at Panmure and Harry Maule of Kelly settled at Brechin Castle. According to the Registrum de Panmure, the senior members of the family seem to have been confident that they would eventually recover their Estates and the leases of these residences would secure their future until that happened.

Yorks Buildings Water Tower, London. c. 1700

Meanwhile, the Yorks Buildings Company, having bought up all the forfeited estates that were exposed for sale, was obliged to pay for these estates by August 1720. They discovered that they could not pay the money to the exchequer on the due date and sought an extra six weeks to pay. This was granted and the company bought five more estates bringing the total purchases up to £303,913. Confidence in the Company was however severely shaken and the share price plunged. Allegations were made of 'jobbery' against the directors. That is to say that they had improperly enriched themselves at the expense of shareholders' funds. It certainly appears that most of the £1,259,575 raised, simply disappeared. The shares which in August 1720 had stood at £295 fell to £14 in November and were unsaleable. The Company tried a lottery as a means of raising extra funds but this too was a failure and further extra time to pay was sought from the exchequer and had again to be granted.

The Company had great difficulty managing the estates and getting them to produce revenue. The tenants on the estates resented the intrusion of strangers, held fealty and continued to pay rent to the native proprietors. At this time, farm rents were paid partly in money and partly in produce. In 1716, the rental income of Panmure Estates was £3,456 but only £1,843 was cash. The rest of the rent was paid in wheat, barley, oatmeal, linen, chickens, butter and so on. Produce was stolen, documents were falsified and there were tales of oatmeal tendered in rent being bulked up with sand and other tricks of that sort. Thus the stage was set for fraud and pilfering on a grand scale, defrauding the London Lairds became a national sport and the management of the forfeited estates became a farce.

On several of the estates, there were mines, quarries, salt pans or fisheries and the Company tried to work these, but a combination of deliberate mismanagement and fraud by local managers and staff led to serious losses which further added to the Company's financial troubles. A lot of estate income came from the estates own meal mills, blacksmiths and wheelwrights shops operating under the hated 'thirlage' system and these could not be made to pay either. The Acts of Parliament relating to the forfeited estates had insisted that all claims against the forfeited lairds had to be met by the Yorks Buildings Company. The local Scots were hugely successful in inventing endless claims against the estates. The Company also had to continue to support the Churches and the Parish Schools out of estate income and

York Buildings Watergate, London. As it is today

everyone tried to ensure that became as expensive as possible. Eventually the Company came to ruin and had to start selling land to survive. The Company in fact survived to 1829 when it was dissolved by Act of Parliament, the Company having been involved in endless litigation since 1719 and the exchequer only received £1,107 as a net return on the forfeiture of fifty estates. Needless to say, lessons were learned and the estates forfeited after Culloden were managed directly by the

Commissioners and seem to have been generally managed to the betterment of the Scottish people particularly in the Highlands.

Lady Panmure died in 1731 having spent a difficult lifetime of devotion to the interests of the family. She added substantially to the family landholding and among other purchases which she made, was the lands and barony of Redcastle or Inverkeilor which she bought on the 8th December 1724. Lady Panmure had no children and Harry Maule of Kelly was heir to the titles. Harry Maule died in 1734. James Maule, his eldest son was a noted historian but he predeceased his father in 1729 and his brother William became heir to the titles. He was a noted soldier rising to the rank of General and served with great distinction in the battles against the French in Flanders in what came to be known as the 'Wars of the Austrian Succession'. He served under George II in the victory at Dettingen in 1742 and under the Duke of Cumberland in the defeat at Fontenoy in 1743. He was elected Member of Parliament for Forfarshire in 1735 and was created a peer of Ireland in 1743.

The Maule family having almost been ruined by their part in the '15, took great care not to get involved in the '45 and in 1764, William repurchased the Panmure estates (excluding the barony of Belhelvie in Aberdeenshire which was sold to other purchasers) from the creditors of the Yorks Buildings Company for £49,157, 18s. 4d this being 30 years purchase of the rental at the time. William died unmarried in 1782 thus ending the male line of the Maules. In 1726, his sister, Harry Maule's eldest daughter Lady Jean, married George, Lord Ramsay the eldest son of William, sixth Earl of Dalhousie, thereby linking the Maules of Panmure with the Ramsay family and the titles and lands of Dalhousie in the Lothians.

The Ramsay years
At the start of the 19th Century, the great estate of Panmure owned much of the land in Carmyllie. Indeed other than the land owned by the smaller estates of the Guynd and Cononsyth, it effectively owned all of Carmyllie. This part of the Panmure story starts with William, Lord Maule of Panmure, a noted soldier and General in the army of William II who had in 1764, successfully bought back the family's estates after the 1715 forfeiture and restored the family to prominence.

When William, Lord Maule of Panmure died unmarried in 1782, the male line of the Maules ended. In 1726, Harry Maule of Kelly's eldest daughter, Lady Jean Maule married George, Lord Ramsay, the eldest son of William 6th Earl of Dalhousie. George and Lady Jean's son Mr. Charles Ramsay succeeded his grandfather as the 7th Earl of Dalhousie in 1759 but he died unmarried in 1764. His brother, the Hon. George Ramsay succeeded Charles as the 8th Earl of Dalhousie in 1764 and he also succeeded to the Panmure estates on the death of his maternal uncle William, Lord Maule of Panmure in 1782.

Earl George had to face a challenge to the titles and lands of large parts of Panmure by a distant relative from an Irish branch of the family, Thomas Maule Esq. who styled himself as a ''Lieutenant of Invalids'' (a term for a wounded former soldier). A hugely complicated case opened at the High Court in Edinburgh in February 1782. This became a great talking point in Georgian Edinburgh and would have been a great source of revenue for Edinburgh's legal profession.

The story behind the case is that Earl William, Lord Maule of Panmure, in his early years had been a Military Officer, rising to the rank of General and serving with great distinction against the Franco-Prussian Alliance on the Continent in the wars of the 1730s and 1740s. As he had been out of Scotland a great deal on Military Service, he had entrusted the family business and papers to a distant cousin and friend, a Mr. Baron Maule who lived at Easter Duddingston, Edinburgh. Amongst these papers were deeds, apparently genuine, and signed by Harry Maule of Kelly and Lady Margaret, Countess of Panmure dated 14th April 1730. These deeds essentially provided that the Ramsay heirs of George Ramsay and Lady Jean (nee Maule) were to inherit the Estates in liferent only. The titles of the Estate were to remain with the ''heirs-male of the family of Maule'' and that the lands and titles should remain with ''persons of the name of Maule''

It appears that for a time, Harry Maule and Lady Margaret had not been on the best of terms with

The Hon. William Maule (1771-1852)

their daughter's family, the Ramsays and these papers had been prepared as a precautionary measure to be a blocking mechanism to prevent the estates from falling to the Ramsays in the event of future difficulties. Crucially for the court case, these deeds had not been registered with the Court of Session. Most of the estates had in any case been forfeited at this time and were in the hands of the Yorks Buildings Company. The estates had only been repurchased by William Maule, Harry Maule's second son in 1764. Harry Maule's estate would have consisted only of the leases of Panmure House and Brechin Castle along with some land purchased since 1716. Matters came to a head when Mr Baron Maule died and these papers were found in his deed box by his son Thomas Maule ''Lieutenant of Invalids'' who promptly launched his claim to the titles and estates.

The outcome of the case was that Thomas Maule "Lieutenant of Invalids" initially succeeded in his claim, but the case went to appeal and the original verdict was overturned granting title to Earl George. As a precaution however, Earl George's second son and heir to the Panmure Estate, William Ramsay, adopted by Royal Assent the name Maule or Ramsay-Maule as a precaution to help thwart this challenge to the titles and estates by Thomas Maule. He thus became known as the Hon. William Ramsay-Maule or Maule of Panmure.

Earl George died in 1787 and the estates and titles were divided between the two eldest sons. The eldest brother, The Hon. George Ramsay succeeded to the titles and estates of Dalhousie and became the 9th Earl of Dalhousie at the age of 17 in 1787. He became laird of the smaller but vastly wealthier, coal bearing estates in the Lothians. He married Christian Broun, only child and heiress of the Coulstoun Estate in East Lothian. Earl George was a great soldier and went on to become the Lieutenant Governor of Nova Scotia and founded Dalhousie University in Halifax, Nova Scotia.

The second son was The Hon. William Maule, born William Ramsay on the 27th October 1771.
He inherited the agricultural estates in Angus in 1787 at the tender age of 15. He assumed the name and arms of Maule of Panmure by Royal dispensation and was to be laird of Panmure for 65 years.

The Panmure Testimonial or 'Live and Let Live' Monument, Monikie

William Maule was quite a character. He was certainly opinionated and he would tolerate no opposition to his will. His capacity for drink was legendary and he was famous for his 36 hour parties. He was a prankster, a gambler and 'fond of the turf' and a playboy. He was known as ''The Generous Sportsman'' in Edinburgh and was written up in the bawdy Kay's Edinburgh Portraits. He was also nicknamed 'Piggy' behind his back because of his 'bulky' figure in his 'mature years'.

Despite his faults, Maule seems to have been a locally popular Laird who was generous to his tenants, charging low rents. He was a considerable benefactor in Angus and Dundee and built the Mechanics Institute in Brechin, the Montrose Museum and he put up money for the improvement of schools and hospitals in Dundee and Angus. After his death, his tenants all subscribed to a fund to raise the Panmure Testimonial or 'Live and Let Live' monument at Monikie in his memory.

In 1789, he entered the army as a coronet in the 11th Dragoons, but his unit was disbanded in 1791. He was then posted as a Lieutenant to the West Lowland Fencibles, being promoted to Captain in 1793 then a Major in the Forfar Fencibles in 1794. During this short army career, he spent some time stationed at Dumfries where it was alleged that he nearly ran Robert Burns down in his carriage. He was said to have a very sleek black carriage or 'phaeton' drawn by six matched black horses which would have been the 'fastest thing on the road' at the time. Burns, claiming to have almost been run down, wrote about Maule :-

"Thou Fool, in thy Phaeton towering ,
Art proud when that phaeton's prais'd ?
'Tis the pride of a Thief's exhibition
When higher his pillory's rais'd "

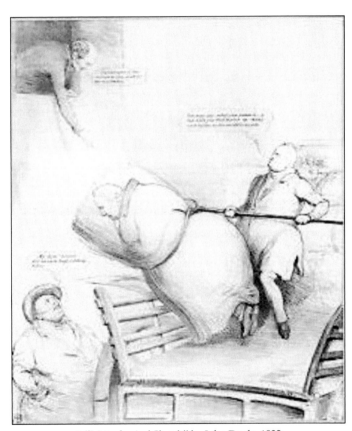

A "Metaphorical Sketch" by John Doyle, 1832

Maule doesn't seem to have taken offence at this as when Burns died; he settled a pension on Jean Armour his widow.

After the army, he then sought election to Parliament. The politics of the family were Tory but Maule, ever the rebel, was quite radical in his political views and was an admirer and supporter of the Whig reformer Charles James Fox who advocated support for the principles of the French Revoloution. Maule even named his eldest son after C.J. Fox. Maule joined the Whig party and was elected Member of Parliament for Forfarshire in the Whig interest at the 1796 election and held the seat right through to 1831. He was raised to the Peerage on the 10th September 1831 by the title of Baron Panmure of Brechin and Navar. He became a Peer by being made a Peer of Ireland, a controversial mechanism that allowed the Prime Minister to create extra Whig Peers. There was much caustic comment about this in the national press at the time. This was epitomised in a ''Metaphorical Sketch'' by cartoonist John Doyle published in March 1832. This cartoon portrayed King William IV wearing a smock and with pitchfork in hand, he is standing on a corn wagon pitching up trusses (sheaves) to Lord Grey. Grey, the Prime Minister of the time, leans from the loft door to receive the trusses. The truss being pitched contains the bulky form of Maule. The King says, *''You may say what you please Grey but to pitch up many trusses such as this would be no joke.* Grey replies *''Depend on it, this exercise is very good for the Constitution.''* John Bull stands by the wagon looking up at the King and says *'' My Eyes! I never did see such truss pitching before!''*

58

Maule was however probably most at home as an agricultural improver, particularly in cattle breeding. His Panmure herd of Aberdeen-Angus cattle was one of the great early herds of AA cattle, a breed formed from the native black polled or hornless cattle that are depicted on the Pictish Stones. His Panmure herd was to produce Panmure 51, the greatest bull of the age and whose blood still runs in much of the AA breed. A portrait of Panmure 51 by John Philip R.A. still hangs in the offices of the AA Cattle Society today.

Maule had married a renowned society beauty, Miss Patricia Heron Gordon of Hallheaths, in Annandale in December 1794, and she bore him 3 sons and 6 daughters. Their relationship was to prove difficult and because of ''reports of her husband's life of debauchery and adultery in London'' which reached her in Angus; she left him in 1817 to live with relatives of her own in Ireland. The chief sufferer of this was Fox, the eldest son of the marriage. Incensed at his wife's desertion, William Maule visited his fifteen year old son, then at The Charterhouse School in London and told him that if he would take his father's side and cease any contact with his mother, he would be allowed ''every advantage befitting his position'' If on the other hand, he continued to see his mother, all his father would give him would be £100 a year and a commission in the army. Fox's reply was that he did not see that his mother was at fault and that he would stand by her.

Maule's entire family life in fact appears to have been rather sour and chaotic and four of his six

William Maule portrayed as the 'Generous Sportsman' in Kay's Edinburgh Portraits

daughters eloped which presumably they saw as preferable to bringing their suitors home to meet their father. On the 4th June 1822, William Maule married as his second wife, Elizabeth Barton, daughter of John William Barton of Hospitalfield, Arbroath, who stood by him in his remaining 30 years of life and outlived him when he died in 1852. This seems to have been a clandestine marriage and undoubtedly against her parent's wishes. There were no further children.

Lord Cockburn who knew him well, on hearing of his death, rather chillingly observed:- *He {William Maule} was popular with those who chose to be submissive and to such was never close in the fist. But the virtues were a different matter. To his 'unfriends' -and he had many- he was insanely brutal. His wife, his daughters, and at least two of his three sons, he compelled to fly from his house, his daughters at midnight, and ever after shut his door and heart against them; neither time nor their worth ever abating his mad and savage hatred. And so it was with everyone who incurred the ineffaceable guilt of daring to resist the capricious and intolerant despotism of his will. He would have roasted every soul of them, and their bodies too. A spoiled beast from his infancy, his oldest son* (Fox), *who presumed to save his sisters by helping them out of the house, was the object of his particular hatred: a hatred which the public eminence of the son rather aggravated than lessened.*

In 1823 when Fox Maule came of age, he hired the eminent lawyer George Cranstoun, then Dean of the Faculty of Advocates, to raise an action in the Court of Session in Edinburgh contesting his father's refusal to grant him 'settled funds' and the denial of his inheritance, his father having by that time willed that his second son Lauderdale Maule should be his heir. The Court ruled in favour of Fox on the 9th June but his father appealed to the House of Lords on the 25th June 1823 and the original verdict was partly overturned. The House of Lords decision seems to have upheld William Maule's right not to provide Fox with income beyond the £100 a year, but on his father's death Fox would regain his entitlement and inherit the titles and the bulk of the estates. Sadly Lauderdale died in hospital at Constantinople in the Crimean War in 1854 and so Fox would have inherited the estates in any case.

A contemporary commentary on this feud was provided by Sir Walter Scott, the lawyer, historian and writer. Scott had attended Edinburgh High School with William Maule's elder brother Lord George Ramsay, later the 9th Earl of Dalhousie. Scott had visited Dalhousie Castle often in his youth and knew the family and their circumstances well. Writing to his friend Lord Montagu on 14th February 1823, he gave the following account:- *''To amuse us within doors we have the cause of young Maule against his father praying for aliment which Cranstoun is just now pleading in my hearing. The liberality of his father has bestowed on him an ensign's commission and one hundred pounds a year and having thus far discharged his duty to his son he denies the right of the court to take the matter further into their consideration. The young man's case is stated with much feeling and delicacy but I doubt, considering the dogged and obstinate temper of the Whiggish tyrant, he had not better gone to the duke's place for the necessary money, for the unfortunate consequence will be that his father will make waste on the estate, cut down and disbark and do twenty times the mischief which old Queensberry made at Drumlanrig.----- Is it not odd that so generous fine and honourable a character as Dalhousie {George Ramsay the 9th Earl. } should have been brother to this he-wolf who would eat his own issue if law would not solemnize such a banquet of Thesytes by a hanging match? So much for living with toad-eaters and parasites in the untempered exercise of every whim that comes uppermost till the slightest contradiction becomes an inexpiable crime in those around him''*.

It is noteworthy in this account by Scott, written in 1823 and with the lairdship of William Maule having a further 29 years to run, that he predicts that Maule would 'make waste on the estate' to deny his heirs their proper inheritance. There is little doubt that when Maule died, the fabric of the estate and its finances were in poor condition. Whether this was merely Maule's debauchery, extravagance and incompetence, or whether he deliberately set out to 'make waste' on the estates might be a subject for some conjecture. At Brechin Castle today, visitors are certainly given the latter version, so one must assume that the family today believe that Maule deliberately tried to destroy the estates. Maule though apparently popular with his tenants at the time, certainly let the buildings and fabric of the estate decline badly and very little was spent on repair and improvement in his time and so when he died in 1852, it was his successors who had to take on the task of rebuilding the estate.

Fox-Maule Ramsay (1801-1874)

As a result of all of this, father and son never met for the remaining 35 years of William Maule's life despite Fox's numerous attempts to bring about reconciliation. Fox was however present with his brothers and other relatives on the day his father died. Fox was the antithesis of his father, they apparently never agreed on anything, but he was well able to make his own way in life. He eventually set up home at Dalguise in Perthshire with his wife the Hon. Montague Abercromby, the eldest daughter of Lord Abercromby of Aboukir and Tullibody whom he married on the 4th April 1831.

Fox Maule, the eldest of the three sons, inherited the titles and the bulk of the estates on the death of his father. He carved out a substantial career in British politics following a spell in the Army. He was apparently a big burly man and was known to his friends as 'the Bison'. He assumed the name Fox Maule-Ramsay in 1861 on inheriting his cousin's titles and estates. His cousin was James Andrew Broun Ramsay, the Lord Dalhousie who is remembered today as the Viceroy of India from 1847 to 1856 and who in his eight years in office, drove forward the building of much of the Indian Railways and also the 'electric telegraph' system, all with aiding the rapid transport of soldiers round India in mind.

Fox Maule, second Baron Panmure and from 1861, the eleventh Earl of Dalhousie, was born in 1801 and was educated at The Charterhouse, London and Edinburgh University. He entered the Army as an ensign and after serving several years in Canada on the staff of his Uncle, the eighth Earl of Dalhousie he retired in 1831 with the rank of Captain. He was elected as MP for Perthshire in 1831 in the Tory interest and subsequently represented the Elgin Burghs and the Burgh of Perth. He was appointed Under-Secretary for the Home Department in Lord Melbourne's administration in 1831. In 1841 he was appointed Vice-President of the Board of Trade. In 1846, on the collapse of the Peel administration, he became Secretary at War with a seat in Lord Russell's Cabinet. In February 1852, he was appointed President of the Board of Control.

Fox was elevated to the House of Lords in 1852 on the death of his father. He was sidelined in the Earl of Aberdeen's coalition, but eventually that collapsed at the height of the war in the Crimea. Lord Palmerston then became Prime Minister and in 1855, Fox resumed his former office of Secretary at War at the height of the Sebastopol campaign and it is this period in office for which he is chiefly remembered in British History. His correspondence from this time was published as 'The Panmure Papers' and these two volumes are a primary source for much of the history on the later stages of the war in the Crimean Peninsula.

Fox resumed his role as Secretary at War against a background of much public disquiet about the war in the Crimean Peninsula. The Crimean war was the first to be reported on by telegraph and Fox regularly complains in his letters about the Times revealing intelligence to the enemy. He says in one letter that ''there is no need for the Russians to have spies in England as they can have all the intelligence they need in the Times for 5d''.The British newspapers were carrying accounts of mismanagement and the squalid conditions and disease that the troops were suffering from. At the time, Fox was blamed for many of the problems in the Crimea and he rather became a scapegoat for all that was wrong about the Crimean campaign and it ended his political career. In fact he did what he could to introduce major reforms to the structure and organisation of the army and improve conditions for the men.

Fox Maule-Ramsay, From 1861, 11ᵀʰ Earl of Dalhousie

Fox Maule had good personal motive to improve conditions in the Crimea as his younger brother, Lt-Colonel the Hon. Lauderdale Maule had died of cholera there. Lauderdale had risen to Lt-Colonel in the 79th Regiment of Foot, and then retired from the army in 1852 to become Member of Parliament for Forfarshire. He had returned to the Crimea as Surveyor-General of the Ordnance, contracted the disease while carrying out his duties at Varna and died at Constantinople in August 1854. The handsome Carrara marble memorial to him in Panbride Church was erected by his friend, the wealthy Russian exile and steel manufacturer, Prince Anatole Demidoff.

From a historical perspective, there is little doubt that Fox's reforms left the British Army in a more efficient state than before. He started a competitive examination for commissions and stopped the use of the lash. It was during his tenure as Secretary at War that the Victoria Cross was introduced and Fox himself read out the names as Queen Victoria presented the first medals.

It was also with Fox that Florence Nightingale took up her campaign to improve conditions for the men, particularly in the military hospitals. After the horrific conditions she had seen at Scutari and the way wounded soldiers were being treated, she tried to instigate improvements and came up against the Bison. It seems that after a difficult start, they managed to come to a reasonable working relationship.

Florence Nightingale had of course the advantage of having Queen Victoria and other reformers such as Sydney Herbert on her side and in the end it was said that "the Bison was no match for the lady"

In Scotland, Fox was enthusiastic about field sports and shot on his estates with many of the leading politicians and businessmen of the age. He was a leading freemason and held many senior positions in Freemasonry and in 1867 became the 68th Grand Master Mason of Scotland. Fox was also involved with many other organisations. Panmure Curling Club was formally founded at Panmure House in 1854 and Dalhousie Golf Club was named after him and he was the first patron. He was Lord Rector of Glasgow University 1842-44, Lord Lieutenant of Forfarshire 1849-74, Keeper of the Privy Seal for Scotland 1853-74, a Commissioner of the Royal Military Asylum and a Governor of his old school, the Charterhouse in London. He was also a Knight of the Thistle and a Knight of the Order of the Bath.

In Scotland, Fox was prominent in Church affairs and greatly approved of the democratic principles of the Free Church of which he was an enthusiastic supporter. In contrast to his father who refused to allow the building of Free Churches, he provided land and assistance to build Free Churches around his estates and in Carmyllie; he provided land on the farm of Wardneuk to build the Free Church there. Fox was a great friend of Dr.Thomas Guthrie, then minister of the Greyfriars Church in Edinburgh and one of the leaders of the Free Church following the 1843 Disruption. Dr. Guthrie was the son of a merchant and the Provost of Brechin and he had been minister at Arbirlot before the Disruption. Dr. Guthrie often preached at Lochlee, the tiny church next to Invermark, Fox's shooting lodge. A stained glass window in the Maule Memorial Chapel in Glen Esk commemorates both Fox and Dr. Guthrie.

Fox inherited the estates in a very run-down condition as very little had been spent on improvements by his father. In defence of his father William Maule, there possibly might not have been huge monetary resources available to improve the estates. Fox on the other hand had inherited the coal bearing Midlothian Estates from his cousin in 1861 as well as the Angus estates and would have had the money to improve them. He was also by this time, selling a great deal of land for housing on the edge of rapidly expanding Victorian Dundee and the sale of land for the Victorian developments in Carnoustie, Monifieth and Broughty Ferry would

Panmure House, c. 1860

have earned Fox a great deal of money. The quarrying operations in Carmyllie would also have contributed.

With this money, Fox started to improve the Estates and he started with the re-modelling of Panmure House, the plans for which appear to have been drawn up in 1851 before his father was yet dead. The Montague Bridge spanning the Monikie Burn in the Panmure policies was built in 1854 in memory of his wife Montague who died in November 1853. After that, further improvements were made in the Panmure policies and the surrounding farms. Little if anything beyond the Free Church seems to have been done in Carmyllie in Fox's lifetime.

Fox was troubled through his middle and later years with recurrent bouts of gout which particularly affected his hands and his ability to write. He died on the 6th July 1874 at Brechin Castle and was buried at Panbride. As he had no children and his brothers had predeceased him, the Barony of Panmure became extinct and the Estates and titles fell to Fox's cousin, Admiral George Ramsay who was second son of Lt-General the Hon John Ramsay, 4th son of the 8th Earl of Dalhousie. Admiral George became the 12th Earl of Dalhousie.

Admiral George Ramsay was born at Kelly Castle on the 26th April 1806 but had no expectation of inheriting a great Scottish Estate. He had entered the Navy aged 14 in 1820 and had worked his way up the ranks, serving on numerous ships all over the globe. He was Commander- in- Chief of the South American Station from 1866 to 1869 and rose to the rank of Admiral in 1875. He seems to have preferred the Dalhousie Estates in Midlothian with their proximity to Edinburgh and seems to have visited his Angus estates only rarely. He was Laird for only six years but limited improvements were apparently continued on the estates in his period. He died suddenly at Dalhousie Castle, Midlothian on the 20th July 1880 and was laid to rest in the Churchyard at Cockpen, Midlothian, near but not in the Ramsay family vault there. He had married Sarah Frances Robertson of Logan House, Midlothian in 1845, by whom he had four sons and it was to be his eldest son, John William Ramsay that was to be the big improver of the Angus Estates.

John William Ramsay (1847- 1887), 13th Earl Dalhousie

John William Ramsay, the 13th Earl of Dalhousie was born in 1847 and like his father; he entered the Royal Navy at the age of fourteen. He quickly learned his profession and was said to have been by far the ablest cadet of his era and quickly rose through the ranks, being promoted to Commander in 1874.

In that same year, Fox Maule's death unexpectedly brought the Earldom and the Estates to his father and he himself gained the title Lord Ramsay. It was quickly realised that he would himself eventually inherit the estates and it was decided that the Navy was not a suitable training for a Laird and he entered as a student at Balliol College, Oxford.

In 1876, he was charged with superintending the Naval training of the two sons of the Prince of Wales, the youngest of whom would later become George V.

In 1877, he married Lady Ida Louisa Bennet, daughter of the sixth Earl of Tankerville. The Tankerville family seat is the Estate and Castle of Chillingham near Wooler in Northumberland. Chillingham is perhaps best known for the ancient herd of ''Chillingham Wild White Cattle'' which still can be seen in the policies at Chillingham today. Lady Dalhousie was a noted society beauty of the time, she regularly featured in 'Vanity Fair' and she had her portrait painted by Sir John Everett Millais.

In April 1880, he was returned to Parliament as one of the members for Liverpool. Unlike his father, Admiral George who was a staunch Tory, Lord Ramsay gave his adherence to Gladstone's Liberal Party. He was however not to be a Member of Parliament for long as his father's death in July 1880, elevated him to the House of Lords. He served as Secretary for Scotland in Gladstone's short-lived administration of 1886.

Countess of Dalhousie ('Vanity Fair' print, 1889)

63

In 1880, John William Ramsay, now Lord Dalhousie and 13th Earl of Dalhousie, inherited estates which though smaller than in earlier times, still extended to 136,602 acres in Forfarshire and 1,419 acres in Midlothian. The management of the estates during the many years that they were in the hands of William Maule had left them in poor condition and though Lord Dalhousie's father and Fox had started to make improvements, there was still a great deal to do. Carmyllie in particular, seems not to have been favoured by many improvements until this time.

The improvements to the estates are discussed later, but his Lordship spent a great deal of money on his estates at a time when home farming profitability was under severe pressure, with the new steamships bringing cheap grain and other food from America and other parts of the World. Also in 1884, much of the cattle stock of Angus was wiped out by a serious outbreak of Rinderpest. The farm rents therefore had to be reduced substantially to meet the reduced farm profitability, and as a result the estates had come into some financial difficulty.

No doubt with the aim of bringing in some extra money at this time, Brechin Castle had been leased to Archibald J. Coates, the Paisley textile manufacturer in 1885, and the Earl and Countess were using Panmure as their family home. This was really the only time Panmure House was ever properly used as a family home from 1852 when Fox re-modelled it, through to 1955 when it was demolished.

As a result of his worries, his Lordship developed insomnia and bouts of anxiety and his general health deteriorated. In late 1885, Lord and Lady Dalhousie took a long voyage to New Zealand and he was greatly recovered when he returned. In 1886, again for the benefit of his health, he took a cruise as far as the Mediterranean in Lord and Lady Brassey's famous steam-yacht the 'Sunbeam'. The account of this voyage was published as 'The Last Voyage in the Sunbeam to India and Australia' but Lady Brassey sadly succumbed to malaria and died on this voyage. During 1887, his Lordship's health deteriorated again and on the 23rd September, Lord and Lady Dalhousie embarked for the United States of America on the transatlantic liner, the Bretagne. They travelled by rail, right into the heart of the country to visit the youngest of Lord Dalhousie's brothers, Lt.-Col. Hon. Charles Maule Ramsay who at that time had retired from the Army and had acquired a cattle ranch near Miles City, Wyoming. They also visited Lady Dalhousie's brother the Hon. F. Bennet in New York. Lord Dalhousie's health had greatly benefited from the change when he and Lady Dalhousie sailed home from New York in early November. During the voyage home, Lady Dalhousie took ill with a chill which developed into peritonitis and blood-poisoning and she was very ill when they arrived at Le Havre on the 13th November. A doctor was summoned from London but she could not be saved and died at The Hotel Frascatti, Le Havre on Thursday the 24th November 1887. She was only 30 years of age.

Further tragedy followed within 24 hours when in the early hours of Friday the 25th November, Lord Dalhousie was heard to be breathing heavily in his sleep. His valet called a doctor who tried to revive him, but he died from an 'apoplectic fit' shortly after. At the time, all the reports were careful not to say that he had taken his own life but it seems certain that while his mind was confused through grief and anxiety, he had taken an overly large dose of some sort of drug or medicine on top of the large toddy his valet had served to him to help him sleep. Lord and Lady Dalhousie's death left five orphaned sons, the eldest, Arthur George Maule, Lord Ramsay now inheriting his father's titles and estates at the tender age of nine years.

Lord and Lady Dalhousie were interred in the Churchyard at Cockpen, Midlothian, the coffins having arrived at Waverly Station, and being carried by cortege down Princes Street and over the Bridges out to Cockpen. The tenants from Dalhousie, Panmure and the Brechin and Edzell Estates all contributed to a fund to build the Dalhousie Memorial Arch which still stands at the south entrance to Edzell.

The nine year old Arthur George Ramsay now took his place as the 14th Earl of Dalhousie. He was educated at Eton and University College, Oxford. Arthur Ramsay served as a Lieutenant in the Second Boer War (1901-2) where he won the Queen's medal and 4 Clasps. In 1903 he married Mary

Adelaide Heathcote-Drummond-Willoughby, a daughter of the 1st Earl of Ancaster who was a prominent Liberal politician. There is a well-known painting of Arthur at Brechin Castle, painted by the renowned Edwardian society portrait painter, John Singer Sargent.

Arthur George Ramsay (1878-1929) 14th Earl of Dalhousie

Arthur had inherited estates burdened by debt and various blocks of land and individual farms seem to have been sold in the early 20th Century to help resolve the situation. All the land held by Panmure in the Friockheim and Inverkeilor areas seems to have been sold off around this time and for example, Hatton Mill was sold by auction in the White Hart Hotel, Arbroath around the time of WW1 and was bought by the Arnott Family. (The White Hart Hotel was the building which later became Woolworths and is now 'Nickel and Dime.')

Arthur rejoined the Army and served in the First World War as a Captain in the Scots Guards where he was badly wounded early in the war. After the war, though he survived through to 23rd December 1928 he seems to have been unable to make any significant contribution to the running of the estates. His wife, the Rt. Hon. Mary Adelaide, Countess of Dalhousie had a Power of Attorney registered to her on the 18th February 1915 and from that date, she appears to have dealt with all business matters connected with her husband's estates.

In 1922, the decision was taken to sell off more land and all the Panmure land in Carmyllie along with that part of the Parish of Arbirlot north of the River Elliot was sold off, mostly to sitting tenants. This ended the Parish of Carmyllie's association with Panmure Estate, an association that stretched back almost to the time of the 'Norman lordship' of Scotland in the 12th Century.

The remaining parts of the Panmure Estate continued to be owned by the Ramsay Family until 1950 when the sudden death of John Gilbert Ramsay, the 15th Earl, unmarried and at the relatively young age of 45, provoked a 'death duties' crisis for the family. He was succeeded by his brother Simon Ramsay, the 16th Earl who had served with the Black Watch in the Second World War in North Africa where he was wounded while charging a machine gun position and taken prisoner by the Italians. He soon escaped from his captors and having been promoted to Major, he took part in the Allied Invasion of Sicily in 1943, where he was awarded the Military Cross. He further reinforced the family's military credentials by marrying Margaret Stirling of Keir whose father Brigadier - General Archibald Stirling of Keir had founded the Commandos, now known as the Special Air Service, in June 1940. Simon stood for Parliament in the 1945 election and was elected MP for Angus in the Conservative interest. He was appointed Governor-General of Rhodesia and Nyasaland in 1957.

In 1950, Simon wrote to all his Panmure tenants to explain the situation:-
As you will doubtless understand, the question of meeting estate liability on my brother's death has caused me very great concern. I find myself forced to sell a considerable part of the estates that have belonged to my family for generations.
With the utmost reluctance I have decided to dispose of the greater part of Panmure, including your farm. I can only say how much sorrow this has caused me and my family.
In the midst of misfortune, however, I have been able to sell to trustees who assure me that it is their intention to hold the estate intact.

This decision affected 52 farms, 23 smallholdings and a total of 11,070 acres. The purchasers of the estate were the Harrison Family Trust. The Liverpool based shipping firm of T&J Harrison had grown very rich on convoy shipping across the Atlantic in WW2 and the money was invested in the Panmure Estate. In December 1955, the Harrison Trust employed Charles Brand Ltd. of Dundee to demolish Panmure House by explosives.

Panmure was sold to the Robinson Charitable Trust in 1971. David Robinson had made his fortune with his company, Radio Rentals which he set up in the early days of television, to rent television sets to millions of people for whom they were too expensive to buy. The Robinson Charitable Trust sold Panmure in 1975 and the proceeds of the sale were used to endow Robinson College at Cambridge University.

The Commercial Union Insurance Company bought the Panmure Estate in 1975 and sold it on in 2001 for around £21 million when it was bought by a property dealing company called Angus Estates, which was funded by Edinburgh financier and property dealer James Manclark. Angus Estates quickly sold most of the 50 tenanted farms to their sitting tenants and then, over the following decade or so, they sold off most of the remaining bits and pieces to advantage.

In Midlothian, the Ramsays owned Dalhousie Castle up to 1977. They had leased it out throughout most of the 20th Century and it was a school for a time, but it was converted to an hotel in 1972. It was sold in 1977 and it remains today a very luxurious country house hotel. Much of the land has been built upon now and Dalhousie sits today in parkland squeezed between Bonnyrigg and Newtongrange. Dalhousie's original primary asset, the coal revenues, seem to have been largely worked out by the time the Coal Commission was formed to nationalise the coal reserves in 1942

In 2007, the Ramsay family sold their family papers, known as the Dalhousie Muniments, to the National Archives of Scotland for a reputed £1.6 million. These papers included a charter from King David I and letters from George Washington and Florence Nightingale.

The Dalhousies remain in good heart today under the current Earl, James Hubert Ramsay, the 17th Earl of Dalhousie. The current Earl pursued a successful career in the City of London mainly at Hambros Bank and in 2009, was appointed Lord Steward to her Majesty's Household. They still own large holdings of land round Brechin and also the 43,662 acre Invermark estate at the head of Glenesk which is a neighbour to the Royal estate at Balmoral. They have also established a thriving Garden Centre on the edge of Brechin.

The Improvements on the Panmure Estate

As explained previously, Earl William Ramsay-Maule, 1st Lord Panmure allowed the Panmure Estate to fall into some disrepair. He was apparently popular with his tenants because he did not charge high rents, but the fabric of the estates suffered. In fairness to Earl William, income from a purely agricultural estate at that time would have left him with limited funds to finance improvements. His son, Fox Maule therefore inherited the estates in poor condition in 1852 and he set about making improvements, starting with Panmure House. Unlike his father, he had the benefit of substantial income from the Midlothian estate and revenue from land sales for development round the rapidly expanding city of Dundee.

Fox employed his friend the Edinburgh architect David Bryce to re-model Panmure House and plans were produced in 1851 before his father was yet dead. Bryce was the leading architect in Scotland in the middle of the 19th century and designed among other things, Fettes College and George Heriot's school. He re-modelled the Bank of Scotland on the Mound and he designed the Royal Exchange building in Dundee. Fox might well have helped Bryce to win the Bank of Scotland commission as Fox's cousin, James Andrew Broun Ramsay, the 10th Earl of Dalhousie and former Viceroy of India, was at that time Governor of the Bank of Scotland. Bryce also re-modelled Kinnaird for the Southesks in 1857 and worked on Cortachy also.

Typical Panmure Date Stone. It means 'John William (Ramsay) 1882 Earl Of Dalhousie

Working for the architect David Bryce at that time were two younger men, John Starforth and James Mclaren who were to exert a major influence on Angus rural architecture. The eldest of these was John Starforth who was a qualified assistant with Bryce from 1844 to 1853 when he left to set up his own practice. He came from County Durham and his practice was involved with churches, country house work, schools, hospitals, villas, farmhouses and farm steadings. His masterpiece was said to be the striking St. Andrews Church in Moffat, Dumfriesshire, and he apparently designed a major extension to Peebles Hydro. There are unusual two storey estate workers houses near the west gate into the Panmure Estate and these are called the Starforth cottages today. They certainly must have been Starforth's work.

John Starforth published the 'Architecture of the Farm' in 1853, 'Villa residences and Farm Architecture' in 1865, 'Designs for Villa residences, with descriptions in 1866 and the 'Architecture of the Park' in 1890. These publications are essentially architectural 'pattern' books intended for use by builders, surveyors, architects, landlords and estate factors. These books have all but been forgotten today, but many of the designs they contain have certainly been used by, or influenced other architects and John Starforth's influence can be seen in many Victorian rural buildings today. Starforth's colleague at Bryce's, James Mclaren, certainly seems to have dipped heavily into his books, particularly for his earlier work at Panmure. Other Angus Estates too seem to have used his designs such as Fotheringham. In fact, estate factors and architects all over the British Isles purchased Starforth's books and buildings to Starforth designs exist today on farms and estates throughout the country.

Local examples taken from Starforths books include the plans for the Hatton of Carnoustie which appear in the Architecture of the Farm described as ''Design for the residence of a proprietor farming his own estate'' and Stannochy House, formerly a factors house on the Brechin Castle Estate with its distinctive crow step gables, appears in Architecture of the Farm as 'a design for a farm-house' number 2 and is priced at £1,250. The Panmure farm cottages built in Fox Maule's time are adapted from a 'pair of labourers cottages'' at a cost of £380 for the pair. Even Arbroath Town Council dipped into Starforth's work, as the design for the west lodge at the Western Cemetery in Arbroath appears in the Architecture of the Park.

The younger of these two men was James Mclaren who worked as a qualified assistant to Bryce from around 1846 to the early 1850's when he returned to his native Dundee to set up his own practice. He got the plum appointment of surveyor and architect to Panmure Estate on the recommendation of Bryce. Mclaren is best remembered today as architect to the Dundee jute wallahs as he built many of their mansions in Barnhill, Broughty Ferry, Carnoustie and Monifeith. He controlled the Panmure feus, that is to say, if you wanted to buy land to build a house in Carnoustie, Monifieth, Broughty Ferry, Barnhill and even parts of Arbroath, Brechin and Edzell, he was the man you had to see. He therefore was responsible for the layout of much of the Victorian built environment in Angus, especially the south end of the county. James Mclaren was appointed as surveyor and architect to the

Panmure estates in the early 1850's and continued in that role to the late 1880's. It would be his firm that would draw many of the plans for the Panmure improvements.

In Fox Maule's period, Panmure House was rebuilt, the lodges and cottages within the policies were constructed and a number of the farmhouses and steadings closest to Panmure House were built at that time. Several of these earlier farmhouses look to have been influenced by Starforth designs though in simplified form. At Brechin Castle, it was also the buildings in the policies and on the farms closest to the castle that were improved. Little if anything seems to have been built in Carmyllie in Fox's lairdship except for the development of the quarries.

Unusual Panmure date stone, Kirkton of Monikie

When Fox died in 1874, Admiral George Ramsay became laird and 12th Earl of Dalhousie. It is said that improvements to the estates carried on in his time but it is not obvious what they were and little seems to have been done in Carmyllie in his time. It was his son John William Ramsay, 13th Earl of Dalhousie who was to be the great improver of the estates and the Victorian stone houses in the Panmure part of Carmyllie were all constructed in his time between 1880 and 1887.

John William Ramsay, 13th Earl of Dalhousie set about the improvements to his estates with great vigour. He was new to the business of landowning but he worked hard at getting to know his estates and tenants and it was said that he visited every farm, large and small to see what was required. It was not only houses and farm buildings that were being renewed but draining, fencing and dyking were carried out also.

Lord Dalhousie gave a dinner for his Brechin and Edzell tenantry at Edzell Castle in November 1882 when he spoke about his difficulties:-

''I have not been brought up to the business of landowning, and I have sometimes felt that I have taken command of a ship, so to say, in rather a gale of wind.

It would be a small pleasure to me to work my estate with the sole object of getting money out of it; any Edinburgh lawyer could do it--more satisfactory to himself--than I should.

It is uphill work trying to bring round an estate that has been allowed to run down, and that is also heavily burdened with debt--I might say up to the lips in debt. I daresay that many of you gentlemen, who no doubt take a look sometimes at the Forfar Valuation Roll, think I must be a precious rich fellow. Would you like to know exactly how much I have pocketed out of the estates during the last two years? Well, I will tell you. Not a single shilling. More than that, rather less than that. Not only have I been living on capital myself, but I have been borrowing money in order that the necessary improvements on the estate should go on''

Standard Panmure 3 roomed Cottage with 2 roomed bothy attached at Denhead of Arbirlot

Apart from the houses on the Cononsyth and Guynd Estates, almost all of the stone built Victorian houses in Carmyllie have or would have had a carved stone, often a lintel above a door with JW 188- ED. This is often wrongly assumed to be a builder's mark or a factor's mark. The date in the middle would normally be between 1880 and 1887 and the letters stand for John William (Ramsay) Earl of Dalhousie and mean that the farm was part of the estates of the Earl of

Dalhousie at Panmure, Brechin Castle or Invermark and that the building in question had been erected as part of the great estate improvements carried on by him from when he inherited the estates in 1880 till he died in 1887. He is the Laird we have to thank for the Carmyllie we have today.

There are other date stones round the estate. In the Panmure policies and on some of the Dundee road farms, there are stones just with a date or with the Panmure 'shell' coat of arms and a date. At Kirkton of Monikie, there is an attractive date stone built into the wall next to the road dated 1587. That stone appears to be much earlier than the building it is set into however. Mr. Hugh Brunton apparently has a date stone in the 1700's on one of his farms. There are other date stones around, but the common ones in Arbirlot and Carmyllie are JW-date-ED with a date from 1880 to1887.

As far as the cottages are concerned, there were really only 3 roomed cottages and 2 roomed bothies. The 3 roomed cottage in detached form would have been a grieve's house or on the small farms, it was provided as a small farmhouse such as at the Brae of Conon and Hunterspath. In semi-detached or terraced form, it would have been a ploughman's house. The cottages at the Newton of Carmyllie and Wardneuk are good examples. The Sitsundry Cottages at Denhead of Arbirlot were originally a 3 roomed cottage with an attached 2 room bothy. At the Brae of Conon, there is a detached 3 roomed house built as the farmhouse and a 2 roomed bothy attached to a cart-shed. The room dimensions of the 3 roomed cottage and the 2 roomed bothy at the Brae of Conon are exactly the same

Well preserved example of a double set of Panmure outhouses; shed, lavatory and piggery. Crudie, Arbirlot

as for the Sitsundry cottages at Denhead. There are dozens of these cottages round Carmyllie and round the rest of the Panmure Estate. Most have been greatly altered. The Denhead and Brae of Conon cottages were modernised with Department of Agriculture Grants in 1957. If you look closely at them though, they were originally all standard designs.

Standard Panmure 3 roomed Cottage used in detached form as a farmhouse.Brae of Conon

All of these houses would have had an outside lavatory, firewood shed and one or two pig stys. The Brae of Conon farmhouse still has an intact example and another can be seen at Crudie.

Newtonbank (below the Carmyllie War Memorial) is unusual with an arch portico round the front door. If this portico is original, this cottage is probably earlier, as this is what the cottages built in Fox's time at East Scryne and in the Panmure policies look like. Redhills, next to the Church at Arbirlot is the same also. Fotheringham too has cottages like this. This design with the arch at the front door is similar to John Starforth's designs in his books; they would have been the earliest of the "improvements" and were probably built before 1880.

Many of the farmhouses too are of a similar design. There seems to have been a basic design of 2 storey house. Classic examples would be Forehills, Curleys, Wardneuk and Milton Haugh and the now demolished old farmhouses at the Milton of Carmyllie and Blindwells were other examples. The slightly more generous version of this house with a single storey L at the back is what Denhead was like originally. Montquir is the same but with the rear 'L' in the middle. Hillhead is another example but that seems to have been turned backwards with later modification by putting dormer windows on the rear roof slope. Craigmill farmhouse at Panbride has been altered in the same way. The Slade farmhouse is also similar but the

Newtonbank, Carmyllie

'L' is 2 storey though that may not be original. Other examples are the Bank of Arbirlot and Crudie Acres. Crudie Acres looks very similar to Denhead but the rear 'L' seems to be at the opposite side. Millhill farmhouse at Arbirlot seems to be a largely unaltered example of the latter type. From the front Millhill looks today, virtually identical to a photograph of Denhead farmhouse taken in the 1950's.

Most of these Panmure houses are built of grey stone of the type that came from Panmure's own quarries at Carmyllie and Denfind. This stone would have been essentially waste. There are strata of this type of stone (a sort of grey mudstone) above and between the layers of Carmyllie pavement and they would have cut and dressed this for building stone. The Panmure houses are unusual because almost all the other stone houses in Angus are built with the red sandstone natural to the area.

The houses on the neighbouring estates are quite different in design. The farmhouses and cottages on Patrick Alan-Fraser's Hospitalfield estate such as the Brax, Denfield and Drumyellow for example, look completely different and not just because they are of red sandstone out of the Brax and Drumyellow quarries. The Fletcher's estate at Letham Grange also has a different style of farmhouses and cottages (largely Edwardian in taste) and they are also mainly red sandstone. Fotheringham estate on the other hand has a number of farmhouses and cottages that look rather like Panmure designs and these were probably also influenced by the Starforth books.

Unaltered example of the slightly more elaborate Panmure 2 storey farmhouses. Millhill, Arbirlot

It would have been Mclaren's junior staff and assistants who would have worked on the cottages, farmhouses and steadings on the Panmure estates (known as Dalhousie Estates after 1860). These buildings would have been commissioned by the Estate Factor and worked up from standard designs, some of which seem to have been taken from or influenced by John Starforth's books. By the 1880's when the surge in building came along under John William, the Dalhousie Estates Office, run by Mr John Shiell the factor, seems to have engaged an 'in house' architect, by the name of Mr D. Fraser. No doubt it was more economical to do this due to the large amount of building going on. James Mclaren's architectural practice was in any case, by then having problems. Mclaren had fallen out with fellow architect, George Shaw Aitken with whom he was then in partnership and he was involved in extensive litigation in 'the Ferrybank stone affair' He had opened a quarry on his own estate of Ferrybank near Cupar in Fife to quarry the fine grained white sandstone there for building. This white sandstone however quickly proved unsuitable for building as it was unreliable on exposure to the weather and legal claims ensued from this. Mclaren's practice did however continue to act as

Typical Example of a Standard Panmure 2 storey Farmhouse, Milton Haugh

Dalhousie Surveyors and control the Panmure Feus on behalf of the Dalhousie Trustees until 1898 despite the death of James Mclaren in 1893.

During the 1880-87 'John William' period, the estate architects simplified the designs of the Dalhousie buildings, and the many cottages and small farmhouses built at that time carry little decorative embellishment. They are plain but practical houses for the age in which they were built. Only the medium and larger farmhouses continued to carry some of the decorative timber and iron work which typified the high Victorian style that was promoted in the Starforth books.

The main building contractor employed by Dalhousie on the Panmure Estate at this time seems to have been the firm of Nicol of Letham. They indeed must have enjoyed a very busy and no doubt very profitable seven years.

It was not only houses and farm buildings that required improvement on the Panmure Estate. Drainage and dyking was required also. In the report on Carmyllie in the first statistical account from 1791, it was reported that until some years ago, ''the land was thought better adapted for pasture than for grain'', but ''in 1791 there was four times the quantity of grain, especially of barley being raised in Carmyllie than 20 years before''. Some draining, liming and marling had clearly been done as far back as that.

In the New Statistical Account of 1843, it is being reported that ''great additions have been made to the cultivated land of the parish by cultivating wastes, draining mosses and marshes, enclosing fields and planting woodland'' and in ''Lord Panmure's part of the parish, some 800-900 acres have been added to the cultivated land since 1770''. It seems therefore that in Earl William's time, at least some improvements were being made in land reclamation and drainage in Carmyllie, though it is unlikely that the estate was financing much of this and improvements would be being made largely by the tenant's own endeavours. It seems to have been common for the Estate to give new tenants several years rent free in exchange for an undertaking that they would 'break in' their farms.

James MacDonald, writing in 1881 in 'Transactions of the Highland and Agricultural Society of Scotland', reports on 'The Agriculture of the Counties of Forfar and Kincardine'. He reports that the Panmure Estate extended into the parishes of Panbride, Monifieth, Barry, Monikie, Arbirlot, Carmyllie, St.Vigeans, Inverkeilor and Kinnell. He points out that the valuation roll for 1856-57 showed that the total valuation of Carmyllie was £4,786 but by 1880-81 it was £7,971 which suggests that significant improvements had been made before 1880. He also reports that the greater part of Carmyllie has been reclaimed in the last 30 years by the crofters themselves. In the 1880-87 'John William' period, the farm steadings were mostly re-developed just as the farmhouses were but there does seem to have been a big reduction in the number of crofts and pendicles as many seem to have disappeared at this time. No doubt the stone from these pendicles was recycled into the farm buildings and probably into the field dykes also.

There was also undoubtedly quite a lot of land drainage being carried out in Carmyllie in the 'John William' period and this would seem to be marked by the relatively new 2 and 3 inch tiles being laid. The type of drainage laid in a field can tell us when the field in question was brought in to use for cropping. Fields laid with stone or rubble drains would have been brought into cropping from the start of the 18th century or earlier up to around 1826. Before 1826 there was a hefty tax on all clay bricks and tiles so that tile drains were too expensive for draining land. In 1826, drain tiles were exempted from this tax provided they were imprinted with the word drain and most early tile drainage dates from that time. The early types were of 2 piece tile and sole form and were just made the same way as roof tiles but bent before firing. Handmade horseshoe tiles were the next development until 1845 when Thomas Scraggs invented a tile extruding machine and round tiles started to be produced. It was said that a man and three boys could produce 11,000 tiles for firing in a ten hour day with Scragg's Machine. From 1845, the inch and collar tile was produced and mechanically extruded horseshoe and egg-shaped tiles were also being produced from this time. By the 1870s, 2 inch round tiles became the norm and 3 inch round tiles were also being widely used by the 1880s.

Applying this method of dating to Denhead of Arbirlot, the Denhead land in the Parish of Arbirlot was originally drained with stone drains and though there are later 'inch and collar' and 'horseshoe' tiles in places, we can assume that it had first been drained for cropping before 1826, and was indeed probably being cropped through much of the 18th century. Most of Denhead's land in Carmyllie Parish on the other hand, is drained with 2 inch and 3 inch tiles and would seem to have been drained for cropping after about 1870 and was probably part of the 1880-87 'John William' improvements. From the early 1880s, a severe agricultural depression set in and by 1890, 'dog and stick' farming became the norm and this continued until war loomed again in the late 1930s with only a brief uplift in prices during the 1914-18 war. Drainage and improvement of farmland in Britain all but ceased during these years and it was not until after WW2 that farming started to progress again.

John William Ramsay, the 13th Earl of Dalhousie had done a great deal of good work to improve his estates and he largely shaped the area we live in today, but he had spent a great deal of money doing it. The problem was that he had spent this money improving the estate just as agriculture went in to a severe depression in the late 1880s. This undoubtedly explains why the estate was in so much debt as when he died in such tragic circumstances in 1887, it was said that he had spent £150,000 on building and other improvements to his estates.

Authorities consulted for this chapter
Primary Sources
Court papers served in the Court of Session, Edinburgh, supporting a claim to the title and lands of Panmure. Information for George, Earl of Dalhousie, and the Honourable Mr. William Ramsay-Maule, his second son *Against* Thomas Maule, Esq;. Lieutenant of Invalids. February 14th 1782. Copy available at The Angus Archives, Forfar.

Letters of Sir Walter Scott, edited by Sir Herbert Grierson Letter to Lord Montagu 14th Feb 1823 vol. vii. pp 331-2. (Pub. London, Constable 1932-37. 12 volumes)

New Statistical Account of Scotland (NSA), Forfarshire. By Ministers of the respective parishes. William Blackwood & Sons, Edinburgh & London 1843

Old Statistical Account of Scotland.(OSA) 1791-1799.Volume XIII Angus. Sir John Sinclair (Editor). Reprinted Edition. Pub. EP Publishing Ltd. Wakefield, Yorkshire. 1976.

Panmure Papers in Two Volumes. Being a selection from the correspondence of Fox Maule, Second Baron Panmure, afterwards Eleventh Earl of Dalhousie, K.T., G.C.B. Edited by Sir George Douglas, Bart., M.A. and Sir George Dalhousie Ramsay C.B. Late of the War Office with a supplementary chapter by the Late Rev. Principal Rainy, D.D. (Published by Hodder & Stoughton, London, 1908)

Registrum De Panmure. 2 vols. by John Stuart LLD (Editor). Privately Printed, Edinburgh 1874.

Third Statistical Account of Scotland, The County of Angus. Edited by William Allen Illsley M.A. Ph.D pub. The Herald Press Arbroath, 1977.

Valuation Rolls for the County Of Forfar/Angus. ---various

Obituaries
Death of Lord Panmure (The Right Hon. William Maule) Dundee Courier, 16th April 1852

John Starforth The Scotsman, Edinburgh. 19th May 1898.

Catalogues
Cluttons, Chartered Surveyors, *The Panmure Estate*, Sale Particulars (Cluttons, Chartered Surveyors. Edinburgh/London 2001)

George, M.D., Catalogue of Political and Personal Satires (in the British Museum), xi. No. 16979

Printed Source and Further R eading
Barclay, James R and Keith, Alexander, *The Aberdeen-Angus Breed: A History* (The Aberdeen Angus Cattle Society, Aberdeen. 1958)

Black, David D., Town Clerk of Brechin, *History of Brechin* to 1864,
2nd Edition (William Paterson , Edinburgh and Black & Johnston , Brechin. 1867)

Brassey, Annie Allnutt Brassey *(Lady Brassey) The Last Voyage to India and Australia in the Sunbeam.* Published posthumously from the travel diaries of Annie Allnutt Brassey (Lady Brassey) (Longmans, Green & Co. London 1889,

Cockburn, Henry, *Circuit Journeys* (David Douglas, Edinburgh. 1889)

Cumming, Gersholm, *Forfarshire Illustrated.* 2nd Edition, (Dundee 1848)

Edwards, D.H., *In Memoriam, The Earl and Countess of Dalhousie*,(Advertiser Office. Brechin 1887)

Ernle, Lord, *English Farming Past and Present.* (Longmans, Green & Co., Ltd 1912, the edition consulted being the 5th edition edited and revised by Sir A.D. Hall and pub. by Longmans, Green & Co. Ltd 1936)

Escott, Margaret, *Maule, Hon. William Ramsay (1771-1852) of Panmure and Brechin Castle, Forfar Farm Architecture, 1865* ('History of Parliament: House of Commons 1820-32' D.R. Fisher ed.) (Cambridge University Press, 2009)

Finch, Barry J., *Ploughing Engines at Work*, (Percival Marshall & Co., Ltd., London 1962)

Fussell, G.E., *The Farmer's Tools* 2nd Edition (Orbis Publishing, London 1981)

Gow, Ian, *Scotland's Lost Houses*, National Trust For Scotland (Aurum Press London 2006)

Hay, George, *Around about the Round 'O'*, (T. Buncle, Arbroath. 1883)

Hay, George, *History of Arbroath*, 2nd ed. (T. Buncle, Arbroath 1899)

Jervise, Andrew, *Land of the Lindsays* 2nd edition, revised by the Rev. James Gammack, M.A. (David Douglas, Edinburgh 1882)

Jervise, Andrew, *Memorials of Angus and Mearns*, (A & C Black, Edinburgh 1861)

McBain, John, *Eminent Arbroathians* (Brodie & Salmond, Arbroath 1897)

McDonald, J.,*On the Agriculture of the Counties of Forfar and Kincardine* by J 'in Transactions of the Highland and Agricultural Society of Scotland', Fourth Series. Vol. 13, 1881 pp82-86

Paterson, James, and Maidment, James (ed) *Kay's Edinburgh Portraits* Vol. 2, Popular Letterpress Ed.(Hamilton, Adams, & Co., London and Thomas D. Morison,Glasgow 1885)

Peter, David MacGregor, *The Baronage of Angus and Mearns* (Oliver & Boyd, Edinburgh 1856)

Ritchie, Graeme R.L., *The Normans in Scotland* (Edinburgh University Press, 1954)

Starforth, John, Four Volumes: *The Architecture of the Farm, 1853, Villa Residences and Farm Architecture* and *Designs for Villa Residences, with Descriptions 1866* and *The Architecture of the Park 1890* (William Blackwood & Sons Edinburgh and London)

Stephens, Henry, *The Book of The Farm*, 3rd Edition. 2 vols particularly Volume ii, 3407 to 3461 'Draining land' (William Blackwood and Sons1877

Taylor, James, M.A., D.D., F.S.A.*The Great Historic Families of Scotland* Volume 1 (J.S. Virtue & Co., Limited, London 1887) Chapters on the Ramsays and the Maules.

Warden, Alex,*Angus or Forfarshire, The Land and People*, 5 vols (Charles Alexander, Dundee, 1882)

Various internet resources including Ancestry, The Peerage.com, Dictionary of Scottish Architects, Dictionary of National Biography, 1885-1900 Volume 47 and others.

Chapter 6

GUYND ESTATE AND THE OUCHTERLONY FAMILY

The Mansion House at the Guynd

The oldest resident at the Guynd is 'The Grey Lady of the Guynd'. She is of course the resident ghost and was said often to be seen at the old lake in the evenings, though she could be seen anywhere around the Estate. I am not aware that she is the manifestation of any particular long departed Ouchterlony, but the Guynd would not be complete without a resident ghost!

According to the old records, from the time of Malcom Canmore and the arrival of Norman influence in Scotland, the Guynd, like most of the land in the Arbroath area, was part of the landholding of the Abbacy of Arbroath. Before the Reformation, Cardinal Beaton seems to have been able to grant land to various members of his family and the lands of the Guynd were held by Cardinal James Beaton (or Bethune) in 1597. He was the Archbishop of Glasgow and a nephew of Cardinal Beaton. The Guynd was held by the Beatons till 1625 when the Marquis of Hamilton acquired the lands belonging to the Abbey. The Hamiltons then sold most of these lands including the Guynd to the Maules of Panmure in 1642.

Confusion arises in discussions of landholdings in medieval Scotland because of the different layers of land ownership. At the Guynd, the Abbacy then the Beatons, the Hamiltons and the Maules would seem to have held the Guynd in superiority only. They would have received tithes from the 'subordinate' Lairds. The Maules of Panmure would have held these superiorities until 1715 when their estates were forfeited to the Crown as a consequence of Earl James Maule's support of the 'Old Pretender'. The Maules were able to buy back most of their estates in 1764 but the superiorities of much of the Guynd lands had passed to the Earls of Strathmore by that time.

The earliest 'Lairds' of the Guynd recorded are the Strachan Family of Carmyllie Castle, which stood just to the east of the present steading at the Mains of Carmyllie. They were the Lairds of much of Carmyllie Parish and held 'Charters over' lands including the Mains, Newton and Milton of Carmyllie as well as Skichen and the Guynd. They would have held their land, including the Guynd in feu, paying a tithe to their 'superiors'. The Strachans seem to have held land in Carmyllie since about 1325 when they received a charter of the lands of Carmyllie from Robert the Bruce.

Commissary Maule writing in 1611 in his history of the Maule family of Panmure (see Registrum de Panmure) tells us that the Strachans started in Carmyllie as millers at the Milton of Carmyllie. They had 'taks' of the mill and lands first for 5 years then 19 years and eventually became 'heritors'. He says the Strachan's mill at Milton of Carmyllie gave the parish its name. In the old tongue (evidently the Norman tongue) it was Cairmoulin then Carmoulne and was brought to the English tongue as Carmile or Carmyly with the French moulin becoming mill. The Strachans gradually acquired more land in Carmyllie, gave up milling, and moved up the hill to become Lairds. They built the house or castle at Carmyllie when one of the Strachans married Nanz Maule of Panmure, the Strachans up to that time having lived in a house of 'earth and stone'.

The Strachans certainly seem to have held the lands of the Guynd for all of the 16th Century. Around

1500, David Strachan founded a chapel and provided a school 'for the instruction of youth' on his lands in Carmyllie. After the Reformation, the Parish of Carmyllie was formed and in 1609, the Strachans as the main lairds were required by 'The Lords Commissioners for the Plantation of Kirks' to enlarge the old chapel to form a new parish church. This brought them nearly to ruin and to repair their finances; they sold the Guynd to the Ouchterlony family in November 1616. The remainder of the Strachan lands in Carmyllie seemed to have passed to Maule of Panmure around this time.

The Ouchterlonys moved to the Guynd from Kelly at Arbirlot which they had occupied since around 1442 and they appear to have built the original Kelly Castle there. The present Kelly Castle is largely a Victorian reconstruction undertaken by Dundee architect James McLaren for Fox Maule-Ramsay the Earl of Dalhousie and 2nd Baron Panmure in 1862. The Ouchterlony name is derived from Lownie (Auchter-Lowny) near Letham and they seem to have held "Charters of the Lands of Balmadies and Others" in 1226-39. The Estate of Balmadies was in fact called 'Ochterlony' up to the end of the 19th century. They appear to have exchanged these lands in 1239 for land at Kenny at Kingoldrum. In 1394, Alexander of Ouchterlony married Janet, only daughter of Sir William Maule of Panmure and was given the lands of Greenford at Arbirlot as dowry. Over the next 50 years, they seem to have acquired various other bits of land around Arbirlot and they acquired the lands of Kelly in 1442, part of which was acquired in exchange for land the Ouchterlony Family held at Preyston in Ayrshire. Kelly had been held by the 'Norman', Mowbray Family in early times and later by the Lindsay Family, the Earls of Crawford, from whom it passed to the Ouchterlonys in 1442. About 1614, Sir William Ouchterlony sold Kelly to Sir William Irvine and it passed from him to Sir Alexander Irvine of Drum about 1630. Lady Marion Douglas, wife of Sir Alexander Irvine gave to Arbirlot Church, the old silver communion cups which they still have at Arbirlot. The inscription on these communion cups reads:- *GIVEN TO THE KIRK OF ARBIRLOT BE MARION DOUGLAS LADY OF DRUM LYFRENTAR OF KELLY AND CUTHLIE ANNO 1633.* The Irvines of Drum having been financially

ruined by taking the Royalist side in the Civil War, sold Kelly to the Earl George Maule of Panmure in 1679 and Kelly later became the home of Harry Maule of Kelly. Over the years, the Castle gradually fell into disrepair and came to be used as housing for farm labourers and even livestock until it was rebuilt in 1862. Panmure Estate eventually sold it in November 1919 to Archibald S. Briggs of the North British Chemical Company at Dowrie Works, Elliot who had previously lived in it for some years as a tenant.

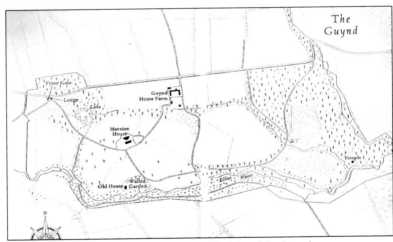

Plan of the Home Farm and Policies of the Guynd

The Ouchterlony family moved to the Guynd around 1616 and they would have built the original mansion there, which is now the 'B' listed 'Garden House', around that time. It would have been a different house from the house that is there now as it has obviously been re-modeled several times from the different types of stonework in the walls. The final re-modeling was carried by the Piersons around 1847, well after the 'New Mansion' was built in 1817. The Piersons re-modeled the old house in the 'gothic revival' style then fashionable and the charming 'minstrels gallery' above a high entrance hall was created at that time. John Ouchterlony, the present Laird made repairs and improvements in the 1970s and the house was habitable up to the 1980s, but has since been subjected to a great degree of vandalism. Today the house is uninhabitable and in poor condition but in its time, it would have been very attractive with a fine view over the Elliot Burn. The first incarnation of this house would have been the house where an early John Ouchterlony (Auchterlonie) of the Guynd wrote his 'Account of the Shire of Forfar' in 1684-5.

Beside the 'old house' there is a substantial stone-walled garden running down to the Elliot Burn which you enter through a yew arch. The lintel above the gate carries a date stone for 1664. This garden is now overgrown but would have been very productive in its day. There is a substantial range of now derelict, south-facing, lean-to glass-houses on the north wall. The O.S. maps of 1860 show that the internal layout of the garden was conventional with intersecting paths dividing the garden into quarters. In the early 1900's, it had ornamental features such as a rose and clematis trellis walk down the centre and topiary yew hedges. In the 1920's, alpine and rock garden plants were growing in it under the direction of Marie Ouchterlony, the Colonel's wife who was by all accounts a keen gardener. The garden became neglected after WW2 when the gardener died but in 1955, it was leased out as a commercial market garden to a Mr. Bert Beard. This venture ceased in the 1960's and the 'Commander' planted the garden out in Christmas trees. These trees became too big and were neglected until the present Laird had them cleared recently.

Lt. Col. Ouchterlony and his daughter boating on the Lake at the Guynd

The ornamental lake at the Guynd was situated north-west of the mansion near the lodge by the west gate. In its time it was a great beauty spot and was well used for picnics by Sunday Schools, Schools and the local community. Shakespearian plays were staged there in the Edwardian era. The lake is now almost completely silted up and it is now overgrown by rhododendron and alder. There are remains of a boat house at the south side of the lake.

The 'B' listed Mansion House at the Guynd was erected in 1817 to plans drawn by Edinburgh architect, James Patterson. Patterson had trained with the celebrated Adam family of architects in Edinburgh and was also the architect for Fasque in the Mearns at about the same time as the Guynd mansion plans were drawn up. The original plans are dated 1799 and are for the central part of the house only. The two wings were added on later plans at the time of construction. A later 'northern range' was added in Victorian times consisting of a coach-house, stable, wash-house, hen-house and other offices forming a rear courtyard. The fan shaped glazing above the main entrance is a particularly attractive feature. There was a tennis court at the west side of the house and this was later replaced by a swimming pool. A few years ago, the present laird removed the old overgrown laurel and yew in front of the Mansion house to open up the view to the south and this restored the 'ha-ha' at the front of the house to its original purpose. The pink sandstone for building the Mansion was quarried on the Estate out of a quarry opened for the purpose at the edge of the Elliot Water.

Plans for the design of the landscape were drawn up by James Abercrombie in 1775, but these plans were not used. The Guynd landscape as we see it today, largely follows a later plan drawn up by another firm of landscape designers, Thomas White and Son. Much of the original planned ornamental planting at the Guynd was destroyed by the great storm of 1953.

The steading at the Guynd Home farm dates from 1847 and was built by James Pierson who had married Margaret Ouchterlony. It would have been a 'model' farm in its day. John Ouchterlony, the present Laird, says that the Piersons had made a substantial profit on speculation in railway shares in the early 1840's. The Guynd quarries (at Glentyrie) though never as successful as the Slade quarries, would also have been producing income for the estate at this time. The Piersons seem to have used that money to improve the estate, as all the buildings at the home farm were built around 1847 except the white, eight sided farmhouse or overseer's house known as 'Parkneuk' which appears to be Georgian.

At the Home Farm there was a saw-mill powered by a water-wheel. A drawing for this water-wheel appears in Henry Stephen's Book of the Farm. Water engineering has long been a pre-occupation at the Guynd as in 1849, the steading and fields at the home farm were supplied with water by a system of stone conduits running from the Elliot burn just below Milton Haugh. This system also supplied water for the dam which in turn provided water to power the saw-mill. A further water supply was installed in 1850 which ran from the Elliot through the Newton of Carmyllie, and then through another stone conduit to supply the lodge, the ornamental lake and the policies and it also supplied water to the New Mansion for laundry and drain flushing.

Parkneuk at the Guynd Home Farm. The overseer's house

The new mansion and all the farms on the Guynd Estate had piped potable water installed around 1857 to plans drawn up by W. Baillie. The water came from the Guynd quarries at Redford and was fed by gravity from a header tank below the quarry and at the west end of what is now Burnhead Terrace. The Guynd would therefore have had one of the earliest piped water supplies in the area.

The piggery at the Guynd was 'state of the art' for 1847 as pigs were then rarely kept on a commercial basis and were mostly fed for domestic consumption in small pig stys attached to or near houses. A recent book called 'Buildings of the Land' by the RCAHMS, features the Guynd piggery. An interesting feature of this piggery is a doo-cot built into one of the gables and there is also a dedicated boiler house for cooking pig food. At the Home Farm, there was also a threshing mill powered by a 'horse gang' and stables for eight pairs of horses.

The National Archives of Scotland hold plans for a steading at the Guynd Home farm though they have not been fully carried out. They also hold plans for a new steading for the Conon dated 1802. The lodge at the Guynd would have been built around 1847 and it like all the Guynd buildings built at this time, carries distinctive decorative pointed finials on the gables.

The Laird at the time the new mansion house was built was John Ouchterlony, the 20th Laird of the Guynd. He was something of a poet, he travelled extensively in Europe and he collected books and prints by Piranesi and Hogarth. He was said to "have peculiar habits" and he was an eccentric. He never married and when he died on the 29th November 1843, the male line of the Ouchterlonys ended with him. Having built a new mansion house, he never moved in to it and he lived and died in the old house. It was said the estate and the new mansion were fast falling to ruin when he died in 1843.

It was a generation earlier in the time of John Ouchterlony the 19th Laird of the Guynd, that the family seems to have been at the zenith of their prosperity. This John Ouchterlony describes himself as a "Merchant in Riga". In a document held by the National Archives of Scotland dated 1773, we find his factor, James Gardyne of Middleton writing on his behalf to the Earl of Panmure. He is asking to buy out the feus of the Guynd, The Tulloes (parish of Dunnichen), The Brax (parish of St. Vigeans) and "Half Lands of the Milltown of Conon". At this time, the Earl of Panmure seems to have had the opportunity to buy back the superiorities forfeited to the Crown in 1715 and Ouchterlony now wished to buy out these 'feus' from Panmure. This tells us that in 1773 the Ouchterlonys had capital available to invest in the Estates.

One of John Ouchterlony, the 20th Laird's sisters, married William Cumming and the Tulloes Estate was inherited by them. It was later inherited by their daughters, Mary Anne and Margaret Cumming who remained spinsters and had a residence called Tulloes Lodge near Cheltenham. The Estate was therefore partly 'broken up' in 1843 on the death of John Ouchterlony, the 20th Laird, and was divided between the families of his two sisters, with Mrs. Cumming's family inheriting the Tulloes Estate and Mrs. Pierson's family inheriting the Guynd and the Brax. The Brax Estate which was Brax farm, Brax Cottage farm and Annefield croft, (Drumyellow was not part of the Guynd as it was part of Grange of Conon and became part of Hospitalfield in 1884), was sold by the Ouchterlonys in 1920. Brax farm was bought by David Weighton who was tenant at the time. The Conon was sold by the Ouchterlonys in 1926 to David Gibb who was the sitting tenant. The Tulloes Estate consisted of Nether, Upper, Woodside and Burnside of Tulloes and North and South Draffinn and Vinneybank. Miss Mary Anne Cumming died and the Tulloes Estate was sold in 1886 by her executors to John C. Brodie an Edinburgh solicitor who owned the neighbouring Idvies Estate. The Tulloes Estate was eventually broken up and mostly sold to sitting tenants after the Second World War.

The Temple at the Guynd was built in 1853 by James Alexander Pierson, John Ouchterlony's nephew and heir. It was built to the design of John Ouchterlony and on his instructions. It is 'B' listed and is in the form of a small rotunda of Grecian style. It is situated in the Harbour Den on a high bank overlooking the Elliot, between the Den of Guynd and the Black Den. Within it is a stone tablet on which is inscribed a verse composed by John Ouchterlony:-

The 'Temple' at the Guynd

'In this lone spot, by mortal seldom trod,
The dust is laid, the spirit fled to God,
Of him who reared these woods, these cultured plains
With verdure clothed, or stored with golden grains ;
O'er these paternal scenes, by time defaced,
Bade yonder mansion rise in simple taste ;
And, deeming naught his own which Heaven bestowed,
Diffused its blessings as a debt he owed.
O empty record! What avails thee now?
Thy anxious days, thy labour-warmed brow ;
See where man's little works himself survive,--
How short his life who bade these forests live.
While they shall rear their ample boughs on high
Through distant ages, and while o'er them sigh
Eve's murmuring breezes, to the thoughtful say--
Like his, so pass thy fleeting span away.'

One would think from these lines that John Ouchterlony had intended to be buried at the Temple, or that his ashes would be scattered there. In fact, John Ouchterlony was interred at the Churchyard of Montrose on his own instructions where there was a fine Corinthian column inscribed to his memory. It was broken intentionally about the middle with the capital lying on the ground to signify that the 'stem' of the 'House of Ouchterlony' has failed. Today the Corinthian column on his grave is just a stump and the broken column has been removed. The stone is inscribed 'sacred *to the memory of John Ouchterlony Esq. of the Guynd. He died on the 29 Nov 1843 in the 70th year of his age'*. His grave can be found in the 'Kirkie-Steps' Churchyard above and to the east of Baltic Street, just a few yards from the rear of St. John's Church, the Old Parish Church of Montrose. John Ouchterlony had intended to be buried with his forebears in Arbroath Abbey. The site of the high altar of Arbroath Abbey was long used as a private burial place by the Ouchterlonys. In 1823, the Crown raised an action of interdict in the Court of Session to prevent its use as a burial place by the Ouchterlonys. The Court granted the interdict, but

John Ouchterlony's grave, 'Kirkie Steps' Graveyard, Montrose

the case was appealed by John Ouchterlony in the House of Lords, who upheld the Crown's interdict against Ouchterlony. One must conclude that the elaborate memorial arrangements of John Ouchterlony were his way of "having the last word" on the subject.

Visitors to the Temple today might wonder why John Ouchterlony had his memorial built in such an isolated and inaccessible place. At that time, it would not have been so isolated or inaccessible. Just below the bank on which the Temple sits, you can see traces of an old road which would have been in use in his time for travel and as a drove road for cattle. This road can be seen on old maps and it was the old 'Hectors' Path or 'Hunters' Path. It ran from the Milton of Conon down the Black Den to just beside the Temple where it branched in two. The left turn would take you east down the Elliot Den to Arbirlot, while the right turn would take you west and over the Elliot to Hunterspath farm and then on over to Panbride and the coast. Near to this road, a spring of clear water issues from the the

Pierson's Memorial near the 'Temple'

foot of the bank on top of which sits the Temple. This spring would no doubt have provided restorative refreshment to travellers in olden times and it is known as St. Johns Well. John Ouchterlony seems to have attached great significance to St. Johns Well and there can be little doubt that he had the Gospel according to St. John, 4 :14. in mind when he instructed the Temple to be built directly above this spring *''But whosoever drinketh of the water I shall give*

Lieut-Col.Ouchterlony with carriage c.1900

him shall never thirst; but the water that I shall give him shall be in him a well of water springing up into everlasting life''.

Just beyond the Temple are other family memorials (not graves). One of these is a block of Peterhead granite, polished and enclosed by an iron railing. It is inscribed: - 'James Alexander Pierson, the twenty-first Laird of The Guynd, died at the Guynd, August the 9th, 1873. Son of James Pierson and Margaret Ouchterlony. Succeeded his Mother in 1849. To his most dear memory this stone is placed here, in faith and hope, by his wife, Elizabeth Townsend, second daughter of James Murray Grant, twelfth Laird of Glenmoriston.' James Alexander Pierson was interred in the family private burial ground at Balmadies.

Further to the east and beyond the Temple, on the 'peninsula' between the Black Den burn and the Elliot, there are traces of what appear to be the remains of a fortification ditch. This is marked on the old O.S. maps as a Roman Camp, though some authorities writing on the subject say it is more likely to be Danish or Viking. As far as the author is aware, no archaeological excavation has been done to evaluate this, but it would certainly have been very small indeed for a Roman Camp.

James Alexander Pierson inherited the Guynd in 1849 from his mother, Margaret Ouchterlony who in turn inherited it from her brother, John Ouchterlony in 1843. James and his wife, Elizabeth would be the first occupants of the new mansion. Elizabeth decorated and furnished the house and laid out the gardens while James put the Estate in order.

The Piersons were fortunate to inherit the Guynd at this time because their own family fortunes had declined and they had sold their own estate of Balmadies in the early 1800's. Balmadies Estate at this time was apparently in a ruinous condition and it passed through a number of owners until it was purchased at a public roup, from the executors of John Rait of Anniston in 1820, by Henry Stephens Esq., the author of 'The Book of the Farm'.

Henry Stephens was one of the agricultural improvers of the Scottish Enlightenment. He had travelled extensively in Europe just after the end of the Napoleonic Wars and studied European farming methods. He created a 'model farm' at Balmadies. He built new steadings and cottages, and a flour mill on the Lunan, and he built the present mansion house of Balmadies. He published 'The Book of the Farm' to great acclaim and it became a 'best seller', remaining in print through a number of editions for nearly 100 years. The recent television series, 'The Victorian Farm' was largely based on 'The Book of the Farm'. Henry Stephens sold Balmadies to the Guardians of Sir Charles Ouchterlony, Bart., in 1830. These Ouchterlonys were distant relatives of the Guynd Ouchterlonys who had made their fortune in India. Balmadies is now the home of the Osborne Family, Georgiana Osborne being the present 'Lord Lieutenant' of Angus.

James Alexander Pierson died in 1873 and the Guynd was inherited by Lieutenant-Colonel John Heathcote Ouchterlony. He was the 22nd Laird of the Guynd and was born in 1841. He had served in

Early motor car at the Guynd c.1908

the Royal Artillery. He was a distant cousin of John Ouchterlony, and descended from a Montrose branch of the Ouchterlonys. He moved to the Guynd from Devon and by all accounts, he quickly became popular in Angus. He was said to be a gregarious, civic-minded man. He had married Marie Wilmot from a wealthy Irish family.

The Lieutenant-Colonel attended the Church of Scotland and was interred at Carmyllie Church when he died in 1922. His wife died in 1913 and she and the succeeding Ouchterlony's have adopted the Roman Catholic Faith from that time.

The Colonel's eldest son, John, known as Jack, made his name as a Military Engineer in Ghana, West Africa but was later killed near Ypres in June 1917 in the Great War. After the war, the Brax estate was sold in 1920 to the tenant, David Weighton and the Guynd was then inherited by the 'Commander', Thomas Heathcote Ouchterlony, the second son who became the 23rd Laird of the Guynd. He was the father of the present and 24th Laird, John Ouchterlony and his brother Angus.

The 'Commander' was a submarine commander in the Great War and had little ambition to become a Laird, preferring a career in the Navy. The Guynd was not paying its way and in 1924, the 'Commander' put it up for sale. This was however, the middle of the depression and no buyer could be found. There was a 'country house sale' held, and much of the furniture and contents of the mansion were sold off. There was also some land sold at this time, including the Conon farm which was sold in 1928. Much of the money was used to meet death duties.

In 1930, the Guynd, together with the Garden house and garden was let to the Cox family of Dundee jute manufacturers by Commander T.C.H. Ouchterlony. They brought the house up to date by installing bathrooms and upgrading the heating system. It had been empty since 1924, as Commander Ouchterlony had preferred a career in the Navy.

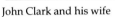

John Clark and his wife   Minnie Clark (now Minnie Soutar)   Jim Prescott with John Ouchterlony

Minnie Clark remembers when she was employed by Mrs Cox as a maid:
The Cox family brought some of their staff with them from Rosemill, near Dundee including my grandfather, John Clark, who was appointed Under Gardener at the Guynd garden while the Head Gardener, Jim Prescot lived in the Garden House.

Clark and his wife lived at Villabank, the Guynd, and I moved from Rosemill to stay with my grandparents at the age of 11 and attended Carmyllie East School under the headmaster, Mr Dewar.

In 1937 when I left school at 14, I was employed by Mrs Cox at the Guynd Mansion house as an 'in-between maid', i.e., I worked with the housemaid in the John morning, then with the table maid in the afternoon and evening. I, along with six other servants, laundry maid, table maid, scullery maid, cook and kitchen maid, 'lived-in', their living quarters being in the basement, with stone floors and stone steps which were scrubbed regularly. I had one day off per week and, if there was no evening meal to serve, we had the evening free. When the table maid left, I was promoted from 'in-between maid', giving me a sense of importance, as I was in charge of the silverware, glasses and crockery and all that decorated the table. Although each maid attended to their duties, all helped if there was an evening meal to serve, finishing around 11pm. One evening, Master Jeff (Cox) commented on the chicken served "Is this the auld broon hen from Dustydrum?" The kitchen maid was in charge of the game, which was kept in a game cupboard or larder alongside the kitchen. Often there was a distinct smell around the larder as there was a belief that the bird had a better flavour if it developed a 'hum' before cooking.

House Staff, Jessie Bell, May Drummond, Alison Lawrie, Minnie Clark with John Ouchterlony
c.1939

The family consisted of Mrs Cox, Miss Mary, Miss Elizabeth and Master Jeffrey. I cannot remember Mrs Cox's husband and I have the impression that he was deceased. I enjoyed working under Mrs Cox and, although she was strict, she treated her staff fairly and I regarded Mrs Cox as the housekeeper. She took overall charge of the household and the garden at the Garden House. Every day she visited the kitchen in the early morning to discuss the menu and report the number of meals required. The furnishings in the house were very fine polished solid furniture, and the soft furnishings included tall chintz curtains with covers on the chairs of similar design.

Jim Prescot and my grandfather had the responsibility of providing produce for the mansion house. While I was still at school, I can remember delivering a message to Mrs Prescot in the Garden House and noticed the luscious growth of vegetables and fruit in the walled garden, including figs, peaches, pears, plums and greengages. Mrs Prescot always gave Minnie a 'reward' such as a bar of chocolate, which Minnie tried to refuse. Mrs Prescot replied, "Never refuse anything except blows!"

John Clark, as well as being under-gardener, stoked the furnaces that heated the boilers for the water and the central heating in the mansion house. A generator supplied electricity for electric light and all were aware when it was in use. It was switched off at 10pm and Mrs Cox expected all her staff to be in their rooms by this time. In the winter evenings, it was easy to detect if this rule was disobeyed because, as soon as the light was switched on, the noisy generator started up again. On our free evenings, when socialising with our boyfriends at the Lodge gate, we timed it exactly how many minutes was required to run the length of the drive to the mansion door!

Guynd Gardens, Centre Walk

While Commander Ouchterlony was serving in the Navy, and although their residence was in Brechin, Mrs Ouchterlony and their son John (born 1936) came for their holidays to the Guynd. Communications when her husband, the Commander was at sea, had been infrequent and there would be concern for his safety. Young John told the staff that they paid many visits to the Catholic Church to 'light candles and pray for 'Ginga'' (his father).
The Guynd estate continued to be managed by the Ouchterlonys including the policies and the lake. There were five 'peckies' employed and the trees, lawns, fences and paths were kept in perfect order.
When the war broke out in September 1939, all large houses were obliged to house refugees and military servicemen. The Cox family vacated the Guynd mansion and took up residence in Fingask

House, Perthshire. My grandfather retired as Under Gardener and the seven staff found various employment.

Ruth Fitchet remembers her visits to Guynd in the 1930s:
I am the granddaughter of William Crighton, who was Overseer on the Guynd Estate from c. 1900 to 1950. When William arrived with his wife Jessie in 1898, they lived in the Guynd Lodge and later moved to the Overseer's house, an unusual octagonal Georgian house, originally the farmhouse. They had two daughters, my mother, Ann and a son, Robert, who was killed in WW1.

William and Jessie Crichton, 1890s

My mother worked and married in Dundee but returned at weekends and holidays to her parents at the Guynd. I was born in 1928 and have many happy memories on the Estate in the 1930s, climbing trees, walking by the lake and making friends with servants in the 'big house' occupied by the Cox family. I was particularly friendly with Mary Fleming, daughter of the cook who, when leaving school, was employed as a nursemaid to John and Angus Ouchterlony's mother in Brechin

It was a laborious task of carrying buckets of water daily from a central tank to the house and then a sense of relief when house tap water was installed around 1933.

In 1939, I was evacuated for a year from Dundee to the Guynd and attended Carmyllie East School

with Mr Dewar as headmaster and Miss Cochrane, the infant teacher. *This was a crucial time for my education as I had to return to Dundee to sit my qualifying exam (the 11+) in a private house since Harris Academy (primary) was closed for a year. Before the Cox family vacated the Guynd House in 1939, I can remember attending the Servants' Ball in the basement and had the pleasure of accepting a dance from David Souter, Milton Haugh!*

Ornamental Lake at the Guynd

My grandfather retired in the 1940s but remained in the Overseer's house until 1950. He was the last Overseer on the Guynd Estate and had given over 40 years' service.

Eventually, aged 47, the 'Commander' met and married Doreen Mary Lloyd of Wimbledon in 1935 and retired from the Navy, settling in temporary accommodation in a house in Brechin. However, when war broke out, the 'Commander' had come out of retirement and had been appointed Naval Attache at Esbjerg, Denmark. He was on naval business in Copenhagen when the Germans invaded in April 1940. Following, it is said, an argument over lost luggage, he missed the last train back to Esbjerg where arrangements had been made to evacuate British Staff. He was arrested in Copenhagen and was held for some time as a P.O.W. He was repatriated before the end of the War and was handed over in Lisbon as part of an exchange of seven diplomatic personnel on each side. He was said to have been very 'gaunt' and in poor health when he came home and a very "different man" to the man who left Angus at the beginning of the War.

Commander T.H. and Doreen Ouchterlony. 1960

During WW 2, the Guynd mansion had been taken over by the Royal Navy to house military personnel stationed at the Royal Navy's Fleet Air Arm air station, HMS Condor. Groups of Polish Officers then W.R.N.S. were billeted there. In 1942, the Admiral in charge of H.M.S. Condor took up residence there with his family.

Mr Bert Soutar, farmer at the Milton can remember:- *'a chauffeur driven Daimler car with a triangular flag on the 'bonnet' arriving in the morning to collect the Admiral'.*

The 'Commander' and Doreen were forced to 'camp' in the basement flat for a few years as it was well into the 1950s when the Navy moved out of the Guynd and they could move into the main house.

Jean Law, Glentyrie, was a cook at the Guynd while the Commander and Mrs Ouchterlony were in residence and she remembers:

After 1951, I was housekeeping at home and looking for fresh interests. The Admiral at Condor

occupied the main part of the building at the Guynd house, with his wife, family and servants. Meanwhile, the Ouchterlonys' had to live in the basement. I remember the large basement stretched the whole area of the Guynd building, with a dining room, bedroom, large boys' bedroom, a substantial kitchen with dining space and a large round table in the hall where there were regular meals. When the boys were small and home from boarding school at Fort Augustus, they were served separately with their meal at 4pm. On occasion, I would take the boys and their cousins for picnics by the lake.

Mrs Jean Stewart (nee Law)

Occasionally I was asked to help the Commander and Mrs Ouchterlony

and it was then I met Heidi Blissenbach, an au pair German girl, who, while carrying out her duties, was learning the English language. Before her spell at the Guynd she was employed by the Hynd family at Boysack, near Arbroath from 1950-52.

Towards the end of 1953, I was offered the job as cook to the Ouchterlony family. I cycled to work past Conon farm and New Mains of Guynd, and working hours were from 10am to 2pm from Monday to Friday and I was paid £2.00 per week. Sometimes payment

Angus and John Ouchterlony, Guynd Mansion

from Mrs Ouchterlony was irregular but eventually I was always paid in full. There were occasions when I had to prepare for dinner parties but usually the au pair served the meal. Nevertheless plain cooking was required with emphasis on the Commander's tastes, such as sweetbreads in sauce, stewed and jellied tripe and oxtail. He was also fond

Angus and John Ouchterlony

of desserts. The kitchen was modern and there was a good cooker. When there were dinner parties, the guests might include, Johnston-Brodies of Idvies, Ramsays of Kinblethmont, Chalmers of Auldbar Castle and possibly the Forsyth-Grants. Fruit and vegetables were collected or delivered from the Garden House where Mr & Mrs Beard were the gardeners and the game was delivered to the kitchen door from the policies.

During my employment, there was a transition when the Ouchterlony family moved 'upstairs' from the basement after the Admirality vacated the main part of the building. The furniture belonging to the Ouchterlony family had been stored in the laundry rooms at the back while the Admirality were in residence. I recall helping Heidi to scrub floors before furnishing the rooms with beautiful furniture.

I realised that Mrs Ouchterlony was a good cook and sometimes when they received invitations, I would prepare some of the food. However the Commander disliked parties and I remember he showed his annoyance when he discovered that his wife had a collection of desserts ready for a party at Idvies House. The Commander did not keep good health, exacerbated from War wounds and, despite his faults; I found he was sincere although I often felt uncomfortable as the atmosphere was strained.

The Commander was very strict with his sons and when they were home from boarding school, he ensured that they were set menial tasks such as weeding the drives, and then they were called to his study where they were set school homework with little pleasure in between.

Mrs Doreen Ouchterlony

After I started work as a cook, Heidi left to return to Germany in early 1954 and Gertlinda (her last name is forgotten and I have lost contact), another German au pair replaced her. However, Heidi could not settle back in Germany and returned to the Guynd house at the end of 1954. On her afternoons off she cycled into Arbroath to attend classes for shorthand and typing. Gertlinda and Heidi worked together with the Commander and Mrs Ouchterlony although the two girls were not compatible. Gertlinda left in early 1956, followed by Heidi who joined the British Armed Forces to carry out secretarial work. She married a NATO member, George Webb, and had one daughter, Patricia. I have kept in contact throughout and she is now widowed and lives in Maidenhead.

The water for the Guynd estate was pumped from the Guynd quarry at Glentyrie. Sy Brown worked every day attending to the pump during 1930s and 1940s but the Shanks engine was replaced by a Lister engine that only required to be switched on and off. At first my brother Ron attended to this duty followed by younger brother Gordon.

Mr William Crighton had been overseer at the Guynd in the 1930s and 1940s and lived in the white eight-sided house but retired before my time of employment. Jack Dey, a 'peckie' (an estate worker) lived in the Guynd Lodge for many years. Tom Smeaton was the farmer at the Home Farm and 'Teenie' Duncan (a keen WRI lady) lived in one of the Home Farm cottages. Mrs Stewart, Bonnycheer, occasionally helped me as cook and took over my job when I left in 1958. At my marriage in the same year, Commander Ouchterlony escorted me to the wedding and rendered a speech of good wishes.

The 'Commanders' legacy to the people of Carmyllie was the donation of the land for the construction of the present Carmyllie Hall in the 1960's. The 'Commander' is still remembered for his Lee-Francis motor car with the registration plate ASR 1. The 'Commander' passed away in 1971 and Mrs. Ouchterlony in 1987. The farms on the estate, New Mains of Guynd, Tillyhoit, Glentyrie and the Redford Smithy were sold in 1977.

The 'Commander's' ashes were scattered near the Temple where there is a memorial inscribed :- Thomas Charles Alexander Heathcote Ouchterlony, Commander Royal Navy, 23rd Laird of the Guynd, 23rd October 1888 - 3rd October 1971, R.I.P.

While the Guynd has been the 'Country Seat' of the Ouchterlonys since 1616, the family earned their living in business in Montrose. They were essentially an extended Montrose trading family and the Guynd was but one of their country residences. Kintrockat at Brechin was another and West Seaton too was for a time, an Ouchterlony property. The family also had fine town residences at numbers 200, 190 and 186, in the High Street of Montrose.

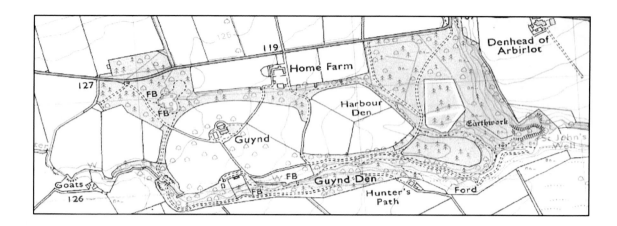

Finally, there is the story of the Pictish Crown. It is said that at the beginning of the 18th Century, a crown of gold was found in the Black Den by a labourer. The Black Den is at the east side of the Guynd next to Denhead. The discovery was connected to an old legend that a Pictish King had lost his Crown while fleeing from battle. It is said that the finder cut the crown in half and sold one half locally for £20 Scots. The other half was apparently sent to a Jewish merchant in London on the promise of a much better price. Needless to say, neither the money nor the other half of the gold crown were ever seen again!

David Duncan, Overseer, The Guynd in his carriage c.1905

The Ouchterlony family around the world

Various members of the family were ministers (of religion) or soldiers. Others were goldsmiths, and gunsmiths. Others still were shopkeepers, brewers and threadmakers. Ouchterlonys too became Baillies and Provosts in Montrose. However, the main business of the Ouchterlonys was as shipowners and traders out of the seaport of Montrose. At various times, Ouchterlonys shipped all kinds of cargoes all over Europe and to and from the Americas. Ouchterlonys settled in the Baltic area in Riga and Sweden and in Boston too. Their main business was however, the 'Baltic Trade' which was the business of shipping grain and malt from Angus and the Mearns to Riga, Danzig and the seaports of Sweden and returning with cargoes of flax for the linen trade in Angus. For this purpose, various members of the Ouchterlony family owned extensive barns, maltings and corn and malt drying kilns in Montrose. Members of the Ouchterlony family were engaged in the 'Baltic Trade' in Montrose from around the middle of the 17th Century to the last John Ouchterlony of the Guynd who died in 1843.

Major John (Jack) Ouchterlony. Killed in Action at the Battle of Messines 1917, aged 32

The Ouchterlony family has produced a number of interesting characters who have made their mark overseas. Mention has already been made of Major John Palgrave Heathcote Ouchterlony D.S.O., the present Laird's late uncle who was known at home as Jack. He was commissioned in the Royal Engineers in 1901 and appointed head of the Military Roads Department in Ashanti, then part of the Gold Coast, now part of Ghana, West Africa. The present Laird has a delightful album of photographs taken by Jack in Africa which include pictures of road building, overturned steam rollers and the like. Jack was born on the 10th June 1884 and had married Kathleen Spackman of Christchurch, New Zealand, at St. Marys Roman Catholic Church, Cadogan Street, London in September 1909. There was one daughter.

In the Great War, he was twice mentioned in despatches and was awarded the Distinguished Service Order in June 1917. He was tragically killed during the capture of the Messines Ridge, just two days before his 33rd birthday on the 7th June 1917.

The loss of the eldest son must have been keenly felt at the Guynd as they had already lost their third son Guy (born 1890) in a tragic accident just a few years earlier. Guy had taken employment with the Canadian Bank of Commerce and had emigrated to Canada where he had married a Miss Winifred Powell at Guelph, Ontario. He had been in his garden on the shore of Lake Ontario when he heard screams from two young girls whose punt had slipped its moorings and was being blown out into the lake. Guy swam out intending to rescue them, but the intense cold of the water gave him cramp and he drowned. He died on the 2nd August 1913 having only been married a few weeks and he left a widow and an unborn son. His son Dr. (Guy) David Ouchterlony was born in April 1914 and became a talented and distinguished musician in Canada He was an organist, a choirmaster and a music teacher and composer.

One of the Ouchterlony's Town Houses, 190, High Street, Montrose

Another Ouchterlony who served the Empire was Sir David Ochterlony, 1st Baronet GCB (1758-1825). He was born and educated in Boston, Massachusetts where his Montrose born father, a captain in the merchant service, had settled and married. David had entered the British Indian Army at the age of 18 and had gone to India as a cadet where he worked his way up to Major-General after serving in a number of battles and uprisings. He was appointed the official British Resident of Delhi in 1818 and scandalised British India by 'going native'. He was reputed to have thirteen Indian concubines

The Ochterlony Monument,
Calcutta

(wives) and in Delhi, he took all thirteen on a promenade around the walls of the Red Fort every evening, each mounted on her own personal elephant. He also apparently took to smoking exotic substances in a hookah water pipe. After his death in 1825, a column was erected by the British East India Company in central Calcutta in his memory, for his leadership of the East India Company's forces in the Anglo-Nepalese War. In August 1969, the now independent India rededicated the column to the memory of the martyrs of the Indian Freedom Movement and it is now known as ''Shaheed Minar'. The present Laird, John Ouchterlony has an oil portrait of Sir David in the hall at the Guynd. Sir David's grandson, Sir Charles Metcalfe Ochterlony, 2nd Baronet (1817-1891) eventually returned to Scotland to buy the Estate of Balmadies.

Two Ouchterlony brothers, John and James from the Montrose branch of the family, went to India to seek careers. John joined the Royal Engineers and became a military engineer in the Madras Engineers. He was quickly posted to and involved in the Chinese War and was promoted to Lieutenant. He surveyed the Island of Chusan (now Zhoushan) for the Army and it was later published as '*A statistical sketch of the Island of Chusan with a brief note on the geography of China*'. He later wrote and published what is still today the standard text on the Chinese war, also known as the Opium war, a particularly unattractive chapter in British history. The book is called '*The Chinese War, being an account of all the operations of the British Forces from the Commencement to the Treaty of Nanking*'.

Ouchterlony was clearly also a highly competent artist as the 53 illustrations in *The Chinese War* were taken from his own drawings made at the time. At the end of the war, he stayed for a time as the first 'Acting Engineer at The New Settlement of Hong-Kong' before eventually returning to Madras where he continued his army career. He surveyed the Nilgiri hills in South India for the army and while doing so, he recommended to his brother James that tea and coffee could be grown there. John's survey of the Nilgiris was published after his death in 1863 but he also had a number of other books and papers published on India.

John's brother, James Ouchterlony had established himself as a successful lawyer and magistrate in Madras but he abandoned his legal career and on his brother's advice, he leased 21,000 acres of largely uninhabited land from the local maharaja and established a huge tea and coffee growing business in the 'Ouchterlony Valley in the Nilgiri hills near the hill resort of Ooty. They had named some of their plantations to remind them of Scotland and they were called Kelly, Guynd, Lauriston, Tulloos, Balmaadies, Burnside and Compton amongst other things. The plantations survive today but most are held by the Manjushree Plantations Company while the Balmaadii Plantation is today an independent producer of organic coffee.

A further Ouchterlony of some note but this time fighting against the British Empire, was Major-General Alexander Ouchterlony of the Russian Imperial Guard, who rose through the ranks of the Russian Army and was said to have been on close terms with Tsar Nicolas I. Ouchterlony was mortally wounded at the Battle of Inkerman on the 5th November, 1854. In 1853, the Montrose newspaper reported that Maj-General Alexander Ouchterlony of the Russian Imperial Guard was in Montrose visiting his Aunt, Henrietta Ouchterlony and 'other relatives'. Maj-General Ouchterlony's father, Robert Ouchterlony was born in Montrose in 1761, the son of John Ouchterlony, Merchant and Mary Ruperta Skinner. Robert Ouchterlony had emigrated to St Petersburg to better conduct his Baltic trading business and he died there in 1830.

Family tradition is that one of the reasons why the Ouchterlony family came to be scattered round the world from early times, is that the family were said to be very active in the Jacobite cause and were thought to have smuggled Jacobite spies and fugitives in and out of the country on their vessels. With their trading and seafaring connections to continental Europe, they would have been regarded by the Georgian Authorities as being highly dangerous and apparently, after Sheriffmuir and Culloden, a number of them slipped away overseas to avoid arrest. There remain today a substantial group of Ouchterlony relatives round the Baltic, particularly in Sweden and there is another group of Ouchterlonys in Canada, mainly around the Toronto area. The present Laird's younger brother, Angus Ouchterlony also now lives in Canada.

A Representation of Sir David Ochterlony with his 'Bibis'

THE COMING OF AGE CELEBRATIONS FOR JACK OUCHTERLONY AT THE GUYND

6th September 1905

The coming of age of Lieutenant J.P.H. (Jack) Ouchterlony, eldest son of Colonel Ouchterlony of the Guynd was celebrated by a dinner for the principle estate staff and tenantry along with neighbouring farmers and friends. Floral arches were erected above the entrance gates and there was a spacious marquee in the grounds. Jack was presented with a sporting gun and 500 cartridges by the tenantry and the estate staff presented him with a cartridge magazine.

Colonel Ouchterlony presided and the guests included Mrs Ouchterlony, Misses Nora and Mary Ouchterlony, Lieutenant Ouchterlony, Masters John, Guy and Arthur Ouchterlony and the following house party:- Sir David Ouchterlony. Miss H. Ouchterlony. Miss A.E. Ouchterlony; Major Sandford and Mrs Sandford, Beezlack; Mrs Sinclair, Mrs Johnston and Mr Turton. Amongst the tenants and others present were:- Mr John Anderson, Mains of Guynd; Rev. James Forrest of Harthill and Conon; Mr John McRobbie, Conon; Mr David Weighton, Brax; Mr D. Fleming, Brax Cottage; Mr D. Smith, Annfield; Mr J. Croll, Brax Quarry; Mr James Buchan, Redford; Mr William Mudie, Redford; Mr Benjamin Norrie, Denhead; Mr William Paterson, Bonnycheer; Mr D. Whyte, Villabank; Mr D. Buchan, Redford; Mr D. Hume, Mains of Carmyllie; Mr D. Maxwell, Panlathy Mill; Mr John Soutar, Miltonhaugh; Mr D. Lumsden, joiner: Mr. James Webster; Mr Alexander Sturrock, Glentyrie; Mr R. Cuthill, Villabank; Mr Peter Whyte, Villabank; Mr Charles McDonald, Westhills; Mr Charles Binnie, Glentyrie; Mr J. Prescott, Mr William Chrichton, Mr J. Cuthill and Mr R. Norrie. Mrs Binnie, Glentyrie, the oldest tenant on the estate, had the seat of honour next to the Colonel. The wives of the tenants were also present, the company numbering in all about eighty. After dinner, there were speeches by Mr Weighton, Brax, Mr David Duncan, overseer on the estate, Lieutenant Ouchterlony, Mr Anderson, Mains of Guynd and The Rev. Mr Forrest.

The company then adjourned to the mansion house where a large number of merchants, shopkeepers and trades people from Arbroath presented Lieutenant Ouchterlony with a handsome suitcase. They were entertained to cake and wine and it was then announced that tea would be served in the marquee at six o'clock. Before tea, Lieutenant Ouchterlony planted a tree in the grounds to mark the occasion. After tea music and dancing was started and kept up to a late hour.

The rejoicings were continued the following day with a large garden party for friends and included parties from most of the principal Angus estates. Dancing followed thereafter.

On the Friday, the children from the East and West Schools, numbering about 250 were entertained at the Guynd to a sumptuous tea on the lawn followed by games. Later, a cinematographic entertainment was provided in the granary at the home farm which was greatly enjoyed.

Carmyllie Heritage Society has an on-going project to identify those in the photograph.

The Coming of Age celebrations for Jack Ouchterlony at The Guynd, 6th September 1905

Authorities Consulted for this Chapter

Primary Sources

National Archives of Scotland (NAS) GD 45/16/1307 Memorial on behalf of John Ouchterlony, Merchant in Riga, to The Earl of Panmure (Part of the Dalhousie Muniments.)

NAS, RHP 2606, Plans for the Guynd Water. 1857 drawn by Wm. Mackie

NAS, RHP 2606, Plan for supplying the Farms and House of the Guynd with water (W. Baillie 1857)

NAS, RHP 2619, sketch of design for a two-plus pair (of horse) farm offices for the Guynd, no date.

NAS, RHP 2619/2, Plan and Elevations of a Court of Offices adapted for a Farm from 130 to 160 acres, 'The Conon' 1802.

Old Statistical Account of Scotland (OSA) 1791-1799.Volume XIII Angus, Sir John Sinclair (ed) Reprinted edition (EP Publishing Ltd. Wakefield, Yorkshire. 1976)

Registrum De Panmure. by John Stuart LLD (Editor). Privately Printed, Edinburgh 1874.

Roll of Honour, Arbroath & District 1914-19 (T.Buncle & Co. Arbroath)

Valuation Rolls for the County Of Forfar/Angus. ---various.

Catalogues

Buildings of the Land, 1750-2000, by Miles Glendinning and Susanna Wade Martins (RCAHMS 2008)

Chinese Wars, being an 'Account of all the operations of the British Forces from the commencement to the treaty of Nanking' by Lieutenant John Ouchterlony, F.G.S. of the Madras Engineers and late acting Engineer at the New Settlement of Hong Kong (Saunders & Otley, London 1844)

Madras District Gazetteer, 'The Nilgiris' by W .Francis (Asian Educational Services. Madras 1908)

Newspapers

Arbroath Guide. 13th September, 1905.

Printed Sources and Further Reading

Cumming, Gersholm, *Forfarshire Illustrated* 2nd edition (Dundee 1848)

Fraser, Duncan, *The Smugglers* (Standard Press, Montrose 1971)

Hay, George, *Around about the Round 'O',* (T. Buncle, Arbroath. 1883)

Hay, George, *History of Arbroath* 2nd edition (T. Buncle, Arbroath 1899)

Jervise, Andrew, *Memorials of Angus and Mearns* (A & C Black, Edinburgh 1861)

Low, James. *Highways and Byways of an Old Scottish Town,* The Closes of Montrose (John Balfour and Sons, Montrose 1938)

MacGregor, David, *The Baronage of Angus and Mearns* (Oliver & Boyd, Edinburgh 1856)

McBain, *Eminent Arbroathians* (Brodie & Salmond , Arbroath 1897)

Miller, David, *Arbroath and its Abbey* (T.G. Stevenson, Edinburgh. 1860)

Rathbone, Belinda, *Living With The Laird* (Harper Perennial, London. 2007)

Smith, R.V., *Ochterlony and his Bibis* (in 'The Hindu'. 8th May 2011)

Stephens, Henry, *The Book of The Farm*, 3rd edition, 2 vols. Vol.1, p 295, fig.152 gives a drawing of the waterwheel (William Blackwood and Sons,1877)

Thurston, Edgar, *The Madras Presidency with Mysore, Coorg and the Associated States* (Cambridge University Press 1913)

Warden, Alex J. *Angus or Forfarshire, The Land and People*. 5 vols. (Charles Alexander & Co   Dundee 1882)

Watkins, Walter Kendall, *The Ochterlony Family of Scotland and Boston, New England* (Privately printed, Boston, USA 1902)

Chapter 7

CONONSYTH MANSION and ESTATE

Cononsyth derives its name from the 'side of Conon', although further research indicates that 'Sythe' could be derived from a surname of a person. Conon was a medieval seat before parishes were formed in 1603. Cononsyth Estate and Backboath though originally associated with Inverkeilor, were brought into Carmyllie when the parishes were formed. Cononsyth estate lay on the north-west tip of Carmyllie parish bordering Kirkden, Inverkeilor and St Vigeans parishes. If the shape of Carmyllie parish resembles a fist then Cononsyth estate is part of the arm above the wrist.

Boundary of Carmyllie Parish

In 1793, Ann Skinner the widow of John Ogilvie of Inchewan, gave her son David Ogilvie, full ownership of the estate subject only to his mother's life-rent. The estate centred round Park Conon and included Easter and Wester Ruives (Borders), Firth of Aberbrothock, 'as belongs to the estate of Collistone' and also the Barony of Cononsyth including the 'Mains and and Manor place', formerly lying within the Parish of Inverkeilor but now lying within the parish of Carmyllie.[1] The Barony of Cononsyth had 'ferm touns' at East (later known as North Cononsyth) and West (South Cononsyth), tenanted by the Brown family, James Brown being the tacksman (lease holder) and probably subletting to his family.[2]

At the beginning of the nineteenth century there were three major revolutions taking place that ultimately spurred the changes in the ownership of Cononsyth Estate; Firstly, agriculture improvement; secondly, an increase in the production of coarse linen and thirdly, an increase in demand for grain beginning with a trade embargo during the Napoleonic Wars. The Browns were farming North and South Cononsyth when the run-rig system was changing to units that were more productive by enclosing land, and Cononsyth Estate would have farms with boundaries such as South Mains, Mid Mains, North Mains and the Mains.

Cononsyth Mansion,(*Forfarshire Illustrated. 1843*)

In Dundee's hinterland during the eighteenth century, there was a rapidly growing industry of spinning and weaving the coarse linen known as Osnaburgs, exported to the western Colonies, mainly for slaves' clothing. Wealthy manufacturers emerged, one of whom was James Brown of Cononsyth, a spinning mill operator and a dealer in the yarn trade. At the beginning of the nineteenth century, Brown had sufficient capital to operate water-spinning mills at Trottick, Friockheim and Arrat[3]. Increased production of yarn became possible through the invention of water-powered spinning mills that prepared flax into yarn mechanically. This was a major breakthrough as the time taken to spin yarn was reduced from six months to two months.[4] During the Napoleonic Wars, spinning yarn for Osnaburgs became very profitable as there was a trade embargo with Europe and Britain had a monopoly of trade across the Atlantic.

---

[1] NAS *Register of Sasines*, RS3/519/110, 1793
[2] Ibid, RS3/519/108, June 1, 1793
[3] Gauldie, Enid, *Dundee Textile Industry,* introduction, xx
[4] Law, p.122

Steam power was still in its infancy in the first decade of the nineteenth century and there were five failed attempts at operating steam mills in Dundee. In 1806, James Brown of Conousyth built the Bell steam mill in Dundee and it was the first successful steam mill of any size in the town. [5] In 1809, his sons, James and William, set the mill in operation.

In 1807, James Brown had a few advantages enabling him to purchase Conousyth; Firstly, he made a lot of money in the linen trade; secondly, he was a long-term leaseholder on the Estate and thirdly, he had the backing of the New Bank in Dundee, established in 1804, that lent money to trustworthy customers. Ann Skinner had died leaving her son David with free ownership and in 1807, he sold Conousyth Estate to James Brown as sitting tenant, probably at a reduced price. The exact price is unknown but part of it (£10,900) was left on loan to Brown who granted a bond in security of the loan. The estate comprised of the Barony of Conousyth including the Mains and Manor place (that James Brown 'as presently possessed and his subtenants'[6]) together with 'houses, biggings, yards, orchards, tofts, crofts, woods, pendicles and also included the lands of Smithyton'. Estates at that time required access to water mills and Conousyth was guaranteed the use of 'Mains of Leyes, with Manor Place, Mill, Mill lands, multures and also Easter and Wester Borders within the Barony of Leyes'. [7]

The Conousyth mansion's architecture is Georgian in style indicating that it was built early in the 19th century. However, there is little evidence that James Brown provided the capital to employ an architect and erect the new mansion, as he was owner for only the four years from 1807 to 1811. Brown died in 1811 and his son Andrew disposed of the estate the following year. It is suggested that David Neave (1773-1841), a well-known Dundee architect, was associated with the Brown family as there are similar buildings in the Perth Road in Dundee. [8] Another stronger possibility however, could be that the mansion was built when the Smart brothers of Montrose took possession in 1812 and employed the Montrose architect David Logan with whom they were familiar. Examples of David Logan's classical style are seen at the Sheriff Court House, Arbroath (1803), Montrose Academy (1815) and Forfar old Academy (1815) and Conousyth mansion shares similar features.

The Brown family's main interests lay in the steam mills in Dundee and in 1812, Andrew Brown conveyed Conousyth Estate to Alex. and William Smart, corn merchants, Montrose by feu

Conousyth Mansion/Farmhouse (*Colin Gibson*)

arrangement under a Bond for £15,000 with obligations, being that part of the purchase price unpaid and remaining due to David Skinner [9]. Again, there is no record of the full price.

The Smart family of Montrose owned Conousyth Estate for nearly sixty years from 1812 to 1871; longer than any other proprietor from 1793 to 1989. Their occupation as corn merchants was at that time, a highly profitable business. The government, dominated by landowning interests, was able to introduce the Corn Laws, that sustained a high price for grain after the Napoleonic Wars. This allowed an accumulation of revenue for landowners and traders, until the Corn Laws were repealed in 1846 permitting a more competitive grain market. Alexander Smart junior was proprietor of Conousyth in 1838 until 1851; thereafter an Alexander Smart Trusteeship was formed and retained the property for another twenty years.

During the Smart family ownership, a small number of interesting details have been retained; the collected rent per annum for Conousyth estate was £233.6.8d in 1823; [10] in 1836 the mansion was classed as 'modern' and Alexander Smart resided with his family for four months in the summer.

[5] Gauldie, p.15
[6] NAS, *Register of Sasines*, RS35/68/184, 1807
[7] Ibid
[8] In conversation with Graham McNicol, Feb 2013
[9] NAS, *Register of Sasines*, RS35/68/184, 1812
[10] Warden, Vol.lll, p.101

Cononsyth mansion 'though placed on high ground, is well sheltered and considerably ornamented with thriving wood' and had a panoramic view 'particularly of the vales of Lunan and the Brothock'.[11] Alexander Smart followed by his son was one of three Heritors of Carmyllie Parish, along with Lord Panmure and John Ouchterlony. In 1869, the Trusteeship of Alexander Smart formed a lease for 19 years with James Gouck, South Mains, who is Colin Ritchie's (farmer, South Mains) great-great grandfather.[12]

James Strachan, a native of Aberdeen had taught at a side school on Cononsyth estate c. 1793.[13] A 'side' school appeared to be more common in the Highlands of Scotland serving the needs of children in remote areas, but it could be that a school (run privately) would be in demand within walking distance, in the north-west of Carmyllie parish. By 1871, only the schoolhouse was habitable and Mr Scott the tenant of Mains of Cononsyth was also tenant of the schoolhouse, indicating perhaps that the school was in the proximity of the Mains. It could be suggested that the school referred to in the *Third Statistical Account (1967)* was the same school that reported: 'there are still parishioners whose parents attended the school near Dumbarrow bridge in the eighties [1880s]; the building is still there and used as an implement shed'.[14]

Throughout the next hundred years, a number of Dundee private businessmen were for short periods, proprietors of Cononsyth Estate. In the twentieth century, it was owned and managed by William and James Rettie (associated with William Low Stores) who were connected to Bruce Rettie, Solicitors, Dundee.

After 1871, John Ewan, a mill spinner and merchant in Dundee was the new Laird of Cononsyth Estate which consisted of six farms, two pendicles, house and land and an old Schoolhouse:[15] William Scott was tenant farmer of the Mains but James Steven and widow Fraser also resided around the Mains farm buildings with a piece of land. William Scott also paid rent for North Mains, a cottage and the Old Schoolhouse. Alex Ford farmed Mid Mains while James Gouck, as mentioned, farmed South Mains, James Clark was tenant of the Ditch at the northeastern tip of the Estate, and Robert Davidson paid rent for Blackhillock pendicle bordering the Ditch. David Young was tenant farmer of Smithyton and Alex Gold resided at Christianhall pendicle. In 1876 William Scott was paying by far the bigger rent of £583.5.4 per annum but there were two occupiers in the Old Schoolhouse paying a small rent of £2.4/- and £1.10/-.

In 1884, John Ewan was still proprietor of Cononsyth Estate although his postal address was Edenhall, Broughty Ferry. Added to the Estate were the farms, South Mains of Smithyton, houses and land at Lovat and Dunbog and Summerhill pendicle but the old Schoolhouse was no longer inhabited.[16] In 1889, the next generation of the Gouck family, South Mains, was given a further 19 year lease.

David Whitton was tenant farmer at Mains of Cononsyth from c. 1884 to c.1896 paying £425.00 rent annually. David Whitton was probably the first tenant to live in the mansion house, since the owner's residence was now in Broughty Ferry. In 1885 there were two cottages at the Mains, one for a grieve and another for a farm servant. One cottage was added at North Mains and another at Mid Mains.[17]

Farming Family residing in Cononsyth Farmhouse c.1890

---

[11] *NSA,* Carmyllie Parish, 1836
[12] Conversation with Violet Ritchie
[13] Warden, Vol iii
[14] *Third Statistical Account*, May 1967
[15] Valuation Roll, Carmyllie Parish, 1871-72

[16] Ibid, 1884-85
[17] Ibid, 1885-86

In 1893, the proprietors were Trustees of the late John Ewan of Cononsyth per Shiell and Small, Solicitors, Dundee. Four years later the new laird was John Alex Wilson, Aerated Water Manufacturer, Dundee per Dickie & Paul, Solicitors, Dundee. Andrew Osler had the tenancy at Mains Cononsyth for six years until 1903 paying a reduced rent of £303.00 per annum.

By 1901, William Bruce Dickie, Solicitor, Dundee was Cononsyth estate proprietor per Dickie & Paul, Solicitors, Dundee. It would appear that Ann McLeod, as mentioned by David Young (below), changed the name of Dunbog pendicle to Dunvegan when she became owner around 1900. Homer Smith also became owner of the house and land at Lovat.

In 1903, David Young, tenant of Mains Cononsyth, paid an even lower rent of £290.00.

Old Farmhouse within the Farm Steading, Mains of Cononsyth

Mr David Young, grandson of David Young remembers:

'I was eight years old when my father gave up the tenancy of Cononsyth to farm at Nethermuir, Aberlemno. I was born in Cononsyth Mansion in 1923. My grandfather, David Young, took the tenancy in 1903. I remember a Mrs McLeod who was then 93 years old living in Dunvegan house that had drystone walls and a thatched roof with a hole for the smoke to escape. She was sitting in bed smoking a clay pipe. She and her husband had travelled from Skye in the latter quarter of the nineteenth century where there was no longer a living from their croft.

Remains of Coachman's Bothy, Stable and Coach-house leading to the Mansion, Cononsyth

Previous tenant farmers of the Mains had lived in the farmhouse within the farm buildings while the proprietor of Cononsyth estate had used the Mansion as a summer residence. There may be some truth that David Whitton was the first tenant to live in the mansion house. I was told that the Coach house alongside the farm buildings was private and reserved for the Laird's use only. The building comprised of a stable, accommodation for the coach and the Coachman's (Strapper's) bothy. The 'Strapper' was required to collect or deliver the Laird and his family to and from their destination.

When my grandfather arrived in 1903, a Shanks' engine, manufactured in Arbroath, was installed in the engine shed, carted from Arbroath in two parts. The chimney had been built c.1870, when Mr Scott was tenant, and coal provided a furnace for a steam engine to generate power for the threshing mill. The chimney had been a few feet taller than it is today. The Shanks' engine was driven by paraffin fuel then oil. Later there was an inside mill powered by electric and tractor driven power could operate the mill too.

Mudie the Blacksmith at Redford came to Cononsyth smiddy on a Wednesday afternoon to shoe horses and mend machinery.

When there was a scarcity of water in the summer, a horse and cart loaded with a water tank drove to Redford village

Steam Engine Room and Chimney, Cononsyth

and filled up the tank from a 'spiggot' available to the public. Cattle were kept in open courts in the steading, leaving the cattle and those who worked there open to the elements. Needless to say, it was difficult to employ a cattleman for any length of time.[18]

In 1907, the Estate was addressed as Cononsyth by Guthrie and was owned by William Rettie, Wholesale Provision Merchant (later William Low stores) Balcairn, Dundee per William Bruce Dickie & Sons. Around this time the proprietor had set out some land with plantations and in 1907, he let the shootings (costing £290.00 per annum) to James Kyd. Solicitor, Dundee.

Cononsyth Steading before a storm in the 1980s

Familiar tenant farmer names appear in 1907 when John Dowell farms North Mains and James Ritchie takes the tenancy of South Mains the following year. In 1919, William Gardiner junior, was tenant at Smithyton until 1931 when he moved to the Mains and was replaced at the Smithyton by Albert Milne. After WW2, part of the estate was sold including the Ditch, Mid Mains, North Mains and Smithyton.

William Rettie remained proprietor of a very much reduced estate until 1942, replaced by James Low Rettie until 1946 when the final owner was Bruce Walker Dickie, Whitehills, Inchture per William Dickie & Sons, Solicitors, Dundee with Philip Rettie paying a rent for the shootings. Later South Mains was sold to the tenant and the final part of the estate, the Mains and the mansion was sold to the tenant, William and Eileen Craig, in 1989. Eileen Craig, daughter of William Gardiner, remembers:

When my father was farmer, the maid's room (downstairs) was made into a bathroom. Later, bathrooms were added to the cottar houses. One of my duties before the mains water was installed in 1956, was to cycle down towards Smithyton to turn on the water switch to supply water to the farm complex. In February 1953, a violent windstorm destroyed most of the plantations. I was returning with my parents from the weekly shop in Arbroath only to find all the trees in the driveway were flattened, as was most of the shelterbelt north of the mansion. After I married Willie, we returned around 1970 to Cononsyth to farm with my father.

Cononsyth Mansion, 2012

---

[18] Testimony, David Young, Oct 2012

98

Another storm in the 1980s caused more destruction when we heard a tremendous crash during darkness that resulted in the west facing part of the stone built steading collapsing. New sheds have been built to accommodate modern farming but the shell of the Mains farm buildings remain where traces of an earlier lifestyle can be seen.[19]

In conclusion the rise of the linen industry allowed wealthy merchant James Brown, to purchase the estate early in the nineteenth century, followed by corn merchant Alexander Smart and his brother from Montrose who were family owners for over sixty years. From then, short ownerships were administered from Dundee, usually in direct contact with Dundee solicitors. After World War 11, tenants gradually purchased their farms; the final farm including shooting rights was sold in 1989.

David Young, Eileen and Willie Craig, 2012

---

[19] Testimony, Eileen Craig

Chapter 8

FARMING

Patrick Bell's Reaper

Cultivating the land was relatively new in Carmyllie Parish compared to the neighbouring parishes and until the late 18th century, 'there were many farms in the parish occupied by farmers in the neighbourhood who used them for grazing their cattle in the summer.'[1] Commissary Maule, historian of the Maule family of Panmure, wrote in 1611 that 'Carmyle was 'ane pair' place, fit only for bestial (cattle) in summer'.[2] By 1770, landlords who were keen to secure more tenants, compelled the farmers to reside on the Carmyllie farms with the result that the land was drained, lime and marl(*e*) were added to the soil and gradually crops increased in quantity and 'were not inferior to those produced on the [other] grounds of the neighbourhood'.[3]

The chart shows that in 1836, the raw produce in bolls, a boll being a Scottish measure of capacity where 1 boll=140 lbs or 63.6 kg and 0.25 boll=1 firlot or 35 lbs or 15.9 kg. The quantity of oats was three times more than barley and six times more than wheat and potatoes. Oats were not only the required food for the farmer's household and farm workers but were also the staple food for horses. Barley could be fed to the cattle or sold. Wheat fetched the highest price, rising from £2 to £4 per quarter of a boll, selling to bakers or households for bread making.[4] Turnips and hay were fed to the livestock and pasture was required for summer feed and over-wintering sheep.

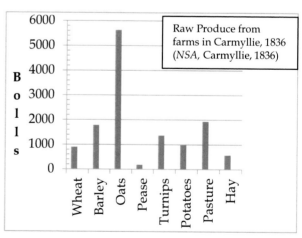

The improvement of agriculture also involved forming boundaries. But only fields with reasonable depth of soil and some drainage were enclosed, leaving many patches with little soil or covered with moss that were difficult to cultivate. The principle landlord of Carmyllie, Lord Panmure, saw an opportunity of increasing the rental income by offering a short-term lease of approximately 4–10

---

[1] *OSA*, Carmyllie, Rev Patrick Bryce, 1790

[2] Stuart, John (ed), *The Registrum de Panmure,* (privately printed, 1874)

[3] *OSA*, Carmyllie

[4] James Kydd Cash Book, received £8.10/- from Mr Herald, Baker, Arbroath for 4 qrs bushels Wheat @ £2 per qr., Sept 1835)

acres to tenants who could earn income from handloom weaving in winter, slate quarrying in the summer or seasonal farm work. It is assumed that the tenants erected a house and outbuildings themselves and with livestock and a small acreage, aimed to be self-sufficient. The names of these pendicles (small pieces of land for cultivation or crofts) give a clue to the condition of the soil such as, Mosston, Mosside, Mossend, Muiredge, Backmuir, Muirheads and Skichen Muir. The high number of pendicles was peculiar to the parish in comparison to the neighbouring parishes and continued in this fashion into the twentieth century.

The chart shows the high number of small farms in Carmyllie in 1870. Although there are fewer under five acres, there are over three times more under 20 acres. After the demise of hand-loom weaving (see Chapter 4), many of the smaller pendicles combined with a neighbouring unit to form a more viable acreage. Yet there were 26 farms between 20 and 100 acres leaving 20 farms over 100 acres, the majority of the farmers cultivating smaller acreages.

There was a period, up to the late 1850s, when farm rents were stable, cereal prices high and cattle were in demand to feed the increasing urban population, due to the industrial revolution. Farmers utilised a portion of their income to improve the land by draining it and feeding it with lime, dissolved bones, bone dust, blood manure and guano (sea bird dung).[5] Lime and coal were paid in one invoice by James Kydd, farmer to Mr Salmond (94 bolls lime cost £9.19.3 and 8 barrels coal £9.9/-).[6] Before the Carmyllie railway, built in 1855, coal and lime were collected from boats beached at Easthaven near Carnoustie and brought to Carmyllie by horse and cart.[7]

The effects of the repeal of the Corn Laws in 1846 affected the income of farmers when cheaper cereals were imported from the Americas and colonial countries and lowering the price of oats, barley and wheat paid to the British farmer. Prices varied with the market but there was an average decrease of oats selling at £1.13/- per quarter (One quarter of a boll=1 firlot) in 1846 to 15/- in 1864. Similarly barley decreased from £2.2/- per quarter to £1 and wheat selling £3.6.10 in 1846 proved uneconomical in Carmyllie by 1864[8] and towards the end of the 1880s no wheat was grown.[9] Carmyllie farmers' good husbandry could not compete with those farmers on better soil who had higher yields and earlier harvests. However, homegrown produce supplemented bought-in feed for livestock rearing which was still a viable option. In addition, the railway opening from Elliot junction to Redford in 1855, proved beneficial to farmers. In 1858, James Kydd paid £3 to John Murry for two wagons of (yard) dung and to Robert Wallace for 'carriage railway from the common'[10], and in 1862, £1.5.8d was paid to William Gold 'for railway carriage lime'[11]. From 1859, there were sales of potatoes by the ton as well as selling 'in the drill'.

Andrew Maxwell Soutar, Mrs Mary Soutar, Jessie and Patrick, Forehills c.1882

Chart: No. of Farms / Acreage of farms in Carmyllie in 1870 (Agricultural Returns AF39/14/1) — Acreage (1 to 5, 5 to 20, 20 to 50, 50 to 100, Above 100)

[5] James Kydd's Cash Book, 1846 and 1864
[6] ibid, Jan, 1853
[7] NSA, Carmyllie, 1836. A new road was projected to East Ha'en and 'were it executed, it would be of great benefit....in shortening the carriage of lime and coals.'
[8] James Kydd, Cash Book, (1832-1865)
[9] Agricultural Returns, AF39/14/2, 1894
[10] James Kydd, Cash Book, 20 Nov, 1858
[11] Ibid, Sept 10, 1862

The chart shows the number of farmers in the three parishes in 1867, Arbirlot, Carmyllie and

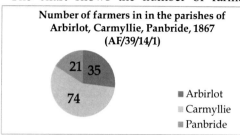

Number of farmers in in the parishes of Arbirlot, Carmyllie, Panbride, 1867 (AF/39/14/1)

- Arbirlot
- Carmyllie
- Panbride

Panbride. Carmyllie had twice as many farmers as Arbirlot and three times as many as Panbride. The acreages of crops in the parishes of Arbirlot and Carmyllie were similar, Arbirlot (4,934), Carmyllie (5005) and Panbride with a smaller acreage of 3,001.[12]

Yet the chart proves, although Carmyllie and Arbirlot parishes covered similar acreages, Carmyllie had a high proportion of small farmers. Cultivation of crops in 1867 showed variations too. Oats and grass under rotation were the most productive crops in Carmyllie, possibly as grassland farming was more suited to the area and was compatible for cattle rearing and dairy farming.

Considering Panbride had a lower acreage, the parish, together with Arbirlot was more productive with wheat and barley. Harvesting cereals was a crucial time for farmers. The welfare of the community depended on a 'good' harvest, oats providing the staple diet for households and livestock. When the crop was ripe, favourable weather could be short so time was of the essence; hence the invention of the reaping machine was so beneficial in

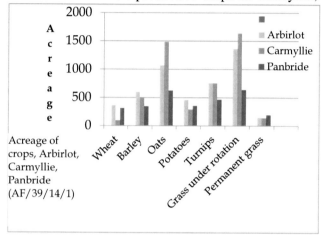

Acreage of crops, Arbirlot, Carmyllie, Panbride (AF/39/14/1)

- Arbirlot
- Carmyllie
- Panbride

many ways. Yet, although the Rev Patrick Bell's (1799-1869) invention became available in 1828, the use of the reaper was still in its infancy in the 1860s and Carmyllie farmers were still cutting corn with the scythe.[13]

When the corn was cut, more intensive work was required to 'bunch' it and set the sheaves together in stooks to dry and allow the kernel to harden. To show gratitude for the farm servants' hard work, Mr Kydd provided beer from Mr Taylor, the brewer.[14] Ten years later, Bell's reaping machine was working on farms in the parish[15], and as seen from the illustration, the grain was laid flat in regular

Carnegie Fullerton and his father, Forehills, c. 1920 (Fullerton family)

Binder, Mains of Cononsyth 1930s (Craig Family)

rows. David Hume employed 'bandsters' separately from farm servants, who followed the reaper, gathering and binding sheaves.

---

[12] Agricultural Returns. AF39/14/1, 1867

[13] James Kydd, Cashbook, 'Paid Silvester Brown £3 for corn cutting', 3 Oct, 1857 and 'Paid Georgre Kydd, £5.14.10 for cutting 12 acres corn', 30 Oct, 1859 and 'Paid Mr Kydd for cutting corn, £7.6.6' was the last entry, 15 Nov, 1862.

[14] Ibid, Bear cost £.1.3/-, 30 Oct, 1858

[15] David Hume Cashbook. 'Files to Reaping Machine, 5/6d', Aug 23, 1873

Presumably, 'bandsters' were experienced, operating rapidly and moving from farm to farm.[16] Farm workers followed the bandsters, lifting the sheaves into stooks.[17] However bandsters were replaced after further improvement was made to the reaper towards the 1890s when a binding system was added, bunching the corn on the machine before ejecting the sheaves. Initially the sheaves were bound by wire but this proved unsuccessful.

One of the reasons was that the sheaf was difficult to cut when 'feeding' the threshing mill.[18] From the 1890s a knotter was added and the sheaves were bound with sisal (string) and from then on, the reaper was known as 'binder', pulled from the front by horses then much later by tractor until it was superseded by the combine harvester in the 1950s.

Cattle were by far the predominant type of livestock in Carmyllie in 1870, exceeding cattle numbers in Arbirlot by over 25%. Carmyllie also had more dairy cows than Arbirlot. Both parishes had a high number of sheep. Horses provided the power required to till the soil, pull burdens and provide a means of transport. Most pigs were reared for domestic use rather than held for trade, so both parishes had roughly equal numbers.

Mr & Mrs Anderson, New Mains Guynd, c. 1900 (Andy Milne)

George and Jessie Fullerton, Forehills, c. 1920 (Gibb family)

With the decreasing prices for cereals after 1846, Carmyllie farmers concentrated on trading with cattle and catching the market with letting of grass and sales of turnips and potatoes. In 1864 James Kydd received £67 from Robert Falconer for 13½ acres of turnips[19] and £35 from Mr Carrie and George Ross for letting 5 acres of potatoes[20].

Additionally, grass parks were rented for the season. In 1861, James Kydd rented a park at Panmure and paid £55 to Mr Cunningham the Panmure factor.[21] Renting grass parks at Panmure was attractive as the grass was ready for grazing earlier in the spring while higher up in Carmyllie, stock was still indoors eating expensive feeding.

Yet transporting animals was usually an all-day task. Farmers, labourers, and dogs 'drove' cattle and sheep along tracks and roads for several miles to fields. With little traffic on the road this operation was possible although a knowledge of the route was an advantage in order to guard open entrances to fields and gardens. The movement and turnover of higher numbers of livestock ran the risk of damage and disease so farmers were obliged to pay insurance[22]. Later a fee (5/11d) was paid to the Contagious Disease Act account.[23]

16 ibid 'Bandsters (Carrey) 3 weeks 1 ½ days @ 28/- £4.10.9, (Gardyne) 3 weeks @ 27/-, £4.1/-', 22 Sept 1876

17 Ibid, 'Mrs Hunter, 99 hours lifting @ 6d per hour, £2.9.6'

18 Muriel Thomson recalled a report that David Maxwell, Newton of Carmyllie, had difficulty with wire sheaves (1985)

19 James Kydd, Cashbook, Apr 1864

20 Ibid, Nov 12, 1864

21 Ibid, 10 Oct, 1861

22 Ibid, James Kydd paid £1.17.10 for 'farm insurance' (22Nov, 1862)

23 David Hume, Cashbook, 3 Dec, 1874

After 1870, farming became economically more challenging. When new leases were given (normally for the duration of 19 years), there was a substantial increase in the half-yearly rent. James Kydd's rent in 1864, was raised from £88 to £115, a rise of over 25%.[24] Yet two years previously, he had the foresight to invest in a major drainage scheme to improve returns from the land. He paid Captain Fotheringham £26.11.3d for 'drain tiles' and later in the month cleared a bill for 'drain digging' for £42.8.3.[25] Farmers paid full-time labourers wages twice yearly at 'the term', Whitsun (end of May),

David Hume, Mains. c.1910 (Gibb Family)

and Martinmas (end of November) while outworkers were paid on seasonal basis. After each 'term', the farmer would start afresh, usually with a different set of servants. At the same time, farmers settled their accounts with such trades as wrights, blacksmiths, saddlers, drapers and shoemakers. This practice was constant throughout the nineteenth century and up to the 1930s, although wages were paid on a monthly basis by the 1920s.[26] Larger tenant farmers employed on average six persons, usually men but one or two could be women, perhaps employed as housekeepers, but undertaking seasonal work.[27] Each farm servant paid according to his or her status (see Chapter 9, p.120). In 1856, Joseph Tosh was paid £10, Robert Norie £9, James Murry £5.5/-, John Dakers £3.3/- and Margaret Brown £3.15/-. Twenty years later in 1876, there was over a 25% increase when Robert Horne was paid £14.7/-, Robert Ford, £16.5/-, A. Mathieson £9, D. Kydd £7, Isabella Sime £9.10/- and Annie Douglas, £10.[28] The tenants on smaller farms would work as a family unit and employ outworkers seasonally, whereas those living on pendicles found work locally and farmed their plot intermittently.

John L. Soutar, Miltonhaugh
1920s (Gibb Family)

In Carmyllie, there were approximately 6,219 acres under crop and 94 farmers in 1910[29]. The main crops in the parish remained similar to the 1860s, with oats and grassland covering over half the acreage, while turnips and hay were more than a quarter, leaving the remainder to barley, potatoes and a small acreage of wheat. The larger tenanted farms would probably grow most of the latter while smaller tenancies required their acreage for oats, turnips, hay and grass for stock rearing. It is noteworthy that there were 74 farmers in the parish in 1867, cropping almost 5000 acres while in 1910, there were 94 farmers sharing 6,219 acres under crop, 20 more farmers cropping over 1000 more acres. The acreage had increased as uncultivated land in Carmyllie had been under reclamation. For example, John Fyfe, a shoemaker in Letham village in the early decades of the nineteenth century, responded to the offer by the Panmure Estate to reclaim land at The Birns and part of the Dilty Moss, free of rent until cultivation was possible.[30]

---

[24] James Kydd, Cashbook, 18 Mar, 1865
[25] Ibid, He paid Captain Fotheringham £26.11.3 for 'Drain Tiles' and later in the month cleared a bill for 'drain digging' for £42.8.3.
[26] David Hume, Cashbook, 1927
[27] Ibid, Wages paid for 4 men and two women, 1875
[28] ibid Jul 1874
[29] Agricultural Returns AF39/14/2, 1910
[30] Personal interview with Anna Hair (nee Fyffe)

Half of the farmers in Carmyllie farmed under 20 acres and they strove to be self-sufficient but rent still had to be paid and so employment was sought elsewhere, with farm day labouring, quarrying, dressmaking or tailoring supplementing the income. Successful trades such as blacksmiths or joiners were able to retain a piece of land to be largely self-sufficient and they would farm when time and

Jessie Smith & George Fullerton. 1905 (Gibb family)

weather permitted. In general, the crofter relied on the larger farms to provide resources such as extra implements, service of a bull and feeding. The cow was an essential livestock asset to the crofter as it supplied milk, butter, cheese and whey[31] and provided the cow kept good health, it produced a calf each year. Often the tethered cow was seen grazing on the roadside grass in summer and on occasions, the crofter or his wife would scythe roadside grass for hay.[32] Yet it required nutritious fodder during the winter to keep the cow 'in milk' and it was important to build a store of winter feed during the growing season and all opportunities were taken. If a farmer had a burn or a ditch running through his land then he could cash-in by allowing crofters to scythe grass on the 'bankin' (side of the burn).[33] Sometimes the crofter would pay the farmer for 'grazing of Quey' [cows].[34] It was also common for crofters to buy potatoes in the drill from the larger farmers.[35]

Most Carmyllie farmers were to face two distinctive changes in the first half of the twentieth century, one after WW1 and another at the outbreak of WW2. The first concerned the tenants on Panmure estate. Taking into account that there were a small number of tenants on the Guynd estate and Cononsyth, there were at least 70% of the tenant farmers in Carmyllie paying rent to the Panmure Estate until 1922. That part of the Panmure Estate north of the Elliot water, which included Carmyllie and some Arbirlot farms, was sold, mostly to sitting tenants. However, there were a few exceptions as the Dundee Water Commissioners bought the Birns, Dykehead, Skichenmuir, West Skichen and East Skichen and Wedderswell (the latter two were under Dundee Water Commissioners from the first decade of the 20th century) from the Panmure Estate by 1919. The water drainage from these farms flowed into reservoirs for Dundee City water supply and farmers had restrictions when grazing animals.[36]

Lena & Lizzie Soutar, Milton. c.1930 (Gibb family)

---

[31] Whey, an extraction from butter and cheese making and was used in recipes or fed to animals such as pigs.
[32] Conversation with Mrs Nettie Gibb, Montquhir (1998) and Gordon Law, Glentyrie (2012)
[33] David Hume Cashbook, Robert Sturrock was charged £1 for 'burnside grass' and A. Lumgair 7/- for 'grass on ditch side', 23 Nov 1874 and Nov 20, 1875
[34] Ibid, D. Boyle paid £2.10/- , 2 Dec, 1876
[35] Ibid, Mr Gibson bought '4 drills of Potato at 10/- per drill' in October 1874, 17 Oct, 1874
[36] Valuation Roll, 1929-30

At the sale in 1922, most pendicle tenants on the Panmure Estate were hardest hit as the quarry industry closed down only to start again after WW1 on a smaller scale, employing fewer men. Few of these part-time farmers would find it viable to purchase small acreages. One or two were enterprising and purchased nearby pendicles. For example, William Boath, Muiredge bought neighbouring pendicles and his unit remained sustainable until the 1960s [37]. Other larger farmers bought nearby patches of land, such as the

Bringing home the 'neeps' Slade Farm 1930s (McDonald Family)

Lochlair farmer who enclosed much of the land at the edge of Dilty Moss. Some houses remained such as Mosston and Muirheads, but other holdings such as the Wagon, Berryhillock, North Mains and Tutties Neuk were merged into bigger units and the farm names are almost forgotten. In addition, Slade farm merged Windyedge, Boath's pendicle (owner of the Whin Inn), Lavrockhall along with two pendicles in Redford village into one unit.[38] Certainly, the practice of merging smaller farms into bigger units was not new, as it was always the case that if a farm is unsustainable another farmer can see opportunities to expand. The landless crofter had a number of alternatives, find farm work locally, move to the town or emigrate.

Those farmers who took the challenge and bought their farms after 1922 were now more dependent on banks and lawyers than to the Laird. Mrs Nita Smith (nee Gibb) relates their family's negotiations to become owner-occupier:-

My grandfather, John Gibb, farmed Montquhir from 1900, and in 1922, when Dalhousie Estates sold off part of their estate that included much of Carmyllie lands, John Gibb, as tenant, bought Montquhir farm. The purchase, made possible by Granny Gibb borrowing money from her two sons, Bill and Tom. Uncle Bill was repaid with interest before he left for Australia in 1926 and my father was repaid before he married in 1930. Another of my father's brothers, Dave, had a milk round in Arbroath and lived in the second Montquhir cottage while my father looked after the farm. Our cottages had no indoor bathroom but we did have running water supplied from a tank at Muirheads. This smallholding was once farmed by the Laird family, who lost three sons in WW1. My father bought Muirheads after the Lairds moved on to Bankhead of Kirkbuddo in the 1920s.

The first tractor, Slade c.1941 (McDonald family)

From the mid-1880s, farming profitability deteriorated very badly, particularly grain growing. Cut-price grain was flooding in from America and Canada on steamers. The difficult years of the 1930s Depression were particularly trying for farmers and it was not until the eve of WW2 that farming profits improved. In these years, Carmyllie farmers like elsewhere in Britain relied more heavily on livestock, the cattle trade and dairy farming. Less land was under the plough. Low input livestock farming often called 'dog and stick farming' became the norm at this time. Livestock had its problems too and much of the cattle stock of the country was devastated by Rinderpest, a highly contagious cattle plague that was thought to have been imported with live cattle from South Africa. It was reported

[37] Ibid, 1938-1939
[38] Presbytery of Arbroath, Teind Roll, Parish of Carmyllie, 1927

that a farming family in Carmyllie, Mr and Mrs Cochrane at 'West Conon', a smallholding that once stood opposite the Community Hall was ruined by Rinderpest in the mid 1880s and they were forced to emigrate to New Zealand.

As modern bureaucracy arose, more overhead expenses occurred such as Health stamps, Fire Insurance, Income Tax, Consolidated Rates and Horse Insurance, together with 'float' transport to an increasing number of livestock markets.[39] To own a motor car in the Parish of Carmyllie in the 1920s would have been a luxury and costly[40], but essential when travel to town was difficult. In 1934, David Hume sold an Overland car for £5 and bought an Austin for £33[41]. On the farm in the 1920s and 30s, draught horses continued to be the centre of power for farm work but this was not without problems. A

Mrs Davie, East Hills c.1942 (Arthur Jarret)

disease, 'grass sickness', was prevalent in horses and was generally fatal with no known cure, so to cover the risk, farmers paid a horse insurance that doubled in price in two years.[42]

Another major change affecting Carmyllie farmers took place at the beginning of WW2. Britain's shipping imports across the Atlantic were in disarray, because of the successful German U-boat campaign so the Government turned to the nation's farmers to 'dig for victory' and feed the nation. This crisis highlighted the run-down condition of agriculture, exacerbated by the unproductive years between the wars. District Agricultural Executive Committees were established to improve husbandry and efficiency. To speed up operations, mechanisation was encouraged which also assisted with the shortage of labour. The basic change was from draught horses to tractor power. New skills had to be

Carmyllie Mart, 1960s

learned as farm work became more specialised. When a tractor was bought, a toolbar and a plough were included to make ploughing possible. [43] More production of food required compulsory measures to grow specific crops and cultivate more land. In Carmyllie an increasing acreage of potatoes was grown and less oats, although there was also concentration on livestock rearing such as cattle, pigs and poultry. Farmers were compensated by the Government provided demands were met. Oat production declined naturally with fewer draught horses although both tractor and horse worked together until the tractor became more versatile with the use of rubber tyres instead of iron wheels.[44]

Jimmy Gordon was born in 1929 and was an auctioneer with the Strathmore Auction Co Ltd from 1945 and remembers dealing with livestock when food was rationed, and his work at the Carmyllie Mart. *My first job in the mart was tattooing fat pigs, which were often entered in one or two lots as many ploughmen and farmers reared a pig for their own consumption. In the early stages of my work, the Ministry of Food controlled the mart since food was rationed during World War 2*

Jimmy Gordon

---

[39] David Hume Cashbook, 1927-1938

[40] Ibid, Annual Car licence£14, 2 new tyres £5.12/- and Car Insurance £12.9/-, 1927

[41] Ibid, In 1934 David Hume sold an Overland car for £5 and bought an Austin for £33

[42] Ibid, Paid Vet, £7.93 Horse Insurance, 11 Jan, 1936. Paid Warden Horse Insurance, £15.5.6, 10 Dec 1938.

[43] Ibid, 1942, Tractor £170, toolbar 52.9/-, Plough, £44.6/-, Tractor Expenses£7.1.7 and Del charges, £13.10/-, total £287,
 10 Apr, 1942

[44] *Third Statistical Account*, p.59

and after until 1954. When farmers were ready to sell cattle, they booked with the Ministry of Food two weeks before taking them to the market. The cattle never entered the ring, as such, instead, when cattle were sold, the seller and the butcher were present together with the Ministry of Food inspector. After the meat was butchered the government had control of the distribution, reaching as far as such places as Liverpool or Bolton as well as locally.

Another early task involved measuring fields for potato crops with chains, usually in June. First I pulled the chain for the measurer then I graduated to measuring the field myself. We often measured the acreage of land for potato merchants or farmers who seasonally rented land. Selling Irish cattle however, occupied much of the Mart's time, even before I was employed in 1945. Dealers bought these Irish cattle 'off the street' in Ireland usually two years old plus, big boned and under-nourished, shipping them to a wharf in Glasgow where they were tagged and loaded on to railway trucks and brought by rail to east Scotland, dropping off 300-400 at Forfar station at one time. I remember the mart employers waiting at Forfar station, and before the train came to a halt, they opened as many trucks as possible so that the mart could draw off the cattle for sale in the mart. Opposition was rife and if they did not move quickly at this stage, then more truckloads would be consigned to Scott & Graham (the rival Forfar mart) or private dealers. I had my

David Hume, Mains with Auctioneer Sam Smith, Carmyllie Mart. In the background is the refreshment hut replacing the roadside stall selling food and drink. Photographer Ian Wight, Arbroath Herald. 1960s

share acting as a clerk. When selling the cattle the auctioneer required a clerk by his side recording details of the sale, but there was also a roup roll clerk in the ring recording too in case the Auctioneer's clerk fell behind with the information. In the ring there was also a martman marking the cattle with a particular colour relating to the buyer, so that in the buyer's pen, all the cattle would be marked with the same colour.

Carmyllie mart (built on land owned by Charles McDonald, Slade) had its share of the Irish cattle trade. Irish Cattle were consigned on a Pink Movement Licence issued for 7 days and because they were imported from another country, these cattle had to be kept on the same farm for three months before selling on to prevent the spread of disease. I recall my early days at Carmyllie mart when most farmers 'drove' their cattle there. The mart was restricted to once a month from March to November, as Carmyllie Mart was without a concrete base and regulations stipulated that 21 days must pass to allow the disinfectant to become effective. The original pens were proving too small for the bigger cattle in size and greater numbers so Strathmore

Dairy Herd at Glentyrie c.1980

Bringing home the hay, Forehills (Gibb family)

Auction Company provided larger pens for the purpose. As well as farmers droving their cattle to market, cattle came in railway trucks to Redford station where they were kept in the surrounding fields until mart day. Cattle were also dropped off at Guthrie station where farmers drove them the three-mile journey to Carmyllie. The tin-roofed mart held the ring and an office, and to the side there were separate premises for the bar, selling alcohol but no food, run by Bob Davidson, Zoar, Forfar. After the cattle were sold, it was mandatory that the 7-day licence be issued to the buyer's farm, usually carried out by Jack Whitton, the local policeman.

All breeds of cattle were bought and sold at Carmyllie Mart, whereas Kirriemuir Mart tended to trade in black cattle only. Yet Carmyllie had its own niche in the trade because local farmers could buy these hardy Irish beasts in the autumn and they would thrive over winter, feeding on 'neeps' and straw, and when selling in the Spring, they left a good margin on turnover before the cattle were 'fattened off' on fresh grass.

Although no sheep were sold at Carmyllie Mart, its popularity continued as it was within a short distance of its customers. I recall that there were many small farms in the area where men had an outside occupation, and I dealt with the wives when visiting the farms, for example, Chasser of South Park, to book in four or five cattle. Cattle floats belonging to Alfred Wilkie and Mennie of Friockheim and Stewart Brothers of Arbroath would lift the cattle if going a distance but gradually, as more transport was available, movement to larger and more regular markets was more possible. Yet I think the lack of indoor pens also caused the closure of Carmyllie Mart and the other marts such as Edzell and Kirriemuir. Exposure to the weather rotted the pens easily and the relentless cold was uncomfortable for the animals and men. Most local farmers agree that the Carmyllie mart closed in the late 1960s and my colleagues and I think it was possibly 1971 that there was a complete closure.

In 1967, Scott & Graham amalgamated with Strathmore Auctions and that led on to a merger with Dundee Market where I would act as auctioneer sometimes. After the Dundee Market, the farmers and merchants would meet in the City Square to do business and refresh themselves in the Cafe Val D'Or. I claim a connection to Carmyllie in that my great uncle, James Peter ran the joinery business with Will Buchan at Redford and also had a Tailor shop in Arbroath. My father was named after him – James Peter Gordon. I can remember attending my great uncle's funeral at Carmyllie church in 1942.

Mr & Mrs Gardiner, Tillyhoit

William Gardiner, tenant farmer at Tillyhoit, gives a vivid account of farming in Carmyllie from the 1930s through to the 1970s.

Threshing day c.1900 (Carcary family)

In 1919, my grandfather was farming at New Mains of Guynd and my father lived in a cottage, married with two sons. In 1919, my father and mother came to Tillyhoit where I was born in 1922 followed by three more siblings, completing the family of six.

Tillyhoit Farm, situated on high ground overlooking the Tay estuary, was on the Guynd estate belonging to T.C. Ouchterlony. I remember each tenant farmer on the Guynd estate took turns to collect the coal from the train at Denhead station and deliver to the Laird's house and the tenant's farms and cottages.

When I began farming, I was working a pair of horse with an additional horse from New Mains of Guynd in busy times. I could plough one and a half acres per 9-hour day, rising at 5am to feed the horse and allowing the horse to rest for 1½ hours at mid-day.

The type of farming was mixed arable, growing oats, wheat, neeps, tatties, grass and fattening cattle for the market. Some oats and tatties were sold, usually at the market, as well as cattle. I recall 'droving' cattle to and from Carmyllie and Arbroath markets. On one occasion, the journey to

'Mid-Yokin' time. Seated from left, Arch Paton, Joe Swankie,
Pete Watt & Jock Leslie (Gibb family)

Arbroath proved too much for two cattle and Wilkie's small float from Friockheim was called to the rescue at Loanmouth beyond the Crofts. I also remember, with amusement, how Grant of Broughty Ferry sent a horse-driven float to collect one of Tillyhoit's horses that was taken back to the Ferry tied to the back of the float! Bunched wheat straw was kept to 'theak' the stacks and cover the tattie pits. The remainder of the oats and tatties were kept to feed the livestock together with neeps, hay and straw and kale for the 'kye'. The family kept a cow and often two, to provide milk and butter for ourselves. This was stopped in 1955-56 when the Doctor advised Mary that our son would react better to bought, treated milk. Pigs were also kept for family use. One pig was killed in the 'back-end' (autumn) and strung up on a ladder at the back door. Cutting up the pig into different parts was attended to immediately and could take well into the evening. The hams (never rolled) were hung up on hooks in the kitchen. There would be enough hams to provide the family ¾ of the winter when another pig was killed, this time in the slaughterhouse and half of the pig came home and the other half was sold to the butcher. Hens were kept for eggs and the occasional hen for the pot. Surplus eggs were sold when my parents visited Arbroath market on a Saturday or my mother sold eggs to the visiting vanmen. Later the Egg Marketing Board collected the eggs in the late 1940s and 1950s.

The family were almost self-sufficient although from the 1930s various vanmen called. Carnegie Soutar the baker came twice weekly and also Ken Duthie the grocer at Friockheim and Walker the butcher from Arbroath later replaced by Fleming. Harry Ross from Carnoustie sold fish and fruit and 'Apple' Thomson, with only one arm, came on a seasonal basis with a flat horse cart. In addition, there was a selection of trades and shops in Redford, such as a blacksmith, joiner, shoemaker, dressmaker and post office as well as two shops.

As each of my brothers left school, I took my turn to work with my father at Tillyhoit. Then the older brother left to work, usually on farms, elsewhere. Neighbours came to help on threshing days when a dozen people or more were required including at least two women to 'louse'. Threshings provided the farmer with oats to sell, and oats, straw and 'caff' for the livestock. Tillyhoit had five threshings in the winter, sometimes working for half a day. The housewives provided a 3-course meal at dinner time plus 'piecies' in the morning and afternoon. If working later in the afternoon, a cooked tea was produced too. Bigger farms at the end of the winter season could have the mill for two days to clear up the stacks. I recall that the steam mill arrived late at night and the millman biked home to Culloden in Arbroath and back at 5 am to start his day.

'Fergie' 35 tractor 1962. (Law family)

I worked at Dustydrum and then later at Cononsyth and lived in the bothy at each farm, returning to Tillyhoit when I married in 1954. Mary and I lived in the cottage at Tillyhoit for six years, moving to Carnoustie in 1960 where we kept pigs and cattle. I travelled to Tillyhoit every day for seventeen years to help my father and returned to take over the farm in 1977. If the roads were treacherous, I would travel to Arbroath then to Carmyllie. I recall how the type of labour changed through the years, especially during and after the Second World War, from working horse, carts and binders to tractors, bogies and combines. Previously, the extended family was called in to plant tatties in the spring then gather them in the Autumn. Later on, tattie merchants rented the tattie field and brought their own squads to deal with to the crop.

I saw that the tractor had the ability to plough deeper which quelled the weeds yet also brought a redder clay soil to the surface. Although this did not improve the soil initially, over the years when mixed with other soils, conditions improved. I thought the grey Fergie was 'magic' even if there was no cab and thick coats had to combat the cold weather. Facing all weather conditions from fetching neeps in deep snow and ice for the animals to setting up bunches to make stooks in wet weather was hard to bear. When the combine appeared in the area in the late 1940s, my father remarked 'That'll never dae!' Nevertheless, my father and I worked the horse alongside the machinery. To this day I am fond of my horse and treat him/her more as a companion.

Carnegie Farm, 1967 (Reid family)

Mary was capable and a great asset to the farm. In Carnoustie she 'held the fort' while I, after helping with the early morning chores, travelled daily to Tilyhoit. Later her young family helped morning and evening with feeding and mucking out pigs and calves. She was a trained dressmaker and with this talent made all the clothes and furnishings for the house and family. We moved back to Tillyhoit in 1977.
The earlier days were the most enjoyable since there was always lots of company when planting and gathering tatties, at harvest time, threshings and clatting neeps to mention a few.[45]

An enterprising farmer, James Allison, who farmed Drummygar, Clearbank and East Ward, diversified and founded Allison's Transport after the war with a capital of less than £400. The fleet grew from 10 vehichles in 1951 to 200 in 1966 and operated haulage services all over Britain, based in Dundee.

Allison's Transport lorry 1950s

During the War, most farm produce was sold direct to the Ministry of Food and there was a ready market. David Hume, Mains of Carmyllie sold 4 fat cattle to the Ministry of Food for £167.16/-6d in Apri 1943. He sold 2 fat pigs to them for £19.11/- the same month and he received potato subsidy of £155 and wheat subsidy of £36 later in 1943. On occasions, the Ministry of Food paid directly to farmers for cattle and potatoes into the early 1950s and pigs were sold to the Ministry until 1956.[46]

Although Government compulsory orders were withdrawn after WW2, farming did not revert to the 1930s. Less heed was paid to rotational cropping and mechanisation changed agriculture for ever, enabling deeper ploughing, speedier sowing and harvest
with fewer gambles with bad weather conditions, together with improved fertiliser that multiplied crop yields. The Government continued to encourage food production by giving subsidies for ploughing, drainage and purchasing lime and manure. Marketing Boards were introduced for marketing potatoes, wool and milk. Deficiency payments were introduced for grain which supplemented returns from crop sales and brought the farmer's return up to a level set in the 'Annual Price Review'. A system of subsidies was introduced for cattle that subsidised keeping cows. There was a subsidy on the calves known as 'the punch' where government officials visited the farm to

---

[45] Testimony, William Gardiner, 2009
[46] David Hume Cashbook, 1950-1961

punch a hole in the calf's ear and then a subsidy was paid. Sugar Beet was an additional highly mechanised crop grown for the sugar factory at Cupar in Fife, which ended when the factory closed in the 1960s.

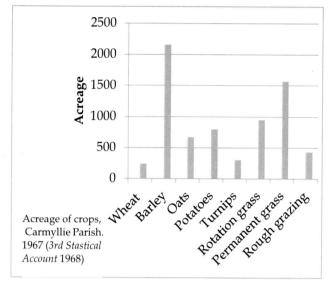

Acreage of crops, Carmyllie Parish. 1967 (3rd Stastical Account 1968)

Assistance from the Government brought irreversible changes. Farmers were investing more in machinery and committing themselves to specialised crops, requiring for instance, drills, planters, fertiliser and pesticide sprayers, grain drying facilities, combine harvesters and balers. If concentrating on say, barley and potatoes, more fields were required to justify the expense so, as farm animal prices fluctuated, some farmers chose to be livestock free. On the other hand, at least eight dairy farms remained in Carmyllie in the 1960s: Milton, Hayhillock, Wardneuk, Montquhir, Miltonhaugh, Skichenmuir, Glentyrie and Conon. They had invested in milking machines, renovated byres and purchased in silage machinery and started to tuberculosis test their cows.[47]

The chart indicates by the 1960s the acreage of barley had increased three times more than oats, partly because demand for oats was less but also barley varieties had improved to give higher yields. Oats produced lower yields, ripened later, and were more likely harvested in deteriorating weather.[48] Turnips and hay became less popular for winter livestock feed being replaced by grass silage, that is, cut grass harvested by machines in summer. A number of beef cattle along with arable farming were also being run in Carmyllie hence the higher acreage under grass.

Mention must be made of the combine harvester that was a revolution in agriculture. This replaced the binder, the building of 'stooks' and the carting of sheaves to the stack yard. There were no more stacks to become infested with rats and mice and await the expense of the threshing mill. All was now dealt with in one operation at harvest time. The first combine harvester was arousing interest in the area at the end of the 1940s when Carnegie Fullerton was promoting the machine. His son, Carnie, relates his father's involvement.

Last of the stack-yards, Muiredge, early 1960s
(Harrow family)

'Neg' Fullerton operating a John Deere tractor binder in Australia, 1920s

Carnegie Fullerton ('Neg' as he was called by most people), born 1902, was the eldest son of George and Jessie Fullerton, Forehills. He attended Greystone School, leaving during WW1 to work with his father until he emigrated to eastern Australia in January 1924, to work with relatives on cattle and sheep farms. In 1926, 'Neg' joined the Australian Division of Massey-Harris and became involved in assembling the

---

[47] Cows were tuberculosis tested in 1950
[48] *Third Statistical Account,* p.64

first reaper-harvester, the forerunner of the combine harvester, produced by the company. On his return to Carmyllie in 1932, he joined the Massey Harris factory based in Manchester where he gained more experience assembling, operating and repairing the combine harvesters that were imported from Canada in huge crates. Later, after WW2 he branched out on his own and initially was repairing tractors and contracting for farmers locally, yet he was eager to introduce the combine harvester to the area. Around 1949/1950 very few farmers owned combines hence 'Neg' took the initiative and hired a Massey-Harris 21 (12' wide cutter head) bagger combine (the grain collected in bags on the machine) from Andrew Small, Craigie Farm, near St Michaels in Fife. The combine was transported via road and ferry across the Tay to Angus. The 'header' was removed and placed on a trailer. Carnie recalls (in 1950) that the whole deck width of the Scotscraig or Abercraig ferry was

occupied by this 'wonder' machine when moving it back and forth across the Tay, to combine harvest crops in Carmyllie and the surrounding parishes. Up until then, crops had only ever been harvested with binders. These large machines came from Canada whereas later, smaller Massey-Harris 726 (8' 6" wide cutter head) model combines were made in Kilmarnock to cope with smaller field entrances.

'Neg' continued his enthusiasm for the combine and sold two locally to Reekie at Parkconon and Caldwell at Grange of Conon. These combines arrived in the huge crates from Arbroath Railway Station on three-wheeled Railway Scammell lorries

'Neg' hired this Massey Harris combine from Fife

- one at Ferndene in Carmyllie and the other at Grange of Conon farm. There the crates were broken open and the final parts added to the main chassis over a few days and the combine set to harvest work on their own farms. In fact, the oldest garage at Ferndene today is made from 75% of one of these old combine crates.

Nonetheless, the surge of farm machinery use had its downsides. Not only was less employment required but also the habitat for wildlife was diminishing. The corncrake could be rescued as the binder approached or the lapwing's nest in the drill was more visible with slow moving machinery.

As there was a revolution in agriculture, so the farming household was changing too. With the motor car, opportunities for families were extending beyond the parish. Visits to cities such as Edinburgh, Aberdeen and Glasgow were possible as were Agricultural shows at various venues. Farmers' daughters too could venture to new horizons.

Mrs Nita Smith (nee Gibb) describes how her life was enlightened when she trained professionally.
Many people still reminisce about the prolonged winter of 1947. The storm began during school term and I remember the Forfar Academy bus stuck on the Newton brae and never moved for six weeks. Snow drifts alternated with icy conditions and gradually covered the bus completely. Transport and

Sledge at Montquir, 1947

communication were cut to a minimum resulting in urgency for dairy farmers to improvise transport in order to deliver milk to Arbroath. At Montquhir, a sledge was built, driven by a horse that had a dual purpose, the milk cans were delivered to town then provisions such as flour and bread were bought and returned to the community. Sledge travelling had an advantage as it travelled to town almost as the crow flies since the snow was well above the fences, dykes and even telephone wires. Again the community came together to help each other. Mrs Clark at Greystone Post Office, notified us of the provisions her customers required together with some local farmers, then we delivered to the Milton, which was a collection point. I cannot recollect how I was able to reach Forfar (perhaps by train from Kirkbuddo or Arbroath) since I had to stay in Forfar for a few days with school friends in order to sit school exams.

The year after 1947, I left school and prepared to sit my driving test. I had no driving lessons and the only tuition was given by my parents, so the day before my test, Dave Robbie, Robbie's Garage, Arbroath, accompanied me round the town. I was delighted to pass first time and the ability to drive was an asset living in a rural area and sharing a car with the family.

After 1948, there was plenty of work at Montquhir, housekeeping and attending to the dairy yet I was unable to find fulfilment. Nonetheless I entered competitions and was successful at the Angus Show, Flower shows and the Women's Own magazine when I won medals for baking and needlework. I think my secret success was the Canadian flour and the baking tips obtained from my mother's cousin (we called him uncle, died in 1954) Carnegie Soutar who had baker shops in Friockheim and Arbroath, followed on by his son George.

Proving my talents encouraged me to look for further training and with my father's blessing I entered the Domestic Science School at Atholl Crescent, Edinburgh in 1955 and enjoyed a three year course, staying in 'digs'. I have to be thankful for the household practice I carried out at home since the teachers at the College remarked that 'I was a natural'. After I completed the course in 1958 with a good qualification, I applied for a teacher's post and was appointed to Stobswell Girls School, Dundee. Here I found much satisfaction. I and another teacher split large classes into two where there were five kitchens, three sewing rooms available and a flat at the back of the school where we taught housewifery. My salary started around £48.0.0d per month and I became a proud owner of a Singer Gazelle car. I held the teacher's post for three years. During this time, I was married to Rae in 1960 and left my teaching career in 1961 to start our family.

The wider use of the motor car gave the opportunity to a variety of farmers' sons/daughters seeking a wife/husband not necessarily within a radius of a few miles. Young Farmers' Clubs engaged members from all who were interested in farming life from town or country. Social gatherings and entertainment were popular. New farmers' wives were settling in the parish with town or country backgrounds.

Arbroath Young Farmers Club. Top, early 1950s Middle, 1959 Bottom, 1962

John E. Kneen M.R.C.V.S.

In 1955 John Kneen, the local vet, came to work with Archie Robertson in Arbroath, working mostly with farm animals. John remembers:

The main health issues were 'choke' in cattle and pneumonia, Irish cattle being very susceptible after a long journey and living in full farm courts. Foul foot was another cattle problem, an infection gathered from gravel penetrating the foot and the animal moving around on wet dung ground. Staggers in cattle was brought on by too much lime in grass. Interestingly early in my career there was no vaccine available for the common 'husk' or lungworm. Sulphonamide drugs were predominantly used while Penicillin and antibiotics were barely into common use. Horses were prone to grass disease and ragwort poisoning was fatal causing liver and brain damage. Pigs were prone to anaemia and treatment, through iron injections, only came into use in the late 1950s.

Arbroath Slaughter House, handling stock from Arbroath, Carnoustie and Friockheim area, required daily inspections of any suspect animals with abcess, pleurisy or TB. Every week 50-100 cattle were dealt with in the slaughterhouse and local butchers would take 3-4 animals while smaller shops would cope with one.

In 1957 I married Maureen and she was a great benefit to the practice, acting as secretary and keeping irate farmers calm at the end of the phone. In the latter part of practicing as a vet, the mobile phone was a great boon, allowing me to attend to emergencies quickly.

When Archie Robertson retired in 1965, I took over the practice and enjoyed being my own boss. Yet a vet can be a dangerous profession as I have had my fair share of being tossed by angry bulls and cows, sometimes to considerable injury.

One fond memory of Carmyllie stands out when visiting Upper Greystone and after completing a numenotomy, to remove a wire from the stomach of a cow, I was invited into the house where a meal was awaiting me of roast beef with the trimmings followed by tea and cakes. To top this, a fortnight later, the identical sequence followed.[49]

Muriel Hume, a farmer's wife, recalls her early-married life in Carmyllie. She reflects on the different culture, looking at the Parish from the outside.

Mrs Muriel Hume

In 1956, I retired from my much loved work travelling all over Scotland as a home service adviser with the North Of Scotland Hydro-Electric Board and the Gas Board, to marry Malcolm Hume, Mains of Carmyllie, and to meet another challenge of living permanently in one place. At first, I was struck by how few farmers' daughters and wives drove a car. Some did not learn to drive until they were married; others relied on their menfolk transporting them to town weekly, usually on Market day. Our weekly trip to Arbroath was very odd. Grandfather drove the womenfolk to town and he met up with his friends at the Mart, while we did the shopping at certain shops, which the family had used for years, followed by a visit to a tearoom until it was time to be driven home again.

With limited transport, the vans arriving at the farms selling meat, fish and vegetables was a novelty to me but of course essential and convenient. The grocer was another surprise. A lady from the shop, who knew what every customer required, phoned weekly for the order before delivery the next day. If my order was not the same as usual she would ask why!

I became aware that when farmers' daughters left school their life seemed to have been already planned. They were expected to take over the general running of the house and help on the farm when required. They were usually in charge of the poultry and in some cases, made butter, taking the produce to sell to town shops. The cow's milk supplied the household as well as farm workers. A group would join the Young Farmers Club and on occasions marry a neighbouring farmer, stay at

---

[49] Testimony, John Kneen

home, bring up children, keep house and carry out farm tasks as required. There was a very definite criterion about what was 'women's work'. Certainly there were a few who took the opportunity to train for a profession, such as teachers and nurses.

When I came to Carmyllie in 1956, the mains electricity from The North of Scotland Hydro-Electricity Board was in the process of connection and I found myself dealing with the laundry without machines and cleaning the flues in the old range(a task I had not encountered since college days). Thankfully, these methods were short -lived and we were soon using a cleaner method of cooking and washing.

We had three children and as they began to grow, I noticed the disadvantage of having no playgroups or nursery school. The children entered primary education straight from a home environment,

possibly unknown to other children unless the parents were friends. The mothers had little opportunity to share problems and experiences and isolation could be a problem. Phoning friends or dropping in for a cup of tea seemed to be irrelevant to the complexities of farming. Nevertheless, the monthly meetings of the Scottish Women's Rural Institute or the 'Rural' were of great value to countrywomen. I had met many SWRI members in the course of my work and I knew that for some it was the only social contact and the opportunity to learn new skills.

Mains of Carmyllie.

Perhaps I felt a stranger being a 'townser' as I had not lived in a rural area nor gone to school there. It was all very difficult for me to acquire the knowledge of who was who and who was related to whom or how long they had lived in the district. Farm names and their location was just as confusing and I found myself lost on a few occasions.

However, gradually I became more country orientated, I learned how to cope with 'crabbit' menfolk when rain or lack of it affected crops, or machines broke down at bad moments. I had to feed men at threshing times, breakfast for the mill men, morning and afternoon 'piecies' and dinner for all the men including neighbours who had come to help. I learned to feed cattle and pigs if it should be necessary, but I hated hens. I had to take pet animals to the vet and to stop whatever I was doing, to bundle the children into the truck and collect spares or at times, take food to outlying fields at busy times. To add to the general mayhem my elderly father-in-law stayed with us and an aged spinster, Aunt Joann. She was a typical example of Victorian age women, that is, they should know their place, cook, sew, keep house and take care of the menfolk and not have too many opinions.[50]

Family day out at the Agricultural show, 1951 (McDonald family)

To sum up, farming in Carmyllie parish adapted and changed through the 120 years from 1850 to 1970, guided by three landowners, the Panmure Estate, the Guynd and Cononsyth for the larger portion of that time. Change was more obvious after WW1 and more so from the beginning of WW2 when the Government's compulsory orders brought control and in return farmers received compensation for production. The last two decades brought a revolution through mechanisation, a better standard

of living and the motor car expanded peoples' horizons.

---

[50] Testimony, Muriel Hume, 2012

Chapter 9

FARM WORKERS

Farm workers formed a high proportion of the population of rural parishes and remained so until the mid twentieth century, although in Carmyllie there were more small farms requiring less hired labour.

Willie Ritchie. Cairnconon c.1910

Within the workforce, there were different skills, ploughman, cattleman, dairyman, labourer (orraman) and shepherd and within this group, there was a pecking order depending on the size of the farmer's labour force. The grieve was entrusted to organise workers and often the first foreman would work with the grieve doing responsible work, such as measuring drills and building corn 'stacks', but the ploughman with his skills was the backbone of the farm. A larger arable farmer usually employed a grieve, allowing the farmer a free hand to conduct business.

Andy Gibb (1923-2011) gives a vivid description of his work: *I have fond memories when working with the farm horses. In the spring time, preparing the soil for cereal sowing and potato planting proved to be a great strain on the horses as they required extra attention, such as careful feeding in the stable, morning, noon and night and measured rest periods. After the fields were sown, the horses' work was less strenuous so a lighter diet was found in the grass fields in the summer. Andy's working hours revolved round the horses' demands. Attention to the horses came first so a 5am or 6am start was necessary to feed the horses, attend to grooming and mounting the harness*

Adam Brown, Glentyrie, c. 1936

on the horse for 'yoking' time at 7am. Dinnertime was at 11.30, giving the horses an hour and a half rest before starting at 1pm. 'Lousing' time was 5pm but more work was required by removing harness, feeding, grooming and bedding. Usually one man was in charge of a pair of horse and could plough an acre per day. One pair of horse was expected to till and sow 50 acres in the farming year.[51]

With urban growth in the nineteenth century came the demand for more food, yet grain prices became depressed, especially in the first four decades of the twentieth century. To supplement the slump in the grain trade, more farmers chose to rear cattle on the farm's own cereals to augment the income. Dairying, a separate skill and supplied a regular income, albeit a demanding routine, milking twice per day, seven days per week and dealing with a perishable commodity. Carmyllie parish had a high percentage of dairy farms; at least sixteen farmers reared and milked cows commercially yet only three dairymen had tied accommodation, implying that the farmer's family had worked the dairy routine themselves or that casual labour had been employed.[52]

---

[51] Testimony, Andy Gibb

[52] Census, 1901. A Dairyman. Dairyman's wife and daughter as a Dairy maid were housed at Milton of Carmyllie.

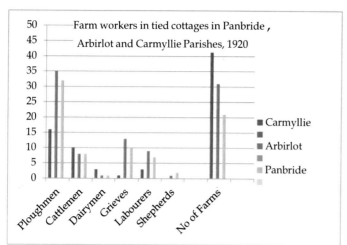

Farm workers in tied cottages in Panbride, Arbirlot and Carmyllie Parishes, 1920

Legend: Carmyllie, Arbirlot, Panbride

Categories: Ploughmen, Cattlemen, Dairymen, Grieves, Labourers, Shepherds, No of Farms

The workers housed in 'tied' houses, had advantages both for the farmer and the employee. Agricultural work at that time was more attractive than in most trades as to be offered a house, a supply of oatmeal, coal, milk and potatoes with the job was commendable. Young couples could plan marriage, accommodation being no hindrance. For the same reason, the farmer had 'control' over his worker, his wife and children who were generally 'on call' all day and every day.

`The chart shows the differing requirements for farm workers in the three parishes of Panbride, Arbirlot and Carmyllie. These parishes are within a short distance of each other and under the same Landlord, Lord Dalhousie, but they have very different labour requirements. There was more than twice the number of farms in Carmyllie parish than Panbride and a third more than Arbirlot yet they had less than half the ploughmen in tied cottages compared to Arbirlot and Panbride. Livestock was an important part of Carmyllie's husbandry as there were more cattlemen and dairymen in tied cottages than in the neighbouring parishes. Grieves, on the other hand,

William Gall, Montquhir, late 1930s

were not numerous in Carmyllie indicating that the generally smaller farms did not require them.

For the most part the farm routine in 1840 remained without change for the next century. Farm workers in general, were on contract for a 'term', six months for single men and one year for married men with families.The farmer negotiated with his farm worker at the end of the 'term' and the employee often had the option to stay on. If he was valued by the farmer, an extra incentive such as an additional firlot (two and half stones or 32 kilos) of oatmeal or more coal could be offered but the half-yearly 'feeing' market set the trend and it was common for workers to seek 'pastures new'.

There was an exception however, in the manner that Ross Robertson the farmer of Lochlair farm in the western extremities of Carmyllie parish employed his workers. He advertised in the local newspaper offering a tied cottage for a farm worker. In one particular case, a successful applicant replied from Inverbervie, Kincardineshire and the correspondence involved instructions to arrive by bus, changing at Forfar or Arbroath and alight from the bus at Carmyllie War Memorial then walk over a mile to Lochlair. This was the May term, so to give a helpful start, the farmer suggested 'I would get one of my men to put in your garden and I have some early potatoes and a few vegetable seeds left over which, I think might be sufficient'[53].

New Mains Guynd (Whitton family)

Another method of gathering an efficient workforce was that a farmer, aware of a neighbour's well-ploughed fields, could negotiate with the skilled ploughman at

---

[53] Letter written by Ross Robertson to John Birse, Inverbervie, 30 May, 1933

the 'feein' market, in the hope that he could be induced to join the farmer's team. Between the wars, negotiations with pay rises were rare, this apparently causing some unrest amongst farm workers as for example, on farms in the east of Carmyllie, eight families left the district and eight families moved into the area within one year.[54] This continual movement of men, women and families and long working hours, allowed farm workers little time to settle in the community and participate in social life. In the 1920s, a Scottish Rural Workers' Approved Society, Carmyllie Branch, was formed with members including Charles Walker, Redford, John Ferrier, Cairnconon, William Fullerton, Redford, Alex Kydd and James Robertson, Slade on the committee.[55] The society was active until WW2, meeting with other branches in the area.

Employment opportunities for women and girls were limited and their wages were generally half of the men's wages. This allowed most farmers to employ at least one maid to live in the farmhouse with meals provided; carrying out housekeeping as well as helping perhaps in the dairy and seasonal work in the fields.

Bothy Men, East Hills, 1930s

Although the farms in Carmyllie had fewer 'tied' cottages, most farms had a non-rated bothy [56] sleeping up to six, three being the average. In 1901, there were 20 bothies in the parish, housing 54 boys and men. [57] Boys, single men or casual workers, were housed in basic accommodation with one or two rooms, stone floors, bare walls and a coal fire/cooker. Furniture was sparse, wooden beds and mattresses filled with 'chaff', a table and a bothy bench with two 'kists,' one a store cupboard for clothes and the other for their utensils consisting of one bowl with the same fork, knife and spoon.

Arthur Jarret (1921-1996) recalls his experiences in the bothy:

In 1933, I left school at 12 and took a farm job for a year but went home every night to Friockheim to my mother. My father re-married and his new wife had no interest in me. Then I was 'fee'd' at East Idvies for £12.00 per half-year and had to work five consecutive Saturdays at harvest time. I appreciated East Idvies because soup was made for us by the farmer's wife and served at dinnertime. The 'orraman' made the porridge in the morning, enough for breakfast and supper. Fresh bread was delivered regularly by the Baker's van.

A' Feein' market was held every six months and two days' holiday was granted for the occasion (May 'term' and November 'term'). The 'term' fairs were normally held in villages and towns,

Cutting hay. East Hills, 1930s (Arthur Jarret)

the most local being Friockheim or Letham. It was not unusual for the farmworkers to change their employment every six months The farm grieve usually accompanied me at the market and gave recommendations to the prospective new 'boss'. The employees wore a bonnet and if they were fee'd

---

[54] School Register, Carmyllie East, 1934
[55] Arbroath Year Book, 1931 and 1940
[56] Valuation Rolls. Bothies were non-rateable until after WW1.
[57] Census, 1901

by a new farmer they indicated this by releasing the stud or 'sneck' on their bonnet. If the farm worker was unable to plough, he was not so easily employed.

The maid from the farmhouse washed the sheets and blankets. I found a woman in Friockheim who attended to my personal washing and my way of transport was my bicycle.

Time off, Conon, 1930s

In the pecking order on the farm, the Grieve was the most important, then the Foreman then the Second man. The Grieve and the Foreman built the stacks and covered the tattie pits, as there would be big losses if mistakes were made. In addition, drilling and seed sowing had to be carefully done. The Cattleman was less important although he had bigger wages since he worked seven days per week. The farmer normally accompanied the cattleman while the cattle were fed, checking the rations of expensive cattle cake. The Orraman carried out a wide variety of general labouring duties, was well down the pecking order, and was ranked just above the 'loon'. Weather conditions had to be 'tholed' but you couldn't show that you were suffering as for example, your workmates laughed at you if you wore gloves to pull 'neeps' on frosty mornings. I lived in a bothy for twelve years, finally finishing up as foreman at East Hills, Carmyllie, until I was married. I enjoyed the bothy life latterly but I was intimidated and bullied when I was younger. The farmer never came into the bothy.

We all looked forward to the monthly dance in the local village hall. There was much discussion about music, dance bands and, of course, who would be in attendance. The maids from the farmhouse dressed up and joined in the excitement.

Two binders at work, Montquhir, 1930s (Gibb family)

When Arthur was interviewed in 1986, he had just retired from employment with Whitton, Potato Merchant, Meigle. He was collected every morning by the firm's van and carried out work in potato fields dotted over Angus. Arthur recalled when he received the pension (age 65), he was most grateful as he was 'better off, financially, than he had ever been',[58]

---

[58] Testimony of Arthur Jarret, 1986

Andy Gibb reminisced about his bothy days too: *I was born at Friockheim Mains in 1923 and was the second member of a family of seven. I attended school at Friockheim then Kinnell and was obliged to leave school in 1936 when I was 13 ½ as help was required on the local farms and my wage (10 shillings per week) was much needed in the family home in the 'lean years' of the 1930s.*

Jim Lyall, New Mains Guynd, 1950s (Whitton family)

Later I was one of ten in the bothy at Fithie. My daily diet was porridge in the morning and brose and 'tatties' at night which could vary when the odd rabbit was caught or a nest of hen's eggs was found around the farm buildings. Milk, oatmeal and coal were supplied by the farmer and part of the grieve's agreement was that his wife cleaned the bothy. I took my own personal laundry home to my mother.

Entertainment in the evenings was provided by the bothy men playing their musical instruments such as accordions, fiddles, mouth organs ('moothies'), spoons or anything that kept the rhythm. Often songs were unaccompanied. Andy took his share by playing the 'moothie'.[59]

One of the many changes in agriculture at the onset of the Second World War was the enforcement of the 'stand-still' order when feein' markets stopped and farm workers' six-month contracts ended, resulting in a more permanent employment with the farmer. This stabilised the workers and their families, giving them the ability to integrate into the community more readily. The main governmental reason however, was to concentrate on 'Dig for Victory' using all available land to grow food with a steady workforce. Mechanisation in the form of the tractor became more widespread although the horse and the tractor worked alongside each other until the early 1950s. The photograph shows the tractor and a mechanised 'tattie' planter with a horse (unseen) and a plough preparing the drills (p.123).

Burnhead Terrace, Redford

Although the tractor and machinery were causing reductions in farm labour numbers, there was still a demand for modernised farm workers' homes after WW2. Angus County Council built groups of houses around rural Angus for this purpose, including the set of eight houses at Burnhead Terrace, Redford.

Jim Lyall, New Mains of Guynd, 1950s

Andy Gibb was employed as a bricklayer during the war as well as a casual farm worker until he found his niche as tractorman at the Mains of Carmyllie. He recalls his long years of employment:

In the 1950s my wife, seven children and me were living at Currend in Carmyllie and I was still employed as a builder's labourer. Other houses that I lived in at Carmyllie were Mossyknowe and Tuttiesneuk. In 1959, when Donald was born, I was offered employment with David Hume & Son at Mains Carmyllie with a 'modern' cottar house. I kept two pigs and a well-attended vegetable garden. Later the ninth and last member of the family was born. I felt contented with my lot and was grateful that there was always seasonal work available for my growing family especially berry picking and 'tattie howkin'. Also all the family enjoyed taking part in local community events.

---

[59] Testimony of Andy Gibb

The tractor now replaced the horse, making the working hours more regular. I enjoyed ploughing and drilling the fields but was not so keen attending to farm animals especially when pig rearing became intensified. However, although I found my work hard, it was honest work.

On my retirement in 1989, I was presented with a 30-year long service medal at the Angus Show from the Royal Highland Society.

Despite the innovation of tractors, much physical labour was still required in the fields until the late 1970s. Families housed on the farm were beneficial to the farmer since children as well as adults were brought into the workforce.

Andy receiving the presentation (Andy Gibb family)

Dawn Robson (nee Gibb) born in 1958, recalls her childhood days on the farm:

Dawn, 1963

I left primary school in a class of three and entered a class at Arbroath High School that was bigger than the whole school at Greystone. This was was quite a culture shock but I settled down and enjoyed the variety of subjects and teachers. It was only when I discussed with my classmates my pastimes at home that I felt slightly alien as in the evenings they listened to music in their friends' houses while we played 'housies' and various games in the farm sheds. On Saturdays, they went 'down town' while we could be helping in the fields

Around eight High School pupils caught the bus at the Monument and the bus was full to capacity by the time it reached the outskirts of Arbroath. When we arrived home after school, the chores (I had to set the tea table while my brothers brought in coal and logs and set the fire) had to be completed. School homework was inclined to be set aside as there was the attraction of fun and games outside. The farmer's wife changed an old henhouse into a playhouse and the inside walls were papered while furniture and kitchen utensils were begged and borrowed and finally a lock was fixed on the door for privacy. At Hallowe'en, there was plenty energy put into 'guising' when we put on fancy dress and visited neighbours as well as houses in Greystone where we performed a 'party piece' and were rewarded, with either sweets or pennies. The annual Guy Fawkes bonfire held at the 'Mains' had a great community spirit that could be seen from a great distance, usually finishing up with hot soup, baked potatoes and refreshments.

Seasonal work in the rural area was easily available from an early age. Strawberry picking was more suitable when we were younger but later I was able to cope with raspberry picking too. At the 'berries' my mother would take one side of the 'dreel' while my brothers and I would attempt the other side with my mother finishing off our side by reaching to the higher berries. The money we earned helped to pay for our school clothes. We had to go out and about to find fruit fields, such as Denhead of Arbirlot, but 'tattie' picking took place at the 'Mains'. Again, when younger we could cope with a 'half bit', gradually taking on a full 'bit' which was measured out by the 'gaffer' (striding out in yards) and placing the 'pinnie' (usually a piece of broom) to indicate the length of the 'bit'. I never received wages for my work at the 'tatties' as the money I earned was given to my father who pooled the family's money together to buy our winter clothes. We were transported to and from the 'tattie' fields in an enclosed float and we sat inside on straw bales. I can just remember when I was very young, there were 'stooks' in the field in front of our house and the threshing mill in operation but it was mostly the combine harvester in the grain fields that I remember. In my teens I was able to find work locally, for example, I helped Mrs Scott at Newton to grade eggs in a large hen-laying unit.

Yet I reflect now on how my mother coped as she was out working every day, either in the fields or as a cleaner in houses, and still able to produce a meal at lunch time and in the evening.[60]

With machinery relieving some of the heavy work on the farm, more adult female workers were picking up seasonal work. Anna Chalmers was more unusual as she worked full-time alongside the men:

I started working full-time with Mr Coventry, Smallburn farm, in the 1950s. I arrived every morning to collect my orders and I tackled a variety of work, feeding cattle, cleaning the byre, bedding, 'clatting neeps', loading trailers, bringing the harvest home, pulling 'neeps', loading tatties, any odd job except ploughing with a tractor. I worked there until

Anna Chalmers, Hillside Cottage, Greystone, 2012

Mr Coventry died in 1979. I live nearby at the family home, Hillside Cottage, Greystone that my grandfather had bought.[61]

Planting potatoes with a Packman Potato Planter at Montquhir (Gibb family)

Mechanisation on the farm required less labour, less 'tied' cottages, less bothies. When Aggie Stott (born 1938) started employment at the Mains of Carmyllie around 1970, transport was more available and she was able to drive herself to work from her home near Forfar, outwith Carmyllie parish. Her description of her work outlines the gradual change from physical to mechanical work on the farm:

At first, the seasons brought a wider variety of employment. In spring, potatoes were planted by machine into two drills, pulled by a tractor at a slow pace. Two of us sat on the machine, which operated a conveyor belt with cups carrying individual potatoes.

Our job was to make sure that each cup held a potato but the machine was efficient and seldom failed, leaving us with a monotonous sedentary occupation! Later this machine was replaced by an automatic planter requiring only the tractor driver. After the potatoes were growing, a few of us would wade through the fields removing 'ground keepers', that is, growth from one or two potatoes that had remained in the ground from the previous crop.

Aggie Stott

Nevertheless in my first years of employment, there were more varied occupations such as 'clatting neeps', preparing and baling hay, then later bringing in baled straw, lifting 'tatties', 'tattie' dressing and lifting 'neeps' for the livestock. I worked from 9am to 4pm and I always had a break in July and August, which was beneficial to me with four small children.

---

[60] Testimony of Dawn Robson (nee Gibb)
[61] Testimony of Anna Chalmers

I have fond memories of 'tattie' lifting by hand, which began in late Sept/Oct. The average pay in the latter 1960s for potato lifting was £4 per day for a full 'bit' and £5 for 'basket' men. Dave Walker, the 'gaffer', was on the field, as the pickers arrived, with a bunch of 'pinnies' (made from broom stalks) under his arm, measuring the 'bits' classified as ½, ¾ or whole bits according to the ability of the picker or sometimes by request. The 'bit' was measured by the stride of the foot, which was not always regular. I remember a tractor driven pulveriser knocking down the shaws before the tractor and digger

Potato picking by squad in 'tattie' holidays (Stewart family)

started. The early diggers scattered the tatties widely but there was an improvement when the elevator digger, taking two drills at one time, placed the tatties in neat rows. After the pickers filled their baskets, I drove a tractor and cart following the tracks of the digger and two men and one boy threw the potatoes from the baskets into the cart.

In the early days, the pickers were mostly local and were transported by tractor and trailer or by an open lorry. Later, squads were transported by lorry from Carnoustie and Arbroath. It was frowned upon if the picker did not complete a day's work as this upset the measurement of the 'bits' on the field and all had to be re-measured. It was accepted that the pickers filled their empty piece bag with

Earlier version of the potato harvester 1990s (Law family)

potatoes to take home, but later when larger squads were required from the town, the pickers took advantage of this 'perk' and returned home with ½ cwt bag with the intent of selling the surplus to chip shops. Consequently, this practice had to be stopped.

In 1982 the potato harvester, often with a pulveriser mounted on the front, put an end to the traditional tattie picking and only two to four people were needed on the machine to pick off rotten potatoes and debris. The potatoes went up on an elevator to be loaded into potato boxes on the trailer. This was a remarkable change of labour on the agricultural scene; from employing a squad of 40-50 people plus the labour required to handle baskets and cart loads, down to a harvester that required one tractor driver and a few helpers on the machine.[62]

---

[62] Testimony of Aggie Stott

Chapter 10

CARMYLLIE TRADES

Farming was the mainstay in the parish and the principle trades that serviced agriculture were blacksmiths, wrights (joiners) and carriers. When transport was limited, trades had to be within a

reasonable distance and so for example, the blacksmiths shops were sited to service the surrounding area. In 1841, there were blacksmiths at Hayhillock in the south-west, Cockelhill (Cockhill) in north-west, Cotton of Backboath in the north and in the villages of Redford and Greystone. Blacksmiths and wrights often worked in co-operation such as when crafting cart wheels for example. This would have happened in both villages where both trades were represented.[63] In 1851, there were still five blacksmiths in

W. McDonald, Slade Farm (McDonald family)

the parish but a blacksmith was trading at Milton instead of Cockhill. By 1861, there was evidence of more activity at Slade quarries as there was an additional blacksmith and joiner employed there. Blacksmiths at Hayhillock, Greystone, Redford and the Milton continued and interestingly, there was a millwright, being a specialised joiner, at Redford with a journeyman and two apprentices as well as a joiner with two journeymen.[64] There were many blacksmiths in Carmyllie because there was specialised smithy work required in the quarry industry as well as the demands from agriculture and the water and corn mills together with the indoor and travelling threshing mills.

Carcary threshing Mill c. 1900 (Olive Carcary)

Blacksmiths

In 1871, Robert Mudie, having come from Abernyte, Perthshire, was a backsmith at Redford with a family of eight, three sons being blacksmiths.[65] By 1891, he had a croft and a smithy and the wright

Mudie family: David, John, Alex, William, William Snr and Robert & George, railway men c. 1920

(joiner) David Buchan had a croft in Redford too. George Black replaced Peter Cameron as blacksmith at Greystone with Robert Sturrock, the Wright.[66] It is thought that George Martin at Hayhillock had concentrated on shoeing horses, agricultural implements and household utensils, as a wright was not in the vicinity.[67] Yet the Martin family remained blacksmiths at Hayhillock for at least sixty years, from 1841 to 1901 and from 1871, farmed 39 acres.[68] By 1911, there was no blacksmith or joiner at Greystone but George Constable was blacksmith at Hayhillock with a croft. By 1930, the new owner at Hayhillock was John Sturrock and remained trading until the early

---

[63] Census, 1841

[64] Ibid, 1851, 1861

[65] Ibid, 1871

[66] Arbroath Year Book (Arbroath Herald) 1891, 1901

[67] Valuation Roll, 1893-94

[68] Census, 1841-1901

1940s. Thomas, William Mudie's son, was the only blacksmith in the parish for a further twenty years and retired in the 1960s.

Thomas Mudie's daughter, Doreen Paul, recalls her father's working days as blacksmith at Redford in the late 1930s:

Blacksmith's bothy, 2010

Between the farm, the petrol pumps and the smiddy, our family work was never done, yet my father's croft was the most demanding. Three men trained alongside my father, working six days per week, accommodated in a bothy at the bottom of the garden that held beds, a stove, table and chairs. My mother gave them their breakfast, dinner and tea in the smiddy house. Shoeing horses was an exacting job and required speed while the iron shoe was red hot and my father would shout 'chap!' which alerted the lads to start chapping the shoe into shape on the anvil with a hammer. Another specialised work for the blacksmith was 'hooping' the wheel, which involved the joiners across the road from Redford smiddy, Willie Buchan and Jim Peters, making the wooden wheel, while the blacksmith made the cog and the hoop to fit. The metal wheel and cog had to be fitted when red hot, then cooled quickly in order to fix tightly to the wheel.

The smiddy furnace caused a tremendous heat and my father called for a drink of water frequently. I was summoned sometimes to 'ca'' the bellows but found no pleasure in the hot 'stoory' atmosphere. Farmers were known to bring their horses to be shod on wet or foggy days so there was an inevitable queue at the smiddy door. My father seldom went out to shoe horses on farms although there were odd occasions, such as, if a horse had bad feet, he would visit the farm to remove the shoes and pare the hooves. Nevertheless, there were many other jobs to be attended to including repairs to farm machinery, gates or any metal objects. The train station at Redford was convenient for the blacksmith as the train wagon delivered the special smiddy coal and perhaps some sheets of metal although there was always a pile of metal at the back of the smiddy.

Hooping the Wheel (Source: 'Scotsman' Trade Review, Apr 1939)

There was never a shortage of water as there was a spring nearby which provided fresh water, enabling a 'spigot' at the side of the road, beside the smiddy, to run constantly. My father had his own generator so electricity was available that

Redford 'smiddy', Tom Mudie, Jim Robertson, Will Rae, late 1920s (Geddes family)

allowed power in the smiddy and the house. I knew when my father was starting the generator in the morning as the smiddy was usually enveloped in smoke.[69]

---

[69] Testimony, Mrs Doreen Paul, 2011

Joiners and Wrights Similarly there was a long established joinery trade in Redford. James Buchan (age 46) and his son, were trading as joiners in 1891 and by 1901, employed two men and two

Joinery workshop remains. (Redford 2013)

Looking inside Joinery workshop (Redford, 2013)

apprentices. Within their croft, there was a joinery workshop with an adjoining shed where coffins were made, James Buchan being the local undertaker. The Black Burn flowed past the workshop driving the waterwheel which powered the sawmill. In 1915, James Buchan rented property from two proprietors, Bonnycheer croft and house from the Guynd Estate, and two houses and land from Panmure Estate. After World War 1, the Panmure property was sold and the new owner of the joinery by 1938 was Mrs Margaret Walker, wife of the tenant, James Peter while William Buchan (James Buchan's son) continued as joiner and tenant. After World War 2, Gordon Gardiner was joiner and property owner including Bonnycheer [70] and employed William Buchan for a time, all carrying out work such as house building and general repairs to farm houses and buildings. Gordon was also the local undertaker producing coffins when required. He retired in the late 1970s, selling the land to a local farmer.

Black Burn used for driving the Sawmill

Carriers

The Carrier Trade was a necessary and sustainable business, especially in the second half of the nineteenth century. In 1851, David Boyle the Greystone carrier, farmed a pendicle, brought up a family[71] and kept his horses fit and healthy. Their biggest customers were farmers and the carrier would charge by weight more than capacity. David Hume paid 2/- for two cart-loads of potatoes transported from the Mains to Carmyllie railway station in 1871, yet he was only charged 1/6d for two carts (commodity unknown) to Arbroath the following Saturday.[72] Sometimes carts were needed only on return journeys. For example in 1874, for three carts of hay delivered from Arbroath to the Mains, the charge was 4/2d.[73]

In 1891, there were four carriers trading in the parish; Andrew Paris, Redford, John Muggins, Greystone and James Hampton, Carnegie Ward all delivering to Arbroath on Saturdays while A. Paterson, Dilty Moss delivered to Dundee on Fridays. Some farmers however, took on to be their own carters, such as Mr Fyffe's son of the Birns, who farmed on the extremities of the parish.[74] By 1910, the horse lorry had taken precedence to the horse and cart for bulk carriage, being more time saving, leaving John Kydd, Greystone as the only official carrier. Later in the 1920s, tenant farmers and tradesmen started to acquire their own motor vehicles.

[70]Valuation Rolls, 1915-16, 1938-39, 1956-57

[71] Angus Census, Carmyllie Parish, 1851, 1861

[72] David Hume, Mains, Farm Account Book, 1871-1877, Dec 1871

[73] Ibid, Feb 1874

[74]Census, Carmyllie, 1861

Coal Merchants and Coal Agents

Carmyllie Parish was fortunate to have access to coal at Redford station after the railway was built in 1855. Previously, ordinary households in the parish used Dilty Moss for a supply of peat while tenant farmers and tradesmen collected cartloads of coal from East Haven, near Carnoustie. Coal along with logs provided warmth to households while farmers, blacksmiths and quarrymen required coal for furnaces and steam power. By 1871, Andrew Paris was trading as a coal merchant as well as a grocer at Redford and this continued until the 1880s.[75] In 1891, Charles Webster was the coal agent, trading under the Dundee and Arbroath Joint railway[76] and was required to record and distribute the coal that arrived at Redford station. By 1901, there were two agents, Alex Webster and D. Fairweather, the latter trading under Smith, Hood & Co but only Alex Webster was trading ten years later.[77] There is no mention of an agent or a coal merchant after World War 1 although Peter Dolan, residing at the Podge, was coal merchant until after World War 2. Lorry deliveries of coal to households had become more prevalent between the two World wars.

Dairymen

There were several dairymen in the parish who delivered milk to town, usually Arbroath. These

David Gibb, Conon (Gibb family)

dairymen were not necessarily farmers and if not, they would buy the milk from the dairy farmer and transport it in large churns every day. When in the town, the dairyman parked his milk cart at the end of the street and customers queued with their jugs while he poured from a measure, the amount required. In 1891, there were five dairymen; James Forrest, farmer, Conon, James Gray, Smallburn, John Jarrat, Mains of Carmyllie, David Maxwell, farmer, Newton and William Carr, Wedderswell. David

Maxwell, junior, recalls his journey in the milk cart to school in Arbroath, feeling very comfortable sitting beside the warm milk cans. Ten years later there were eight dairymen with some changes to names and places, such as D. Gibb, Mains, David Edgar, Conon, David Turnbull, Smallburn, John Gibb, Montquhir, A. Duthie, Skichenmuir, D. Sturrock, Tillyhoit and J. Carrie, West Hills.[78] Tom Rennie, Parkneuk, in the west of the parish, carted his milk into Forfar. By the 1920s and early 30s trading milk in the town became too competitive as a dairyman would lower his price to customers without notice, resulting in some dairymen losing trade. With such a necessary yet perishable commodity, an improved and more just trading

Delivering milk and collecting provisions in Arbroath, during snowstorm 1947. (Gibb family)

---

[75] Ibid, 1871, 1881
[76] Arbroath Year Book, 1891
[77] Ibid, 1901, 1911
[78] Ibid, 1891, 1901

mechanism was required. In 1933, a government agency, the Scottish Milk Marketing Board, was established, controlling milk production and distribution and guaranteeing minimum prices to the producers.

Grocers

Grocers, tailors and shoemakers were sustainable if there were sufficient customers within walking distance. In the three decades around the middle of the nineteenth century, the grocer trade was unpredictable. In 1841, there was a grocer at West Hills and George Anderson was a publican at the Milton but for the next ten years, there was no indication of a grocer or publican at all.[79] Why was there no need for a grocer who sold food and household goods? Tenant farmers would shop when attending the weekly market, but most parishioners were self-sufficient with food from the 'kailyard' and livestock such as a cow, pigs and hens. There was little money to spend as rates of pay from, for example, handloom weaving and agricultural work were at a minimum.[80] In February 1872, Helen Boyle worked 12 days pulling turnips and was paid 1/- per day.[81] The necessities of life such as rent, shoes or boots and fuel (perhaps peat rather than coal) and oatmeal from the miller required money. Even the tenant farmer and tradesman had very few household expenses. In 1871, David Hume, farmer at the Mains, spent in one year 1/8d on ½ lb tea, fish costing 1/2d, 4lbs beef for 3/4d and around Christmas, £1.00 was spent on groceries.[82] The crofter, handloom weaver and farm labourer could rarely afford these goods. However, two grocers were functioning in 1861, one at Muiredge and one at the Milton, with a grocer's boy at the Newton. By 1871, at the peak of the quarry industry, there was a grocer at the Milton, the two at Redford had double occupations, one as a quarrier and grocer, and the other was a grocer come coal merchant. In 1881, both Redford and Greystone had grocers trading. There were also two grocers serving the quarries at the Slade.[83]

Whin Inn ('Arbroath Guide Illustrated Review)
Note the sign advertising 'Bass' beer!

From then onwards, there were grocers in the two villages, two usually in Redford and one in Greystone until the 1950s and there are memories of a 'shoppie' at Newtonbank, north of the Milton until the late 1930s. The grocer shop at the Slade quarries closed before WW1 but a licensed grocer sold porter and ale at Cairnconon, (known as the Whin Inn) which was owned by William Boath.[84] After his death in 1942, the Inn was closed and was sold to Mr Garden and re-named 'Invergarden'. After a change of hands, the house name reverted to 'The Whin'.

In the 1930s, various vans such as grocers, butchers, bakers and fish and fresh vegetables were delivering to households bringing more variety to the diet. This service continued until the 1960s.

Tailors

To call on the services of a tailor to be fitted, for example, with a suit of clothes was a luxury, only to be afforded by tenant farmers, successful tradesmen or manufacturers. Clothes for the majority in the parish were homemade and growing children's outfits were eked out by wearing 'hand-downs'. Hence, the demand for tailoring had been low with few tailors trading in the parish. In 1851, the tailor at Dykehead in the west of the parish was trading both as a tailor and saddler, while there was a tailor at Redford. Thereafter, in 1871, the Redford tailor became a tailor and clothier[85] suggesting that he was responding to the demand for lengths of cloth. In 1872, David Hume, farmer, paid £3.9.6d for a suit of clothes although in that same year he bought another suit costing £2.10/- from Mr Anderson,

[79] Census, Carmyllie, 1841, 1851
[80] See Handloom Weavers and Crofters, p 49
[81] David Hume, FCB, 1872
[82] David Hume, Farm Account Books, 1871
[83] Census, Carmyllie, 1861, 1871, 1881
[84] Arbroath Year Book, 1940
[85] Census, Carmyllie, 1851-1871

tailor.[86] By 1881, there was an elderly master tailor, John Low (age 61), at Greystone while a tailor tailor in the vicinity of Slade quarries, James Cuthhill, and James Peter, in 1919, had a shop in Redford as well as a tailor and clothier business in Commerce Street, Arbroath.[87]

Dressmakers

The Rev William Robertson mentions in 1836 that' Carmyllie inhabitants had been primitive 'in their habits and dresses' compared to their 'polished' neighbours and were singled out as 'the bodies of Carmyllie', but the Reverend declared that [these] 'peculiarities have disappeared' and 'the *hodden* dresses .... are now exchanged for English cloths and cotton'.[88]

It was the custom of the aristocracy to call on the services of a dressmaker at their residence to sew outfits for the family, and the nineteenth century saw an increase in professionals and wealthy manufacturers following this trend. Tenant farmers and successful traders' wives would trade with dressmakers when attending the market on Saturdays. Nevertheless, this was beyond the means of most Carmyllie parishioners and as travelling the minimum of five miles to town was always an issue, self-taught skills were necessary. There was a dressmaker trading in 1851 at Saughmont in the south-west of the parish and one at Tuttiesneuk and by 1861, there were two dressmaker teachers at the Milton while one was trading at Drummygar and another at Mosston and still another at Cotton of Cononsyth.[89] Yet trading as a dressmaker was poorly rewarded as sewing by hand was time-consuming and the hourly rate was low. In 1872, David Hume paid towards a dressmaker's account a total of 10/10d and later in 1874; he paid a draper's bill amounting to 3/6d.[90] Once female members of families mastered the skill, home dressmaking would be the norm and the competent could trade from their own home. In 1881, there continued to be a dressmaker at Drummygar and one at Greystone.[91] By 1930, Mrs Duncan had established herself as a dressmaker in Redford and remained in the trade until the late 1950s.[92]

Shoemakers

Shoemaking however, was a lifetime skill and footwear was and is a necessity, resulting in a number of shoemakers trading in the parish. In 1851, there were two shoemakers at the Goats, one at the Milton, one at Drummygar while William Rait at Redford was employing two apprentices. By 1861, there were no shoemakers at the Goats but there was a master shoemaker spreading his skills at the Milton while at Drummygar, the shoemaker employed one other as well as a bootmaker journeyman. At the height of the quarry industry in 1871, there were six shoemakers; one master shoemaker at Greystone with the others were near the Slade quarries. Drummygar had two bootmakers, Glentyrie one shoemaker and Redford had one master shoemaker employing one shoemaker at the Slade. In 1871, David Hume, tenant at the Mains paid 16/- for a pair of boots, whereas a pair of boots was bought for Mrs Hume in 1877 for 10/-.[93] Ten years later, there was one shoemaker, James Taylor with his journeyman, James Murray, at Greystone and another at Mosston, near the quarries. There was a master shoemaker at Redford with a boy assistant and Alex Webster had established himself as a master bootmaker. By 1891, there were two shoemakers at Redford, Alex Webster and William Brown while James Adam was trading at Muiredge and there remained a shoemaker at Greystone until WW1.

Less trades-people were required in the second decade of the twentieth century due to the decline in the quarry industry and poor farming profitability. Two grocers remained at Redford, one at Greystone and one at the Whin while a coal merchant, dressmaker, joiner and shoemaker all traded into the early 1950s at Redford.

[86] David Hume, Farm Cash book, 1872-1876
[87] Arbroath Year Book, 1922
[88] NSA, Rev William Robertson, 1836, p361
[89] Census, Carmyllie, 1851, 1861
[90] David Hume, FCB, 1872
[91] Census, Carmyllie, 1881
[92] Valuation Roll, Carmyllie
[93] David Hume, Farm Cash Book, 1871, 1877

Corn or Meal Millers

Various mills were dotted over rural Angus, such as lint mills, corn mills and spinning mills, situated beside a flow of water to give power to the mill. There were however only Corn Mills in Carmyllie[94]. Corn mills have been a centre to communities from medieval times, and in Carmyllie the two mills at the Milton and Milton of Conon are seen on Pont's map of 1689.[95] Under feudal law, the *thirlage* system was enforced whereby the Laird of the estate employed the miller to mill his tenants' corn and the tenants were obliged or *suckened* to take their corn to their Laird's mill. This system essentially became a form of taxation and was despised by all. The *suckeners* were also held responsible for the upkeep of the mill. The three estate owners in the Parish, at the end of the eighteenth century, Lord Panmure, John Ouchterlony of the Guynd and David Ogilvie, Cononsyth, all laid claim to a miller

Plan for Milton of Conon, Redford and the Brae to be 'shared' by Earl of Panmure and John Ouchterlony of The Guynd (RHP 2613, 1772)

and a mill. The Milton was under Lord Panmure, the Milton of Conon was 'shared' by Lord Panmure and John Ouchterlony of the Guynd (see plan) while Cononsyth had an agreement with Colliston Mill (see Cononsyth Mansion).

An Act of Parliament repealed Thirlage law in 1779 and the two mills, Milton and Milton of Conon, would thereafter be run on a commercial basis. Andrew Fyfe was a miller at the Milton in 1841 and George Ross was the miller at Milton of Conon for at least 20 years. In 1851, Arthur Guthrie had a journeyman at the Milton although there is no mention of them milling in 1861. William Millar had an apprentice at the Milton of Conon and Margaret Falconer, wife of David Falconer, was tenant and occupier of the farming unit. Ten years later, John Bell was corn miller at the Milton and Robert Ritchie was master meal miller at the Milton of Conon.[96] In January 1872, R. Ritchie, miller, received £2 for 'one bag of oatmeal' for the household at the Mains[97] and in September the farmer paid J. Bell, Milton, £2.10/- for 2 bolls[98] meal for the farm workers. In 1881 the 'oatmeal' miller, John Bell, at the Milton had a croft of 3 acres but milling ceases to function in the 1880s although James Grieve and his grandson remained millers at Milton of Conon in 1891.[99] The last miller mentioned in the parish was George Henry at the Milton of Conon in 1893.[100]

Quarrymasters

William Duncan the quarrymaster with his son William Junior and James Wright, his son-in-law and also a quarrymaster, entered into the community spirit especially from the 1880s to 1910. William Duncan, Junior, was a member of the School Board in 1891 and in 1901 was also a County Councillor representing Carmyllie.[101] He dedicated in 1901, a stained glass window in the parish church in

The Rose Window, Carmyllie Parish Church. 1903

memory of his father. James Wright joined the School Board in 1897 and for ten years was a prominent figure in the parish.[102] In 1901, he was a member of the Parish Council and in addition was

---

[94] NSA, Carmyllie 1836

[95] Map *Old Angus and Mearns,* by Timothee Pont, *c.* 1640

[96] Census, Carmyllie, 1841-1871

[97] David Hume, FCB, Jan 1872

[98] One boll weighs 140lbs or 63kg 503g

[99] Census, Carmyllie, 1881-1891

[100] Valuation Roll, Carmyllie, 1893-94

[101] Arbroath Year Book, 1891, 1901

[102] School Board Minutes, Carmyllie, 1897

president of the Musical Society and vice-president of Carmyllie & District Ploughing Association.[103] While an elder of the Parish church, James Wright donated in 1903, the 'Rose' stained glass window by the renowned artist Stephen Adam.[104]

Tradesmen as Pillars of the Community

Many tradesmen became 'pillars of the community' when the 'fee' system caused most farm workers to move house every year giving them little opportunity to take part in Carmyllie social life. Although the heritors of the estates, school headmasters and tenant farmers were called upon to hold office in various associations, many trades-people took responsibility too. In 1891, Andrew Paris, coal merchant and grocer, was treasurer of the Temperance Society while William Carr, tailor, showed musical talent as a harmoniumist and Choirmaster at the Carmyllie Parish Church in addition to being a conductor of the Musical Society. Charles Webster, railway agent, was secretary to both the Draughts Club and the Musical society. In 1901, William Mudie, blacksmith and David Buchan, joiner, took an interest in the Musical Society as the former was vice-president and the latter was secretary and treasurer. David Buchan went on to be harmoniumist in the UF church and secretary to the Horticultural society in 1911, while James Sturrock, Post office and grocer, Greystone, was congregational treasurer of the Parish church and vice-president of the Ploughman's Association.[105]

Alexander Webster was settled as a shoemaker with a wife and five children in Redford from 1880[106] and by 1910, he was in business as a Carrier, Coal Merchant and was paying rent for a field[107] besides having many interests in the community. He was drawn to politics as he was treasurer to the Liberal Association in 1891, and a member of the School Board. Moreover, he was treasurer to the Ploughman's Society and Labourer's Benefit Society and later in 1900, was superintendant of the Free Church Sunday School and treasurer of the International Ploughman's Society –

Mr and Mrs Alexander Webster

Carmyllie Branch. Webster ran a Carrier service to Arbroath on a Saturday. Later after being a Coal Merchant, he became a Coal agent in 1910[108], being suitably placed at Redford railway station although his principle trade was always shoemaking. By 1922, his son David followed his father's trade and also took part in the community, acting as treasurer to the Ploughing society and secretary to the Scottish Rural Workers[109] together with farming his piece of land. He retired in the late 1940s, being the last shoemaker in the parish.

The numerous trades were vital to the folk of the parish because Carmyllie was an inconvenient distance from any town. The tradespeople not only provided essential services but also participated in the social life of the community.

[103] Arbroath Year Book, 1901
[104] Carmyllie Parish Church Records, 1803
[105] Arbroath Year Book, 1891, 1901, 1910
[106] Census, Carmyllie, 1881
[107] Valuation Roll, Carmyllie, 1910
[108] Arbroath Year Book, 1910
[109] Ibid, 1922, 1939

Changes in Carmyllie over the Years

by Arch Paton, c. 1980

Carmyllie being a quiet place
You'd think t'would never change its face
But if you sit doon and ponder
The changes there would make you wonder

If my memory is no playing tricks
Of grocer shops it once had six
Two at Redford and at Graystone
At Newtonbank there was anither ane
At the roadside near Mossend
Your money you could also spend
While at the Whin, as weel as booze
You could groceries and news

A souter's shop there was as weel
Where boots and shoes were aye for sale
The cobbler worked from morn till nicht
To keep our footwearwaterticht

At Reedford once upon a time
A merchant selt baith coal and lime
And wooden logs and fire bricks
Hid aye a stock of kindling sticks

Twa smiddies then made horse's shoes
And bits for grubbers and for ploos
Knives for grubbers, tines for harrows
And iron wheels for cotter's barrows

Some days saw an early start
To drive your cattle to the mart
And aye the price you got that day
Wad barely pay the neeps and strae

Quarries once were commonplace
But of them noo there's scarce a trace
Their products brought Carmyllie fame
Across the sea as well's hame

Of schools there had been two
Until somebody thought that ane would do
Tomorrow's race should be discerning
When crammed wi'concentrated learning

To keep Carmyllie fold in order
A Bobby was housed within its border
A quieter lot has now been reared
And the Police Station's disappeared

At hairst the cornyards were packed
Wi' corn and wheat a neatly stacked
Noo barley seems a' they're needin
Whether for whisky or for feeding

On every day the good Lord sent
To Forfar and Arbroath there went
Aboot eight milk carts a fully laden
Wi' milk and eggs frae ilk

When lousin time cam roond each day
The men to the bothy made their way
Noo sic a place can no be seen
Even ferms are few and far between

But noo we dinna need to worry
To the supermarket we fill our trolley
Wi' eggs in cartons, butter in wrap
Clean tatties veg and fruit, all on tap

Chapter 11

CARMYLLIE VILLAGES

Greystone Village, 2012

Many visitors to the parish are looking for a village called Carmyllie, as in Arbirlot parish there is a village of Arbirlot and in St Vigeans, there is a village of the same name also. There is no village named Carmyllie but there are two villages in the parish, Greystone and Redford, although in 1836 the Rev William Robertson mentioned there were 'three small hamlets.....containing a population respectfully of 75, 51 and 48'.[1] It is thought that the third hamlet was either the Milton or Drummygar. Bert Souter, farmer at the Milton, remarked that there used to be a row of several small cottages at the edge of the road, running from his farmhouse down almost as far as the burn.

Greystone

Greystone in the west of the parish is the oldest village, nestled in a hollow, relatively sheltered from

James Sturrock, Greystone Post Office. 1930s

the north and east and near to the Kirkbuddo parish boundary. In 1877, there were four houses paying rent from £10 to £25 and 15 houses all paying rent under £4, Panmure Estate being the proprietor. By 1894, land had been reclaimed and within the village, there was a tenant farmer, George Black, two pendicles tenanted by John Muggins[2] and David McKay, a blacksmith, Robert McGregor together with a Wright, Robert Sturrock and Mrs William Sturrock was grocer and Postmistress. The Rev Keith farmed the Glebe.

In 1910 at Greystone, Robert Sturrock who was also a Joiner worked a pendicle. John Kydd a carrier lived in one cottage and transported goods to Arbroath on Saturdays.[3] The other cottages were occupied by; James Taylor, a shoemaker, Andrew Taylor and James Sturrock, both quarriers, William Low, a stonedresser and Helen Brown a teacher. Mrs Elizabeth Sturrock had the Post Office and to complete the village, there was the Free Church Manse, Church and Hall, school and schoolhouse.

---

[1] NSA, Carmyllie Parish, p.359, 1836

[2] John Muggins died in 1913. He was the last male member of the Muggins family who lived in Greystone for over 150 years. John worked at the quarries and was a carrier between Greystone and Arbroath. *Annual Carmyllie Free Church Magazine,* by Rev John Thomson, 1913

[3] Arbroath Year Book, 1910

The village Post Offices were the hub of communication for the community with all letters, postcards, telegrams and later in 1930s and 40s, telephone calls passing through, allowing the Postmistress or Postmaster to gather all the gossip about the community. The Sturrock family were in charge of Greystone Post Office from 1890 for over fifty years. The Rev John Thomson, minister of the Free Church had been well aware of the lack of privacy and while he was army chaplain in France during WW1, he sent postcards to the Manse in a language that appeared foreign but his family could read the plain English when the postcards were reflected in a mirror. Harry Officer's daughter Audrey remembers that before and during WW2, the Sturrock sisters ran Greystone Post Office and all telephone messages came via them. Nothing was confidential!

Mrs Catherine Clark replaced the Sturrock family as postmistress in 1946. She gives a clear account of village life in her memories:

Jack and I married in 1942, but I had to wait four years until Jack was demobbed from his War Service before we could settle down together. However, as Jack's demobilisation was drawing near, an opportunity arose early in 1946 when a postmistress was required for Greystone Post Office. I with my young son Graham, moved from Burnhead to Greystone and remained postmistress for over fifty years.
The shop was open from 7am to 8pm but if someone required an essential item, it could be later than 8pm. The entrance to the Post Office and shop was through the front door to the left, and to the right

Greystone Post Office, c.1946

the family living quarters. In the early days, German Prisoners of War from Kirkbuddo called, asking me to sell their wooden toys. I had a three-ring cooker at the rear of the shop, so I kept an eye on the pot of soup which I always had prepared and this was greatly appreciated by the posties or salesmen and travellers when it was cold. I started early to see to the delivery of newspapers as well as catching farm workers before 'yokin' time. 'Bogie roll' had to be cut down into manageable pieces before selling to the pipe smokers. We stayed open late in the evenings to let the farm workers stock up on groceries and provide some with postal orders for the football coupons. I realised that wives, living in the area with little transport, had no opportunity to shop until Saturday, so I felt I had to provide
for their needs. As well as the Post Office, I stocked groceries as well as some pharmaceuticals, needles, thread, wool and ironmongery from drawing pins to wellingtons. In fact, if a customer required something that was not in stock, I would quickly get it for them from the town. To begin with, a sales traveller from Strachan, Wallace and Whyte came round once a month to collect my order and delivered the following Saturday. Later Jack and I dealt with the Cash and Carry in Dundee where we bought the goods direct.

Being a Postmistress required professionalism and my superiors and customers respected me. When people were in need of a reference for employment, they looked to the Postmistress for a signature. Greystone Post Office, Arbroath, Angus, was attached to Dundee and Arbroath main offices and although the Head Office was in Aberdeen, the money was brought from the Dundee Office. However times were always changing and when I arrived in 1946, a new Welfare state was emerging that added to Post Office duties, such as pension books, family allowance and benefits as well as the continuing Ration books together with postage and parcels and 'I had to learn as I went along'. Inspectors arrived from Arbroath without warning and always found the management in a good functional condition. Representatives also visited from Aberdeen, usually ending with a cup of coffee and a chat. Yet it was the trust that I had in my customers and likewise the trust the community had in me that allowed the management to run smoothly. For example, at Christmas time especially, as people were working all day, they brought their mail and parcels in the evening, which I piled, into baskets. I had the mail and parcels weighed and stamped ready for the postman the next day and workers paid me that evening. Also another example of trust, the postman brought pension books from couples (mostly without transport) to me, stamped the book, gave the money and the book to the postman who returned both to the pensioners on the same day. At one time, there were three postie vans serving the area. Not everyone had a phone in the 1950s and 1960s and although there was a telephone box nearby, sometimes locals would ask me, in times of emergency, for the use of my telephone.

Mrs Clark with her sons

I saw many remarkable incidents and changes in my fifty years of service. My husband and I were barely settled a year in our home when, in 1947, the worst snowstorm in living memory hit the country. The snow started in January and freezing conditions continued for three months, roads were blocked, cleared and blocked again. There was no electricity at this time (Carmyllie was not connected until the 1950s) so residents relied on a supply of paraffin and coal. I did my bit by selling paraffin to those who came with their cans. I was expecting our second child and as the time drew near, the snow levels showed no improvement. Those around me became anxious and advised that I should be taken to Arbroath where medical help was at hand. Mr Soutar, Milton, transported me with horse and sledge across to the Milton 'as the crow flies' (The snow was higher than the fences so they could go across the fields) where I was greeted and given a hot cup of tea and fresh-made scone. From there I was taken into Arbroath by car, a very bumpy ride. I stayed with my relations and my son was born within the week. My first visitor was the Rev John Thomson who had not visited Arbroath for six weeks. Yet there were many snowstorms to contend with, although not on the same scale as 1947. The 'Mains Brae' was always bad. Posties became stuck but they did try to reach the Post Office where they were able to 'dry off' in front of a good coal fire. When the postie found it impossible to reach Greystone, Jack, who made his own skis, would go to the Milton to pick up the mail in a sealed bag.

Presentation to Mrs Clark for 50 years service as Postmistress

As the combine harvester and modern farm machinery became the norm, less agricultural labour was required and I was aware of this in the 1960s as there was less custom at the shop. There followed a big void in the community when Greystone Primary School closed in 1970. I missed my good friend Miss Beattie and the children calling to choose their much thought-out purchase of sweets. Gradually there was less demand for provisions, as I could not compete with the supermarkets. More locals had their own transport and pensions were forwarded through the Bank. However, I still traded on after Kirkbuddo, Craichie and Redford Post Offices closed. In the latter years, Greystone PO opened for half days only.

In 1988, we had a bad experience when there was a burglary around the same time as Kirkbuddo and Craichie PO. Thieves broke in and stole two drawers that contained money and my important PO stamp. One big drawer was found in a burn at the Milton and my purse, empty of course, was found in a shed at Hillhead.

In 1992, when my husband died and my two sons had found their own way, I was alone at Greystone for four more winters. I realised that the time had come to retire into Arbroath where I would be near my own family.

Mr Mackintosh (Senior), Solicitors, Arbroath, dealt with my business when I moved into Greystone PO in 1946 and Mr Mackintosh's son 'saw me out' in 1996.[4]

---

[4] Testimony, Mrs Catherine Clark, 2009

Redford

Redford village, on the east side of the parish, grew in size due to the quarry industry and the railway connection. In 1877, there were five houses, 2 owned by the Guynd Estate and 3 by the Panmure Estate. By 1894, there were 12 houses in Redford[5]:-

Redford Village, 1900. By kind permission of Arbroath Herald, 25 Jan 2013

Guynd Estate	Tenant	Rent
House	Don McKenzie, Police Constable	£ 4.15.0
Smithy Croft	Robert Mudie, Blacksmith	35.02.0
Wright's Croft	James Buchan, Wright	28.00.0
Cottage	George Anderson	5.05.0
Cottage	William Carr, Tailor	5.05.0
Panmure Estate		
Pendicle and House	Alex Booth, Manufacturer	14.00.0
House	Charles Webster, Stationmaster	4.00.0
House	John Anderson, Quarrier	4.00.0
House	D. Fairweather, Quarrier	4.00.0
Pendicle and House	Andrew Paris, Grocer	12.10.0
House and Shop	Alex Webster, Bootmaker	8.00.0
Pendicle	William Brown, Shoemaker	5.00.0

---

[5]Valuation Roll, Carmyllie, 1877 and 1894

James Pierson, Laird at the Guynd, submitted this plan of four attached cottages at Redford in 1862. The cottage on the left had a room, kitchen and a shop facing the road whereas the other had only one room and a kitchen. They had access to a coal house each but there was only one shared wash house. The houses on the 1880 map of Redford are probably on the east side of road and almost opposite the Smithy. The map also shows another Smithy in the northern part of the village. Beside this smithy, there was a row of houses running parallel to the railway, one of which was the Post Office. In 1880, there was no passenger service and no ticket office

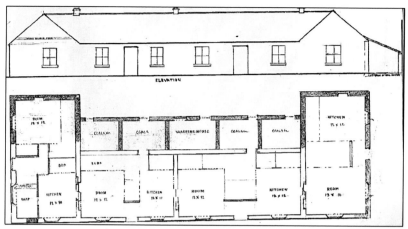

Plans of Cottages at Redford, 1862, RHP 2618

but later in 1900, the ticket office was beside the railway line to the east of the main road. The road to Bonnycheer and Arbroath was altered later and re-positioned north of the railway.

The road through Redford was still unpaved as shown in the photograph (p137), since the railway lines crossing the road are barely visible. South of the railway line beside the Smithy, there was a

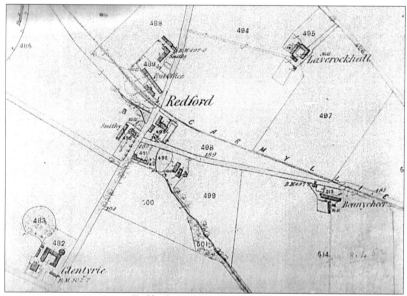

Redford, 1880 (NAS, RHP 2600)

spring with a good supply of water, which served the community. This was in constant use, the picture showing the pipe from the well filling a water tank ('bowser') while the horse waits patiently.

By 1910, the Guynd Estate property at Redford was reduced to the smithy and croft. The smithy was tenanted by William Mudie who was now paying rent for smithy, croft and house separately. At the croft, James Buchan the joiner paid a combined rent for his house and croft, but the workshop was separate and he also rented two more houses and some land from Panmure Estate. Various other tenants of Panmure Estate residing in the village were John Morrison the Policeman, John Carrie, Dairyman, Charles Smith, Shepherd, David Laing the Stationmaster, Mrs Annie Binnie the Postmistress and George Walker, Labourer. Alexander Webster started as a bootmaker with a shop but later had a Coal Merchant business along with a piece of land.

Doreen Paul (nee Mudie,) daughter of Tom Mudie the blacksmith at Redford, recalls a variety of activities that took place in Redford village during 1930s and 1940s:
'*I remember some of the village characters, such as Frank ('Moley') Mitchell whose General Store, opposite to the smiddy,*

Mrs Mudie and Doreen

138

sold everything from needles, pins, eatables and clothes, to bicycle parts. On the left of the 'general store' was Peter Dolan the Coalman's office, and next to that, on the edge of the road, was a wooden house, which was another shop run by Mrs Walker and Janet for many years. Dave Webster was a shoemaker who, as well as making boots, repaired footwear and stitched together damaged horse harness. His family were in charge of the business for decades but after the Second World War, demand fell and he retired in the late 1940s. Similarly, Miss Duncan the dressmaker supplied the

needs of locals for many years but she closed her business around the same time. Mrs Isabella Smart (who later became Mrs Fairweather) was in charge of the Post Office, opening early in the morning to receive the daily newspapers from the bus and she closed late in the evening, seven days a week. Mrs Christison, as well as having a large family, found time to act as a local midwife and make large pots of soup for the schoolchildren. Peter Dolan, the coal merchant, seemed to have a permanent position sitting on an old tree trunk watching the day go by. Mrs

The ticket office, Redford Station c.1920

Kippen (Kippen was the local 'Bobby') was a trained nurse who was called upon in emergencies.

In the mid 1930s, I remember my father or mother pumping the petrol by hand from the petrol pump and selling to motorists and farmers for their agricultural needs. However, during the Second World War, the sale of petrol was restricted and two soldiers were billeted into Redford Smiddy to 'police' the rationed petrol. The old petrol pump was replaced by a new one. The soldiers had a 24-hour duty and worked 12 hour shifts, selling petrol at a set price of 2/- per gallon. Farmers and agricultural businesses were given extra petrol allowance for their tractors or engines while private motorists found it difficult to get fuel. The two soldiers lived in the smiddy house and I had to vacate my upstairs room to give them accommodation. I recall two particularly 'colourful' Polish soldiers whom,

'The Day of Rest at Redford Smithy', 1913 (Geddes family)
Back Row: Unknown, James Geddes, Unknown, Unknown, Nell Mudie
Front Row: John Mudie(m. Betsy Geddes), Unknown, William Mudie, Unknown, Jess Walker (shop owner) and her father, Charles Walker

although they spoke little English, spotted Mrs Mudie's sewing machine and asked permission to sew a pair of shoes for her, which they completed. One day I ran to investigate a 'commotion' in the garden, only to find one of the Poles chasing the maid, Peg McNulty, round the garden shouting 'I love you! I love you!' I quickly put this nonsense to an end!!

Gordon Law, Glentyrie, remembers Jim Fairweather who was roadman for many years. After Jim cut the grass on the road verges, Peter Dolan's daughter, who helped her father with his pendicle at the Podge, would gather the dried grass from the verge, adding to the forage for their animals.

139

The village policeman was really the Parish policeman and the first policeman was John Morrison. He occupied the Police station and house at Redford, rented by Angus County Council in 1910 from the Panmure Estate.

Jack Whitton was the Carmyllie Policeman for twenty-one years from 1950 to 1971. His widow Nancy recalls Jack's experiences:

Jack and I married in 1949 and lived in furnished rooms in Montrose for one year before coming to Carmyllie Police station in 1950.

The police house had a small kitchen with a boiler in the corner. Paraffin lights were used as there was no electricity but Nancy was grateful that water was heated by means of a coal fire. To help with the supply of fuel, there was a bonus sometimes when the Arbroath-Carmyllie train passed and as it neared Redford station, Danny the fireman tooted and large lumps of coal were thrown across the fence ready for Jack or I to collect! There was a cell in Friockheim police station, but no cell at Carmyllie. If the occasion arose, when Jack arrested an offender, a van came out from the Arbroath office to pick up the culprit.

Nancy, August 2009

Jack was on duty eight hours daily but was on call 24 hours. He kept a logbook that was checked periodically by the Chief Constables.

A police magazine came out every fortnight with a list of fugitives. A pair of binoculars was kept in the house to check for runaways, usually escaped boys from Rossie Boys School near Montrose. Jack wrote a report that was sent to the Arbroath office twice yearly. He noted that Carmyllie was always at the bottom of the crime list and was assured by his seniors that was the best place to be.

The three policemen from Friockheim, Carmyllie and Arbroath Landward met at Colliston twice a week with their logbooks where they exchanged notes. They could communicate by phone but were obliged to meet twice per week. Arbroath office phoned if they found anyone in the area with an outstanding warrant. Arbroath was more or less the County station and Forfar was the Headquarters.

Old Policeman's House, Redford, 2011

Jack wore his uniform (including the baton) every day even in hot summers. Three years before his retirement he was allowed to discard his jacket if need be. Jack was more than half way through his service before he had a weekend off, but was allowed one day every eight days provided he was home before midnight. Annual leave consisted of two weeks of summer holidays and one week in either spring or autumn, during which time the policing was manned from Arbroath.

Jack rode about twenty miles by bicycle around Carmyllie. In the early 1960s, permission was given to buy a motorbike. He referred to a map showing the boundaries, which often overlapped, stretching out to Wellbank, Inverarity, Glamis, Letham and Kirkden School, which marched with Guthrie.

Firearms were checked regularly although Jack's work was mostly involved in agriculture. He attended statutory sheep dipping on farms to ensure that all sheep were disinfected. There were also regulations with swine fever and in the 1950s and early 60s there were outbreaks of anthrax in cattle and sheep. There were outbreaks at such places as the Crofts and Montquhir where the police attended at the disposal of the infected animals. There was no entry or exit to the farm and the cattle carcass was burned or buried in a deep hole. The police remained at the scene until the animal or animals were destroyed which stretched into the early hours of the morning or could take several days, depending on the number of cattle. Jack remembers the smells varied from delicious roast beef to repugnancy.

Some farmers reared turkeys for Christmas and Jack had a busy time with the 'turkey trot', checking that none had 'flown' by mistake! Also there were a few Christmas tree plantations which Jack checked regularly for unlawful disappearance of the odd tree.

Top. Redford village from the south c.1930
Bottom. Redford village from the north 1950s

There were the regular children troubles, which were usually dealt with when Jack reported them to their parents. When the tinkers arrived at Balnabreich farm in the spring there was often a warrant to be issued for, say, a bag stolen at a dance. However, Jack found this was not straightforward since the tinkers would drop into the Gaelic language when accused. Jack solved the problem by involving his Gaelic speaking colleague from Glamis to assist in the situation. Nevertheless, Jack appreciated their style of life and in return, they were amiable towards him.
If there was a house or farm fire, Jack had to remain until it was extinguished. He was also called to farm or road accidents and, sadly, some fatalities. He knew everyone in the Parish and often roadmen had information that Jack sifted through.

When Carmyllie mart was held in the spring and autumn, Jack was on duty to check the Irish cattle certificates as well as the alcohol licence, which was held by Strachan, Balmoral Hotel, Friockheim. Jack held Scout meetings in the mart before the closure in the late 1960s.

The local policeman was on duty at social events, such as whist drives and dances which were usually held in the East or West schools then later in the new hall which was opened in 1960. Community police or 'special constables' were available for assistance or called upon as witnesses.

While in the process of building a new Carmyllie police station in 1957, Jack, I, and our young family were not certain that this would be our new home until we actually took up residence. I was 'on duty' too as I was there to take messages and phone calls but was very seldom in touch with people 'on the wrong side'. Jack and I were called upon frequently to sign personal documents. There was an office in the new station, which had a separate entrance but again no police cell.

When Jack retired in 1971, police cars were covering a wider area and a policeman was no longer required for the Parish of Carmyllie. The police station house was sold as a private dwelling. Jack continued to reside in Carmyllie and died in 2006.[6]

'Carmyllie Permanent Way Gang'
Back Row: ?, Charles Potter
Front Row: Charles Walker, David Kydd, James Shepherd

[6] Testimony, Mrs Nancy Whitton, 2009

Chapter 12

WORLD WAR 1 and WORLD WAR 2

World War 1   1914-1918.

The Great War began on the 28 July 1914 and by 1918, Carmyllie had lost thirty men from the Parish and district.

Zeppelin

On May 2, 1915, a Zeppelin passed over the county. The Zeppelin was a rigid type airship with a covered metal frame, filled with gas and named after its German inventor, Ferdinand von Zepplin. The Zeppelin was also known as 'blimp'. The airship passed over Arbroath and Carnoustie and probably crossed over Carmyllie Parish on its way over the Grampians. It dropped five bombs in the neighbourhood, one at Arbirlot, which fortunately did no damage, but 'those who heard the terrific explosions were not likely to forget it'.[7] The airship was of limited value to the Germans as it was easily blown off course and they had difficulty in targeting strategic places such as shipyards and factories.

Conscription

In January 1916, Parliament passed the first conscription laws (compulsory enrolment) ever passed in Britain. At first only single men and childless widowers aged 18 to 41 were called up, but by 1918, compulsory service had been extended to include all men aged 18 to 51. More than 2.3 million conscripts were enlisted nationally before the end of the war in November 1918.

Pte Joseph A Law, Royal Artillery

The Rev John Thomson, while minister at Carmyllie Free Church, (1904-1943) wrote an annual magazine, combining local incidents with national and international events. The following are excerpts from 1908 to 1924:

1908 Carmyllie Quarries closed
1910 Quarries re-opened
1911 Severe drought
1912 Year of the Great Coal Strike
April, The sinking of the Titanic on colliding with an iceberg in the North Atlantic – 1,600 souls perished.
Mrs Falconer, M.P.'s mother, died and Mrs McRobbie, Conon, died, age 59.
1913 Captain Scott and his brave comrades were lost in the snowy wastes of the Antartic.
John Muggins died in Barry. He was the last male member of the Muggins family who lived in Greystone for over 150 years. He worked at the quarries and was a carrier between Greystone and Arbroath
July 15th A cable arrived from the Guynd with tragic news of the death by drowning of Guy Ouchterlony in Oakville, Canada. He had been married for only three months.
Dec 19th Mrs Ouchterlony, senior, died suddenly in London.
1913 Severe snowstorms in January and March.
Collection to DRI was £4.7/-. Seven members [of Carmyllie Free Church] old and young, received treatment in Hospital.
Torrential rain at the beginning of May with severe damage to seed and livestock, particularly sheep and lambs.

---

[7] *Carmyllie Free Church Magazine*, Rev John Thomson, 1915, ed. by Nettie Gibb

1914 Flower Services in Church. Flowers sent to D.R.I. All kinds of gifts sent to soldiers wounded and billeted in Dundee.

Examples of gifts sent to soldiers:

62 lbs jam	*29 doz eggs*	*Oatcake*
4lbs butter	*2lbs Tea*	*Scones*
2 Boxes of Biscuits	*12 cakes*	*Plum Puddings*
10 fowls	*3 large boxes of fruit*	*Sweets*
1085 cigarettes	*Tobacco*	*Toffee*
Chocolates	*Honey*	*Handkerchiefs*

These gifts were divided with the wounded in The War Hospital, Caird Rest, DRI, Dundee. Thank you letters were sent to W.F. Anderson, Schoolmaster, Greystone.

1915 21 May: this date is memorable as it is the day on which, for the first time since the world recorded the passing of time by mechanical means, the clocks were put forward an hour for the first four months of summer

Jim Fullerton, Black Watch, Slade
(Gibb family)

1916 May 31- June1 now known as the Battle of Jutland

June 5   Loss of HMS 'Hampshire' with Lord Kitchener and staff on board off the west of Orkneys.

Regulation of the darkening of Churches

1916 David Kinnear killed on the Somme. Will Duncan died near Arras

July 19 1917. Hope Kinnear and his comrades were gassed in their sleep and Hope only survived a few days.

1917. Rev John Thomson volunteered to give service as a chaplain to the troops in France

Rev John Thomson ((McDonald family)

after an appeal from the Scottish Churches Services. Carmyllie West Church changed the time of the Services to 2.20pm and Rev JA Tweedie, Arbroath was appointed Moderator to the Presbytery. After some delays, Rev Thomson left for France on 29 June. The whole four months were spent in the forward lines in the Somme area and they afforded such an experience of the real meaning of wars. The Rev was in four different places, Brusle, Bernes, Tincrus and Villers Fancon and his work was among English regiments. One could not do enough for these brave men and the Rev got an insight into the conditions under which our men lived, fought and died.

At home, harvest was gathered in good weather, potato crop good.

Dec 30 (1917) There was a special memorial service for those who died in battle. Major Jack Ouchterlony was killed near Leper in France.

1918 The Great War is almost over and the gradual fall of our Empire is not new in our history. This war has seen four other Empires fall a) Russia b) Germany c) Austria/ Hungary and d) Turkey

1918 Carmyllie Quarries closed

Mrs Nita Smith (nee Gibb) at the grave of
Pte William Fullerton in Belgium (2009)

Mrs Nita Smith (nee Gibb) visited the grave of 153566 Private William Fullerton, 43rd BN Canadian Infantry in Belgium who died on 19 May 1916. He was a nephew of Nita's grandfather, born and brought up in Redford, Carmyllie and emigrated to Canada just before war broke out.

At home among the wounded are:

George Constable	*Charles Constable*
Alexander Norrie	*William Norrie*
George Duthie	*Robert Pattullo*

Private James Davie (missing)

R M Hume, Hillhead of Carmyllie, served as 2nd Lieutenant in the Black Watch on the Western Front and was reported 'missing' in April 1918 but was repatriated in January 1919 from being a Prisoner of War.[8]

11 April Sgt James Shepherd awarded the Military Medal for saving the guns of a battery when under heavy machine gun fire.

April Robert Patullo gained a Military medal for destroying a bridge in the face of rapidly advancing Germans.

Private James Irving, Little Lochlair, returned after two years as a German Prisoner of War.

James Irving along with three other POWs from the Parish were presented publicly with a wallet and £5.00.

Outbreak of Influenza epidemic – many deaths

1919 March It was suggested that a War Memorial be erected in the Parish. In a short time, £240.00 was collected and Memorial was built at the Newton 'cross roads' ('Gollywell'). However, the unveiling took place later in 1920.

10 April Mrs May Turnbull was awarded the Red Cross badge for four and half years' service as Matron in Garsick House Military Hospital, Ayr and it was presented by Queen Alexandra, the Queen Mother.

The Military Cross was awarded to David Constable, Saskatchewan, Canada.

A supper was given in the East school to our returned soldiers (about 20 attended) with James Falconer in the chair.

28 June Peace Treaty with Germany was formerly signed at Versailles.

6 July Recognised as Peace Sunday.

11 November The anniversary of the day on which the Armistice was signed by Germany which ended the Great War. By special request of the King, wherever practical, all work and traffic ceased for two minutes at 11am. Our church bell was rung as a signal but it was only towns and cities that the impact of silence would be felt.

1920 11th April. Unveiling of the War Memorial. Bitterly cold day of wind and rain. 100 people were present and a special choir under the leadership of Mr Dalgety from Forfar, accompanied by Mr Sydney, organist of the Parish church, Forfar, led the praise. After an address from Rev Lyon, Colonel Ouchterlony unveiled the Memorial.

1921 Enormous damage to crops due to flooding

 The age long problem of troubles in Ireland and its relation with Great Britain is far from settled.

1922 Sale of part of the Dalhousie Estates which included the Carmyllie lands. Among our losses is the 'enforced severance', of Mr and Mrs Falconer (The local Member of Parliament) from his home at Milton of Conon.

1922 Oct. Through the intiative of Mrs Carnegie of Lour, a company of the Girl Guide Movement was formed for the Carmyllie district.

1924 27th May. The Telephone Exchange at Redford was formerly opened by Mrs Morgan, Grange of Conon.

---

[8] Forces War Records, 9 Mar 2013

In Proud and Grateful Memory of Men from Carmyllie and District who fell in the Great Wars

<u>1914-1918</u>
Sub Lt George Hunter RNVR
Pte William Fullerton Can Inf
Str Robert Smith RN
Pte William Duthie SG
Pte Alexander Kydd RSF
Pte William Duncan SH
Gnr Alex Laird RGA
Gnr Robert Pryde RGA
Pte William Low A & SH
Pte James Laird HLI
Pte George MacFarlane BW
Pte David Laird GH
SS Alex McQuattie F&FY
Pte Robert Milne BW
Gnr Alexander Mitchell RFA
Pte John Peters RSF
Major JPH Ouchterlony DSO RE
Pte James Binnie SG
Pte James Cowie BW
Pte Robert Crichton A & SH
Pte James Davie   (Can) CH
Sgt Major James C Duncan (Can) CH
L Cpl Norman Lawton NZ RB
L Cpl Alexander Sturrock MFP MPC
Pte John Peters BW
Pte William Philip BW

Pte James Soutar BW
Pte David Strachan SG
Pte Charles Sturrock BW
Pte Hugh Robertson NZ

<u>1939-1945</u>
Pte James Ritchie BW
GnrAlexander Quirrie RA
GnrAlexander Peters SHRA

Pte Wm Duncan, S.H.
Drummygar

The comparison of casualties between World War 1 and World War 2 written on every War Memorial is stark – the majority have fallen in World War 1. In the case of Carmyllie and District, 90% of the fatalities were in the 1914-1918 conflict, three from the same family.

The Second World War
1939 -1945

The Home Guard

In May 1940 men, whose occupations were necessary to allow the country to function, such as farmers, certain factory workers and some mechanics, were exempt from the war 'call-up' yet wished to defend the country voluntarily. By July, the organisation was named the Home Guard and men between 17 and 65 could call at the local Police Station for an application form.

Members of Carmyllie Home Guard, 1943 or 1944
From left, back row: Willie Sturrock, George Kinnear, Ack Findlay, J. Douglas, Frank Clark and Dave Chalmers
Second back row: ? Rose, ? Mitchell, Andy Paton, Will Chalmers, Tom Findlay, Willie Gardiner, W. McGhee, George Fairweather
Third back row: Willie Gall, D, Gall, Tom Gall, Stan Mollison, Fred Smith, J. Sturrock, Dave Smith, D. Milne, Dave Mollison
Front Row: Gordon Gibb, Chae Spink, Alf Coventry, Ronald Hume, Jim Smith, Will McGregor, Lawrence Walker

Ronald M. Hume was the Lieutenant in the Carmyllie branch of the Home Guard, known as the 1st Angus Battalion unit from the 1st February 1941. Ronald served as Lieutenant in the Black Watch in WW1.

Under him, a platoon of 30 men was formed in Carmyllie, remaining operational until December 1944. Reference to the Home Guard in the modern age is not always taken seriously, but in 1940 and 1941, known as the 'dark years', the War had caused a great deal of anxiety both to civilians and armed forces, many with memories of World War 1. Numerous men would have enlisted having seen bombing in the area.

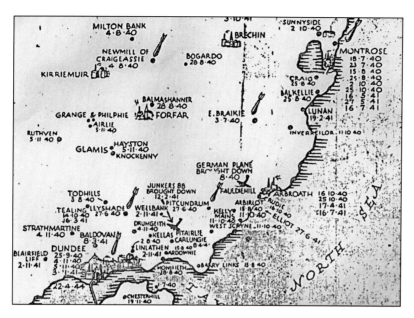

Aeroplanes brought down and bombs dropped in Dundee, Arbroath and Montrose area, 1940-1941 (Source unknown)

In 1940 and 1941, there were a number of bombs dropped locally (approx 40) and several German aeroplanes were shot down in the Tay estuary hinterland in a span of 18 months, most of the Germans flying over from occupied Norway. Although there was no activity in Carmyllie, (the nearest was a bomb at the Bank of Arbirlot and a German plane was brought down at Fauldiehill, Arbirlot) the Carmyllie Home Guard would have been on hand to deal with enemy pilots. They had regular training exercises to develop their skills for Home defence.

Arch Paton, Glebe Cottage, Carmyllie, wrote this poem while serving as a Gunner in World War 2.

Oft in my mind I plainly see
Thousands of miles across the sea
The place I left so long ago
The Heathen Hun to help lay low

It is no place of worldwide fame
Carmyllie is its humble name
To me around that name there clings
Memories of all kinds of things

Towards the southern end is my home
Around these again I'd long to roam
The Guynd, the Milton and all around
To me each inch is well known ground

The auld Kirk stands upon the brae
Towards it I oft did wind my way
Many have passed on and have been laid
Beside it in the auld Kirk yaird

Nestling peacefully in the vale
Is Redford, source of many a tale
Away to the West the quarry braes
There I've spent many pleasant days

I hope my thoughts are not in vain
That soon I'll see them all again
Meantime they will remain the theme
Of many a pleasant thought and dream
(signed) Archie, 11 Oct 1942

(Thankfully Archie did return from the War and served as Church beadle for a further 25 years.)

Women's Land Army

During the War, the Government encouraged all farmers to maximise food production and the Women's Land Army movement was started to help staff the farms as many men were away at war.

When the Land Army started in 1939 it was voluntary, but later conscription was introduced and by 1944, there were over 80,000 women working on the land. Many girls chose the Land Army instead of factory work or joining the uniformed services. If they lived at a distance, accommodation was provided on the farm or in hostels but if stationed nearby, they would walk to work.

Minnie Clark (now Soutar) remembers her time in the Land Army in 1940 at the age of 17:

I was employed by Archie Jackson at New Mains of Guynd while continuing to live with my grandparents at Villabank. I was the only Land Army girl on the farm along with three male farm workers, Wull Esplin, Wull Johnstone and Pat Renshaw.

My duties included planting potatoes, 'clatting' neeps, feeding animals and at harvest time sitting on the binder driven by a tractor. There were two horses as well as a tractor. I can't remember driving tractors or dealing with the horses, but I do recall being asked to take the horse to Tammy Mudie, the blacksmith, all by myself and being inwardly very scared. I was so relieved afterwards that I had completed the task successfully.

As a Land Girl, I was supplied with a uniform from a depot by a supervisor called Miss Ireland at East Balmirmer. I thought there were meetings held periodically for the Land Army but I can't remember ever attending them.

Minnie Clark (now Soutar) wearing the Land Army uniform, 1940

Minnie with friends, 1941

The uniform consisted of:- one greatcoat in khaki but with a white blanket lining for winter, 1 hat and 1 tie, 2 short-sleeved shirts, 2 pairs knee length socks, 1 corduroy breeches, 2 bib and brace overalls, 1 pair shoes, 1 pair wellingtons, 2 pairs boots, 2 green pullovers and 1 long raincoat. We also had an armband, green for every day and red for 'dress' occasions. We gained a half diamond badge each year to be sewn on to our armbands[9].

Our second Land Girl, Rena Tindal, joined the Land Army with her sister Annie in 1944 when she was 17. She remembers; *Although I lived in a neighbouring parish, Miss Ireland supervised me. The official age was 18 but since my sister was older, I was allowed to enlist earlier. I walked four miles to my work in a market garden that supplied fruit and vegetables to Broughty Ferry. The hours of work were from 7am to 5pm although at fruit harvest time the hours extended to 9pm. There were*

---

[9] Testimony, Mrs Minnie Soutar (nee Clark), 2009

short breaks in the morning and afternoon and 1 ½ hours for lunch and there was no food supplied so I carried 'piecies'. We had a a variety of work such as attending to the tomatoes in the greenhouses, digging up leeks from the frozen earth with no gloves and the repetitive job of weeding, the latter cheered on by a singsong or a good gossip.[10]

Ration Books

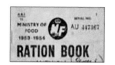

During and after WW2 from 1940 to 1954, everyone was issued with a ration book in order to eke out food supplies. But in rural areas, food was less restrictive and fresh eggs, vegetables, potatoes, milk, butter, and chicken were available 'under the counter'. Farmers collected a supply of oatmeal from the local miller to be shared with the farm workers and many households had a pigsty where pigs were reared. The meat from one whole pig contributed towards the family diet for several months.

It was difficult to get sufficient sugar to make jam yet this could be overcome by requesting extra for 'beekeeping'. Children were restricted to 2oz sweets per week but often looked towards adults for some extra coupons. To supplement the diet, soup, stovies, oatcakes and scones were made in the household kitchen while a bakers' van delivered bread from Friockheim or Arbroath.

At the end of the war, gas masks were returned to the East and West schools. On 8 May 1945, the schools closed for three days to celebrate 'the end of the War in Europe'[11] although the school gardens were still in crop in July 1946 for 'The Dig for Victory' scheme.

Lila & Isobel Purvis, Brae of Conon, Queen's Nurses, WW2

---

[10] Testimony, Mrs Rina Tindal, 2011
[11] School Log Book, Carmyllie East, 8 May, 1945

Chapter 13

SICKNESS AND HEALTH

The Rev William Robertson in 1836, observed that 'in the Parish of Carmyllie, the climate is considerably colder than the surrounding parishes, caused by the rain falling on a stiff retentive subsoil preventing the absorption of the waters, and the surrounding air is kept loaded with moisture'. He goes on to say that 'rheumatic, catarrhal and inflammatory complaints are common and derive from these climatic conditions'.[12]

In 1899, the Nation's health was in a poor condition, largely due to urban growth and slums. This came to the Government's attention when recruiting men for the Boer War (1899-1902) and many were rejected. Instructions were sent to the Medical Officers to take measures to improve the nourishment and health of the children. The School Boards were notified in 1908, that schools would have regular visits from the Medical Officer of Health and meals provided for the needy.

Infectious diseases such as tuberculosis, typhoid, diphtheria, measles, mumps, chicken pox, polio, scarlet fever, and whooping cough were prevalent, particularly in children, although typhoid was seldom mentioned after the end of nineteenth century when sanitary inspectors became more vigilant. By far the most common infection was scarlet fever. In 1894, John Fyffe the dairy farmer at the Milton was charged in Arbroath Sherriff Court for promoting the spread of the infection. His dairymaid was lodging in the farmhouse and was in contact with Mr Fyffe's children who were suffering from scarlet fever. The dairymaid was milking cows in the byre and consequently, potentially infected milk was carried in the milk churns to Arbroath and distributed to individual customers.[13]

Scarlet fever continued to be a major problem and in 1907, the County Medical Officer called at Carmyllie West School to inspect the sanitary conditions of the buildings. In 1915, the infection was so widespread that the West school was closed for a day in order to fumigate the classrooms.[14] The introduction of toilet soap into schools after WW1 and inspections from the District Nurse, helped to keep diseases at bay. Immunisations and diphtheria vaccinations were carried out too by 1941.

Unventilated housing and large families living in close quarters had exacerbated the spread of disease. Skin infections were common too and complaints such as 'itch', impetigo, ringworm ('titter') nettle rash, and scabies were all linked to poor washing facilities and contact with farm animals in rural areas. Most people walked to their work and children walked to school through all weather conditions. In January 1910, some West school pupils were 'unable to walk [to school] because of chilblains.'

Carmyllie Parish had the services of Dr William Barron, residing in Letham village, for an extraordinary number of years from 1896 to 1940.[15] He visited his patients initially with a horse and carriage, taking the old direct route (track) from Newton of Idvies through Ascurry farm to East Hills.

The Spanish influenza pandemic in 1918-19 affected the whole world and killed as many people as died fighting in the Great War and the strongest and healthiest people were usually the worst affected. In Carmyllie Parish, the schools were closed or half-open for over six months and many adults succumbed to the 'flu'.

Tuberculosis was a further scourge to human health and there were many TB hospitals, known as Sanatoria, built to try to nurse and cure patients of this contagious disease, largely with fresh air and nursing, but over 50% of patients died in these Sanatoria. In the 1930s, 40% of all cattle were infected

---

12 *NSA*, Carmyllie, 1836
13 *Arbroath Guide*, 11 Aug, 1894
14 School Log Book, Carmyllie West, 1907, 1915
15 Arbroath Year Books, 1890-1940

with tuberculosis and there were 50,000 new human cases of TB reported every year, the large majority of which would prove fatal. To counter TB in the human population, the BCG vaccine was introduced just after WW2, and these vaccines were administered at school. As milk was the primary source of infection, measures were taken to reduce the infection in dairy cows and the Attested Herd Scheme began in 1935. This was a voluntary scheme but most of the larger dairy herds took part. Later, in 1950, compulsory eradication was introduced in all herds of breeding females including beef suckler cattle as well as dairy herds and by 1960, tuberculosis was almost eliminated. Since then it has made a significant return in certain parts of the country. A further measure to control tuberculosis in the human population was the pasteurisation of milk, introduced around 1948, initially for non-Attested Milk but since 1983, it has been illegal to sell unpasteurised milk in Scotland.

After 1945, penicillin was mass-produced, but up until then there was a genuine fear of toxins entering the body through open cuts and abrasions causing inflammation and swelling. Usually a home remedy was administered in the form of an extremely hot poultice, placed on the wound that would bring the infection to 'a head'.

Mrs Nita Smith remembers her experience when she contacted scarlet fever in 1935:
My earliest outstanding memory was while I was staying in Arbroath with my mother's cousin and her husband (we called them aunt and uncle) I was playing on the swings and broke my arm. I was taken to Arbroath Infirmary and during my stay; I contracted scarlet fever as there was an outbreak at that time. Since we were milk producers and sold direct to the public, I was not allowed home and was transferred to the fever hospital at Little Cairnie. I remember my mother and Mrs Martin, Dustydrum, visiting me on my fourth birthday and in order to restrict all contact, I could only see them through a glass window. As the scarlet fever receded, I developed very bad swollen glands and was removed to Dundee Royal Infirmary where I underwent an operation. Visitors were able to visit but any presents (including a treasured bracelet) were forfeited to the hospital for fear of infection. I recall that my parents paid the cost of all my medical treatment in both hospitals.[16]

Arbroath Infirmary Ambulance, 1930s (Gibb family)

When anti-polio precautions were put in place in 1955, Dr Hird and her assistant Nurse Downie arrived at the East and West schools in 1957 to inoculate pupils born since 1947 against poliomyelitis, commonly known as polio. Later, in 1961, all pupils were inoculated against polio.

A relative of Nurse Robertson, who had served the Carmyllie parish during WW2, visited the Byre Shop in 1990 and remembered Nurse Robertson relating an experience: *We once had to remove tonsils from a girl who lived in the 'Bobby's' house at Redford and the operation took place on the kitchen table. The tonsils were buried in the garden. The young girl left the area when she was eight. I also remember treating people for anthrax, which was usually fatal. However, I was able to cure one case, which was most unusual. The anthrax case was kept in isolation.*

Before the National Health Service was introduced in July 1948, communities raised funds to help hospitals, nurses and those in need of treatment. For example the West Free Church had regular collections and in 1913, '£4.7/- was sent to DRI, where seven Church members, old and young, were receiving treatment in Hospital.'[17]

---

[16] Testimony, Mrs Nita Smith (nee Gibb) 2011
[17] *Carmyllie Free Church Magazine*, by Rev. John Thomson, 1913

Chapter 14

AFTER WORK

Off to town! Forehills, Carmyllie (Gibb family)

In the nineteenth century 'after work' group entertainment in Carmyllie was sparse, chiefly because working hours were long, travelling distance was inconvenient and communications were poor. Musical evenings were common with farm workers in the bothies, especially when there was an accordionist, a fiddler, a penny whistler or any rhythm improvisers in their midst. Certainly the quarry workers living in close quarters at the Slade would have had a 'get-together' after work, although the hours of work were long and there was no entertainment allowed on the Sabbath. Occasionally, there would be the odd picnic in summer or a jaunt to the town.

At the beginning of the twentieth century, the ploughmen formed an Association, which organised an occasional dance. Later, other groups started up such as the Boy Scouts, Cubs, Girl Guides and Brownies, WRI, a Social Drama/Group and the Church Women's Guild. Gradually as the motor car became more available and communications improved, socialising in the evening was an attraction.

Carmyllie Parish Church trip to Crombie, Aug. 1924 (Muriel Thomson)

Attending a concert in the Community Hall, 1977
Included in the picture:
Mrs Fairweather, Mrs Carrie Jarret, Peggy Boath, Rosie Ritchie, Mrs Mary
Dowell, Mrs Violet Ritchie, Willie Boath, Arthur Jarret, Gordon Law,

An evening out at Carmyllie Farmers Dance in the Café Moderne
Tom Mudie, Blacksmith, Will Scott, Newton, David Hume, Mains

Community Venues

'Jubilee Hall', East School, Redford

After Carmyllie East School was built in 1875, smaller social functions took place in the Old Parochial school and to serve the needs of those residing nearer Redford, the 'Jubilee Hall' built in 1887, served this purpose also. Mr John Anderson and his wife Margaret (nee Soutar) celebrated their Golden Wedding in the 'Jubilee Hall' in 1894. [18] Larger functions such as Sales of Work and community dances took place in either the East or West School.

Commander Thomas Ouchterlony of the Guynd, offered land to build a new community hall at a site

---

[18] Arbroath Herald, 1894 (Soutar family)

that suited the community as it was approximately in the centre of Carmyllie Parish. The first plans for the `new' hall were mooted as far back as the 1930s and funds were raised, but the War intervened and it was not until 1960 that the foundations were laid.

In the 1950s, there was an increasing pressure from the headmasters of both the East and West Schools, for community groups to make alternative arrangements as they found that allowing the use of the two schools as venues was becoming increasingly disruptive to the pupils' educational needs. This provided a further impetus to build the community hall.

Hall fund raising event (Sale of Work), East School, Redford, 1948

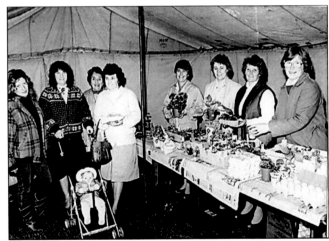

Community Hall Opening Ceremony (1960)
Back Row: TCAH Ouchterlony, Tom Gibb, Ian Sim, Jim Smith, Ron Brown,
Front Row: Mrs Sturrock, John Lawrie, Mrs Ouchterlony, George Morrison, Angus Council and Mrs Sim   (Arbroath Herald, 1960)

Fund raising continues. Carmyllie Hall Fete, mid 1970s

The architect, Peter Young of Roger and Young, Brechin, planned a Scandinavian design with timber roof slates that was the wonder of many a passer-by, as this building was unique.
The hall opened in 1960, and a crowd of over 500 watched the ceremony 'despite the cold wind and showers'.[19] After moving indoors, the opening address was given by Mrs Ouchterlony, Guynd.

The playing fields were levelled and opened in 1963 and have proved popular for many years for organised picnics and later for various hobby clubs. The hall has served the community for over fifty years with meetings and functions held most week evenings. A Hall Committee was formed to organise maintenance, hall lets and fund raising.

Organised Opening of Carmyllie Playing Fields, 1 June, 1963 (Brown, headmaster)

---

[19] Arbroath Herald, 1960

Carmyllie and District Ploughing Association

Carmyllie and District Ploughing Association. 1st Prize, C. McDonald, 1908

Ploughmen and farm labourers began to organise themselves at the end of the 19th century and there was a Ploughman's and Labourer's Benefit Society formed which met quarterly either in the East school or the Parochial school. The Vice-President was Tom Stewart, Redford, Secretary, William Binnie, Crofts and Treasurer Alexander Webster, Redford. [20] Ten years later in 1901, an International Ploughmen's Society – Carmyllie Branch formed with nine on the committee and office bearers. Running alongside the

Society, a Carmyllie and District Ploughing Association had begun with an annual meeting in November and an annual ploughing match in December. The president was Col. Ouchterlony, Vice-President, James Wright, and Secretary and Treasurer, R. McDougall, West Hills. The Ploughman's Society and the Association were still flourishing in 1911 but by 1922, only the International Ploughman's Society continued with Henry Milne as president, Vice-President James Sturrock and Treasurer Alexander Webster.

George Fullerton, Forehills, Ploughing Match Cup, c. 1930

There were enthusiastic entries for ploughing matches from both farmers and ploughmen, all keen to show their expertise against their neighbours. The Ploughing Association held social functions to raise funds for trophies and the hire of a field for the ploughing match. An Annual Dance held in 1905 at Hillhead was thought to have been a Ploughing Society event. Certainly, in the 1930s, there was a large annual gathering of men when the trophies were presented.

In 1931, the Society was continuing in the same way as in the 1920s but by 1940, committee members were reduced in number. The tractor was replacing the horse and the fields were being ploughed and cultivated, deeper and more thoroughly. Shortly after WW2, the Carmyllie Branch of the Society closed but members continued to keep an interest and most joined the Friockheim Ploughing Association.

Carmyllie & District Plouging Association, Trophies presented by Mrs McVicar (East Manse) at the Parochial School
Included in the picture: Geordie Sturrock, Alex Sturrock,Whigstreet, John Sturrock and Gordon Sturrock,Hayhillock, Tom Johnston, Kirkbuddo, Willie Alexander, Tom Gibb (Montquhir) (early 1930s)

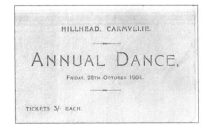

HILLHEAD, CARMYLLIE.

ANNUAL DANCE,
Friday, 28th October 1904.

TICKETS 3/- EACH.

---

[20] Arbroath Year Book, 1891

Carmyllie Scout Association

Lord Baden-Powell started the national Scout movement in 1907 after he had noticed how boys, during the Siege of Mafeking in the Boer War, had used their initiative under pressure to make themselves useful and capitalise on limited resources.

The 1st Glasgow troop of Boy Scouts in Scotland was registered on the 25th January 1908. Captain Robert Young OBE, known to generations of boys as 'Boss Young', led the troop from 1907 until his death in 1940.

There is very little recorded information about the Scout Movement in Carmyllie, yet Scout Archives show that a group was registered with the Scout Association in 1951, registration no. 29031. The 1st Carmyllie troop was attached to the 40th Angus group in the Arbroath Landward District. The group Scout Master was Jack R Whitton, the local 'bobby', and the meetings were held in the refreshment shed at the Carmyllie Mart.

Carmyllie Scout Troop camping at Lunan Bay, c.1951

The 1st Carmyllie troop waxed and waned over the years, depending on the number of boys in the parish and the availability of willing people to give their time to run the troop. At the same time, there was a strong Scout Association established at Leysmill and when there were no active Scout or Cub groups in the area, local boys and more recently girls, would travel the short journey to Leysmill to participate.

In Carmyllie, John Miller was the Scout Leader for a lengthy period in the 1980s and Yolande Gordon was Cub Leader. John Sinclair ran the Cubs in the 1990s and early 2000s before illness caused him to resign.

Cub Scouts parent's night, Carmyllie hall.
'Thanks' badges were presented to Jim Kennedy, Dave Muirhead and Mrs Jean Duke. Joe Whitton was presented with a tankard by John Cross on behalf of the Souts and Leaders from Leysmill. (*Arbroath Herald,* Nov 1981)

Carmyllie Guides and Brownies

After Robert Baden-Powell started the Scout Movement in 1907, there were requests that girls should be involved in a similar organisation. This was referred to as a 'foolish idea', an 'idiotic sport' and a 'mischievous new development'. However two years later, a group calling themselves Girl Scouts turned up at a Crystal Palace rally and Baden-Powell decided to form an organisation for girls but the name 'Scout' must be removed as this might antagonise the boys and further, parents might be alienated as the name could give a 'tomboyish' image to their daughters. In 1910, Baden-Powell asked his sister, Agnes, to look after the new organisation and a few years later his wife, Olave, was appointed Chief Guide.

Carmyllie Guides, 1930s

The first Guide Company in Scotland was the First Peebles, registered in 1910, and founded by Lady Erskine.

In 1922, Mr Smith the West School headmaster, asked the School Board to allow the newly formed Guide Company to use the school for meetings. Later Miss Ouchterlony requested one afternoon per week for the Brownie Pack. Carmyllie Guides were registered as 32nd Forfarshire in the Forfar Rural District and Mrs Elliot Carnegy was District Commissioner. Miss Margaret Imrie, a teacher at Greystone school, had experience in guide work and was appointed Captain, Miss Grey was Lieutenant and Miss Ouchterlony was Brown Owl. In 1924, there were nine girls in the Guides and ten in the Brownies.

Carmyllie Guides & Brownies, 1930s

The next record was in 1933 when Miss McKay was Captain, Miss Cochrane, Lieutenant and Mrs Lionel Hill was District Commissioner. There were thirteen Guides that year and they met in the Old Parochial school (Viewfar) at 5pm. The Brownie Pack continued in 1933, also with Miss Smart (St Ruth's) and Miss Robb (East Hills), taking 16 Brownies in the Old Parochial school on Saturdays at 3pm. A year later, Mrs McVicar (East Manse) and Mrs Scofield (Guynd Lodge) had 15 Guides and 16 Brownies who were still in the care of Miss Smart and Miss Robb. This continued until 1937 when Miss Cox (The Guynd) and Mrs Scofield (Guynd Lodge), ran both Guides and Brownies until 1938. There have been Brownie packs formed in Carmyllie on and off since after World War 1. Mrs Goetz's mother was a Brownie in c.1920. Dorothy Officer remembers that she joined the Brownies in 1932, age 7, and the meetings were held at Viewfar. Rose Goetz (nee McKay) was a Brownie, age 6, in 1936 and her leader was Janet Walker from Redford. Rose walked from Greystone to Viewfar with Dorothy McLaren. She has fond memories of nature trails, reef knots and silver 3d collections.

The Guide Company was set up again during the Second World War. Audrey Greig (nee Officer) who joined in 1944, recalls that they met in the hall at the Old Parochial School and Miss Ironside was the leader. Audrey and Nita Smith (nee Gibb) remember camping at Idvies House with the permission of Col. Johnston Brodie. In 1945, Miss Irons (Crombie Lodge) and Miss Grant (East Schoolhouse) were in charge of the Guides and Miss Sim (Carnegie) the Brownies. Guiders during 1946 were Miss Balfour (Arbroath) and Miss Sim (Carnegie)

Carmyllie Brownie Pack, 1972

and Brownie leaders were Miss Sim and Miss Balfour.

There were no Guides in 1947 but Miss Sim continued with the Brownie Pack. The Guides resumed in 1948 with Miss Sim, and the Brownies also restarted that year with Mrs Cunningham (Forfar). In 1949, Miss Sim ran both Guides and Brownies until 1950 when both groups were suspended.

In 1968, Anne Law (Glentyrie) contacted Miss Carnegie of Lour who was previously a Chief Commissioner for Guiding, enquiring if a Brownie Pack could resume in Carmyllie. Miss Carnegie contacted the local Commissione Mrs Marjory Smith who helped to form a Pack. They met every Monday in the Carmyllie Hall from 6-7pm. Anne Law was Brown Owl and Mrs Minnie Souter (Milton) was Tawny Owl until 1974 when Mrs Alison McDonald (Milton of Conon) took charge and in 1977, the Carmyllie Pack joined with Friockheim until 1990.

the Queen's Guide award to Nancy Wishart, 1976

Carmyllie Girl Guides started again in 1970, with Myra Miller, (Firth) Irene Gibb, (Montquhir) and Mrs P. Murray (Schoolhouse) as Leaders. In 1973, the Guides were under the leadership of Liz Hendry (Schoolhouse) with Doreen Brown (Drummygar) as helper. Doreen took over as leader from 1976 to 1980 and she remembers camping at Ladenford, Kinnaird Castle and the Guynd. She recalls that during the time she was assistant leader and leader, there was an exceptional number of girls who gained their Queen's Guide award, the highest award obtainable. Doreen retired in 1980 when Rita Ollerenshaw took over as leader and continued the good work until 1990 when the company joined with Friockheim.

Scottish Womens Rural Institute Carmyllie 'Rural' Story

In 1897, Adelaide Hoodless of Stoney Creek, Ontario, started the first Women's Institute to address the isolation and lack of further education of women living in rural areas. At the end of the First World War, a farmer's wife, Catherine Blair, started the first SWRI in East Lothian. She was inspired after she heard her dairymaid remark, 'The men are aye meetin' with their neebors in the stable, at the mart or in the pub and passin' the time of day, but for the likes 'o us women there's never a body to speak tae.' Thirty-seven women attended the first meeting in Longniddry and from then on, branches opened throughout Scotland.

Carmyllie WRI Founder Members
Mrs Crighton, Mrs Prescott, Mrs Melville, Miss Ritchie, Miss Ogilvie, Mrs Robertson, Mrs Jarret, Mrs Walker, Mrs Scofield, Mrs David, Miss Gibb, Mrs Dolan, Mrs J Clark   Front: Mrs Petrie, Mrs G Cox (Guynd House) Mrs McKay, Mrs M Sturrock, Miss Cochrane (teacher) Mrs Dolan (1925)

In 1929, County Federations were set up to co-ordinate groups and organise many educational events such as crafts, sporting competitions and choirs.

In 1925, a WRI branch was formed in Carmyllie and agreed to meet on the second Thursday of each month at 7.15pm in the East School. It was forecast that the Carmyllie organisation would not last as a male bachelor was reputed to say, 'It'll nae last, Carmyllie wifies canna agree.' Both statements were proved wrong.

The first Office Bearers were; President Mrs McKay, East Schoolhouse, Vice-President, Mrs Robb, East Hills, Secretary and Treasurer, Mrs Watson, Redford. The Committee were:- Mrs Inverarity, Dummiesholes, Mrs Sturrock, Burnside, Mrs Mudie, Redford, Miss Webster, Redford. The fee was 2/1d and visitors 4d.

On the early syllabus, there were such items as a butter-making class, a dancing class and embroidery lessons. Visits to other 'Rurals' with sketches and songs and demonstrations of cookery and crafts helped to form many good friendships.

50th Birthday Party
Founder members and Former presidents
Mrs Clark, Post Office, Mrs F Mitchell, Guildy, Mrs Mary Sturrock, Burnhead, Mrs Davina Fyffe, Mrs J Walker, Arbroath, Mrs M Birse, Mrs Sheila Hood, Memus, Mrs Tindal, Newbigging (1975)

Each meeting had at least one competition, which helped in acquiring skills for the Annual Federation Show.

The Birthday celebrations in the early years took the form of a whist or beetle drive and dance. In the 1930s, the dancing was accompanied by music from a wind-up gramophone. Occasionally there was a whistling competition and on the odd occasion when men were invited, they took part in knitting, potato peeling and sewing on a button. During the Second World War, due to sugar rationing, the old tradition of a 'dumpling' rather than a Birthday cake was made.

Carmyllie WRI 60th Birthday Party. 1985

Syllabus, 1969/1970

In 1941, members of the local Home Guard were invited to enjoy whist, dancing and supper and the following year, soldiers stationed locally were also invited to join in the fun. 'Black-out' regulations during the War restricted travel in the dark so the WRI decided to hold meetings only when there a good moon to light the way home.

In 1975, at the 50th Anniversary of Carmyllie WRI, Mrs Mary Sturrock, a founder member, gave a speech. She recalled that before the Branch was formed, the Social Club at the West School was not suitable for mothers or older women as in those days, there was no transport other than bicycles or by foot and Greystone was a long walk. In 1925, after difficult communications (no telephone), an introductory meeting was held at the East School, presided over by Mrs Whyte, president of the Federation, with twelve ladies in attendance. Mrs Whyte attended the first WRI meeting, demonstrating how to cure rabbit skins to make fur-backed gloves and foot muffs. There were frequent committee meetings as the lack of telephones made for poor communication.

The programmes of Whist or Beetle Drives with dancing and games continued until the Community Hall was built in 1960, with the exception of 1953 when members saw the film of the Coronation, the royal visit to Edinburgh and the Braemar Gathering. The WRI continued to celebrate their Birthday in the usual way, although the Whist Drive became a separate function. Meetings were held in the new Hall from 1961.

In 1985, at the 85th Jubilee celebration, Mrs Nettie Gibb, who had been president of Carmylie WRI, off and on, since the 1930s, presented an embroidered picture with the inscription:

'Sixty years of Rural Living
Working, playing, learning, giving
Reaching out to other Lands
Intertwining many hands'

In 2005, the 80th Birthday party was celebrated with members past and present and friends, all enjoying an excellent dinner with traditional music and song. Three long-serving members were presented with Honorary Members' Certificates and Badges and the special Birthday cake was cut, made by the President.

Carmyllie WRI continues in good spirit today with over twenty members from both town and country. Nationally, the institute plays an important part in many issues involving women and children.

Jubilee Year
Mrs Nettie Gibb presenting embroidered picture to Mrs Nan Reid, President, 1985

Carmyllie Drama Group

The Carmyllie Players

In 1924 Grace Gray, third teacher at Carmyllie West (Greystone) School, lodged with Meg Imrie in the school cottage. Also staying in the cottage was Aggie, Meg's sister, who acted as housekeeper, and her aged father.

Carmyllie Players (Two versions)
(right image)Back Row: Mrs G. Sturrock, William Lindsay, Miss Imrie, Ronald Hume, Miss C. McVicar
Front Row: H.O.Officer, Lena Soutar, Sandy Imrie, Nettie Fullerton (c.1928)

Mr John Smith was headmaster and all three teachers were musical. John Smith was also organist at Carmyllie Free Church. Miss Betty Gray, sister of Grace, was sure that these talented people were the founders of the Carmyllie Players for whom John Smith wrote the first plays.

They were kept busy entertaining local groups. In 1926, they gave a performance in aid of Church funds. In 1929, a performance, in aid of the 'Soup Kitchen' raised £9.10/- and they defrayed expenses as the smaller than usual attendance was due to 'flu in the village. In 1930, the performance, again in aid of the 'Soup Kitchen', raised £10.05.6d.

The Press and Journal reported in 1928, that a dramatic entertainment in aid of the UF Church was given in the East school at Redford. The Players enacted the Scottish play 'Sauce for the Goose' written by local author, Peter Gray. The actors were mentioned as 'performing with free confidence and portrayed the different characters in an easy natural style'. The cast was:

H.L. Officer	Tam Robertson	Miss Lena Soutar	Maggie McGlashan
Miss Imrie	Mrs Lawrence	Robert Hume	Herbert Lawrence
Miss Fullerton	Kate Armstrong	Mrs G Sturrock	Jean Burns
Miss Imrie	Captain Burns	W. Lindsay	Robert Burns
Miss McVicar	The Maid		

Several years ago, a lady from Dundee wrote to the Dundee Courier explaining that she had found an old newspaper with mention of a performance by the Carmyllie Players in The Good Templar Hall, Arbroath. The cutting read 'A crowded audience was present at the Templar Hall in Arbroath last night on the occasion of the presentation by the Carmyllie Players of the Scottish Comedy 'Sauce for the Goose'. The entertainment was in aid the Ness fund, which had been set up to provide the shelter and toilets in the Victoria Park, Arbroath. This was arranged by Mrs Greig of Seaton and a committee of ladies, and Provost A. McLaren Robertson was the Chairman. Mrs Alison Gibson from Downfield, Dundee was interested in the cutting as her late brother-in-law, William Lindsay of Chamberlainknowe, was one of the cast players.

New Carmyllie Drama Group

In 1999, a new drama group was formed in Carmyllie called 'The Carmyllie Amateur Dramatic Society' known as CADS. They stage approximately two performances a year in the Carmyllie Hall and include youth performances, pantomime and many comedies.

The first performance was 'Last Tango in Carmyllie' and the group celebrated the 10th anniversary with a special production of 'Faulty Towers'.

CADS (2009)

Carmyllie Social Club later Men's Club

In 1926 Harry Officer, Headmaster at Greystone School introduced a weekly Social Club and requested the School Board for the use of the School on Wednesday evenings. This was granted on condition that the Club provided the paraffin for the heater and paid the cleaner. The Club flourished and whists, fancy dress competitions and dances were regular events. Miss Betty Gray was a teacher at the West school from 1934 to 1937 and she recalled: *I was musical and played the piano in the school for parties, carols, hymns and concerts. The Social Club was flourishing* and *I was called upon to play the piano at the after-whist dances. I recall one lengthy occasion, the annual Fancy Dress dance when I joined up with local fiddlers, Jo Fairweather and Andrew Ferrier and 'Harry O' on the drums. It was no easy task as the dances extended to 2am and many sore fingers I had thumping out Eightsome Reels, Lancers, Quadrilles, Strip the Willow, Broon's Reel, La Rousse, and the more sedate Waltz Country Dance or St Bernard's Waltz. They even tackled Foxtrots and One-steps with the latest 'hits' from sixpenny sheet music.*

Social Club Fancy Dress, 1930s

Little is known of a Men's Club until the early 1960s when the Community Hall opened and offered more space and facilities. Just after WW2, the WRI minuted that when there were whists or beetle drives, dancing or games, men participated also. Ronald Brown the West School Headmaster, chaired the initial meetings and junior members could attend from 7.30-9.30pm providing a parent or a responsible adult accompanied them.

In order to take part in competitions with neighbouring clubs, the Carmyllie men had to be members of the Federation of Men's Clubs and that involved Club rules and notification to the Federation together with an entry fee. Club administration was organised by the Secretary, Jack Whitton, the local 'bobby'. There was a keen spirit of competitiveness and every week there were Club games such as carpet bowls, darts, dominoes or whist. Carpet bowls was particularly popular and often a team was

Carmyllie Men's Club, c. 1966

selected to play matches against other clubs. Transport of members and equipment was arranged and up to 30 members would visit other clubs, such as Arbirlot, St Vigeans or Inverkeilor.

Fundraising usually took the form of whist drives, dances or occasional concerts. At the AGM, prizes were presented for competitions won throughout the year. In 1965, Mrs C. Spink made the presentations. After the business, members accompanied by their wives and friends enjoyed an evening of whist, supper and a short dance. In 1967, at a Basket Whist, each player paid 4/- each with the hostess free. In the same year at the AGM, it was moved that the entrance fee be raised to 10/- but that was defeated.

In October 1966, J.F. Clark presented Ron Gibb of the Conon farm, who had been Treasurer of the Mens Club since the start and also Treasurer of the preceding Social Club, with a leather wallet in appreciation of his services. The Club continues successfully to the present day and includes members who, although now living out with the Parish, have a keen interest in the area.

Carmyllie Church of Scotland Women's Guild

The motto of the Church of Scotland is 'Whose we are and whom we serve' taken from Acts 27. Verse 23. Each meeting is opened with a prayer, hymn or a reading and closes with the Lord's Prayer and a Benediction.

An introductory meeting was held in the Parish Church Manse after the Rev James Thomson was inducted in 1948, when it was agreed to form a Women's Guild. Office Bearers were elected:- President Mrs Thomson, Vice-President Mrs Sim, Secretary Mrs Grant and Treasurer Mrs Ronald Hume. In March, the Cords of Membership were explained to members and application forms were signed. It was decided that one meeting on the third Monday of the month would be suitable.

Women's Guild meeting inside the Church Hall, 2008

Members were advised by Headquarters of the amount expected to be paid to Foreign Missions and the maintenance of the Ministry. A decision was made to allocate £20 to these schemes. Allocation of funds to Church schemes was agreed: Foreign Missions £10, Home Mission £3, Jewish Mission £1 and Temperance £1.

Throughout its life, the Guild raised a lot of funds for good causes such as the Church fabric fund and funds to support the Sunday School. The syllabus had a variety of speakers on subjects ranging from the work of missionaries, seaside missions, temperance and moral issues. These rather serious matters were lightened by social events, the most notable was the annual musical evening held in the Church when numerous neighbouring Guilds were invited.

In 1949, a Choir was formed and practised once a month on a Monday evening. This continued until the early 1960s when it was no longer mentioned in the Minutes.
A new Church hall was gifted in 1964 by Mrs Ruth McDonald, principally for the use of the Sunday School, but was also available for Church and Women's Guild meetings.

Women's Guild preparing for a Sale of Work at the Church Hall, 2010

Mrs Thomson resigned from the Guild in May 1966 and Mrs Ruth McDonald took over as President. The Rev Alexander Spence's wife presided from October 1968 and it was agreed to hold meetings in the Manse, due to Mrs Spence's state of health.

The Guild was able to participate in the Quincentenary events in 2000, but thereafter due to gradual ageing and the failing health of the members, the small numbers agreed to try informal meetings to attract new members. This was less than successful and after the membership was reduced to six, it was agreed to disband the Guild in 2012.

The Carmyllie Farmers' Dance

Carmyllie Farmers'
Dinner and Dance
IN THE
Cafe Moderne, Arbroath. Thursday, 7th April.
Music by Cameron's Band
Dinner 7.30 p.m. .... Ticket 15/-

This event was the highlight of the year and usually held on the first Friday in April. It started in 1949 and was held in the Cafe Moderne in Arbroath, later moving to the Seaforth Hotel. At the inaugural dance, the band was Jim Cameron's Scottish Band and his musicians played for many years providing a very strenuous programme of dances. The programme did not change even with the passing years and the company whirled round to Lancers, Quadrilles, Rory o More, Eightsome Reels, Strip the Willow and Broon's Reel and many more with the occasional Slow Waltz to calm things down a bit and let folk get their breath back. It was not for the faint-hearted.

The ladies wore their best ball gowns and the men were resplendent in kilts or dinner jackets and the Grand March which started off the evening was a real fashion show.

Sadly, the ticket prices did not stay the same and they went from 15/- in 1957 to £5 in 1979. It was a dinner dance with a substantial three-course meal to keep up the strength for the dancing. At the end of the evening hot soup in teacups was served before everyone set off on the journey home. On one occasion this was very welcome as, while enjoying the dancing, the snow was falling thickly in many parts of Carmyllie and it was no fun to walk a bit of the way home through deep snow in dance finery.

Café Modern c. 1950 (Gibb family)

Mrs Gibb, Montquhir, organised the Dance for many years and after each dance, she carefully removed the programmes from the walls and returned them to her home. They lay there under the

Carmyllie Farmers' Dance 1958 (Brown and Gibb family)

carpet in the sitting room until the next year. It kept them clean and flat and, as the programme did not change year in year out (despite some of the younger folk suggesting a modern dance now and then, please!) it saved the expense of having them printed each year.

The Carmyllie Farmers Dance has been consigned to history and memory.

Carmyllie Young Wives Group

By 1978, Carmyllie Parish had settled down to one Primary school, and as the school roll was relatively high, there were mothers gathering with similar interests. A decision was taken to set up a Young Wives group, initially affiliated to the Church, and the first meeting was held in Carmyllie Hall on the 16th November 1978 at 7.45pm

Alison McDonald in the Chair led the committee. Other office-bearers were Margaret Martin, Vice-Chairperson, Lorna Johnston, Secretary, Doreen Brown, Treasurer and Committee members, Ann Jackson, Margaret Paton, Alison McDonald, Irene Gibb, Rita Olernshaw and Ethel Alexander. A Bank account was opened in the name of 'Carmyllie Young Wives Group'.

At the meetings, there were talks on various subjects, cookery and demonstrations, occasional visits to factories and social evenings. It was agreed to have a break in July and August. A dance, ceilidh and a barbeque were regular fixtures.

After running for two years, it was questioned whether all the funds should be given to the Church of Scotland in Edinburgh or alternatively, to rename the group and give funds to local charities. The latter was chosen and in 1982, the group was re-named the 'Carmyllie Ladies Group' and open to all ages. Funds were donated to local causes, such as aid to Mrs McGregor's disabled son at West Mains of Gardyne and the Baby unit at Ninewells Hospital.
The group continues to hold a valuable place in the community.

Carmyllie Youth Club

1979-1987
Carmyllie Youth Club opened in 1979 and was organised by Carey Gibb, Dawn and David Robson. There were still sufficient teenagers in the Parish who mixed socially so it was possible to form a club of over twenty members. The Club met on a Sunday evening from 7 to 10pm at Carmyllie Community hall. They played darts, pool, badminton, football, netball and board games.

Occasionally there were trips to the swimming pool at Carnoustie High where there were sponsored swims to raise funds for summer trips. There were exchange visits from neighbouring Youth Clubs throughout the year, together with special competitions with Tayside association of Youth Clubs and beyond. In 1986 the Club organised a sponsored walk round Carmyllie and the proceeds went towards a camping holiday weekend in Banchory which eight members attended.
In 1987, the Club folded due to lack of members and the funds were donated to the upkeep of Carmyllie Hall.

Chapter 15

FAMOUS PEOPLE ASSOCIATED WITH CARMYLLIE

William Small (1734-1775)

William Small was born in Carmyllie, the son of the Carmyllie Presbyterian Church minister, the Rev James Small and his wife Lillias Scott. He was educated at Dundee Grammar School and Marischal College, Aberdeen where he received a MA in 1755. In 1758 he was appointed Professor of Natural Philosophy at the College of William and Mary in Virginia which was then one of Britain's American Colonies before American Independence.

While at William and Mary College, Small had an influence over a young Thomas Jefferson (1743-1826) and introduced him to members of Virginia's society. Jefferson, in recalling his student years, remarked that 'Small was a man profound in most of the useful branches of science, with a happy talent of communication, correct and gentlemanly manners, and a large and liberal mind... from his conversation, I got my first views of the expansion of science and of the system of things in which we are placed.' To this day the Physics department at the College of William and Mary houses the William Small Physical Laboratory, named in his honour.

Small returned to Britain in 1764 with a letter of introduction from Benjamin Franklin and became a Doctor of medicine the following year and settled in Birmingham. As a result he met a prominent industrialist who introduced him to further acquaintances such as, Erasmus Darwin (grandfather of Charles), Josiah Wedgewood, founder of Wedgewood pottery, John Baskerville, printer and typographer, James Keir, chemist and Richard Lovel Edgworth, writer and inventor. In 1767 he met engineer James Watt and probably, as they were both from Scotland, struck up a lasting friendship.

Small founded the Lunar Society – a discussion club of prominent industrialists, natural philosophers and intellectuals who met regularly in Birmingham between 1765 and 1813 and so named since they held their meetings when there was a full moon as there was no street lighting.

Unfortunately he contracted malaria while in Virginia and was cared for by Erasmus Darwin. Sadly the disease hastened his untimely death in 1775.

Reference: William Small, Historical Reviews, Journal of the Royal Society of Medicine, Vol 90, 1997

James Bowman Lindsay (1799-1862)

James Bowman Lindsay was born at Cotton of West Hills, Carmyllie to John Lindsay and Elizabeth Bowman and was the third child of a family of four. He was apprenticed as a handloom weaver and was seen walking to Arbroath with the web strapped on his back in order that he could read a book while travelling. With his keenness to learn, his parents arranged his admittance to St Andrews University where he excelled in mathematics and physics, then changed course and studied theology, the latter giving him an in-depth knowledge of many languages that led him to compile a Pentacontaglossal dictionary.

Windyedge where James B. Lindsay was an apprentice weaver (Muriel Thomson, 1980s)

While on leave from the university he set up a school in a barn at Dilty Moss, teaching local children for a nominal fee.

Changing course away from theology, Bowman-Lindsay joined the Watt Institution (the precursor of Dundee University), and lectured in magnetism and electricity. At this time, the candle-lit jute mills in Dundee were bedevilled with fires and there was an urgent demand for safe lighting. In 1835, he demonstrated the electric bulb in the Thistle Hall, Dundee, and this was a great advancement for industry. Diversifying again, he taught in a 'prison' school (a school for criminal's children), at a salary of £50 per annum. He went on to experiment with telegraphy, transmitting messages through and across bodies of water. In 1858, the Government granted him a pension of £100 for his services to science. He died in 1862 and was buried in Western Necropolis, Perth Road, Dundee, where his grave features a large granite obelisk, erected by public subscription.

Reference: James Bowman Lindsay, Local History Centre, Dundee

Patrick Bell (1799-1869)

Patrick Bell was born on his father's farm at Mid-Leoch, Auchterhouse, and worked with his brother on the farm. The scythe and the sickle had been used to cut the grain for generations and at the end of the eighteenth century, prizes were offered by agricultural bodies for a machine that would relieve the backbreaking effort of reaping crops, much to the objection of farm labourers who believed they would be deprived of work.

Later, Bell attended St Andrews University to train in divinity and during his holidays, he experimented in his father's farm shed after observing the action of shears while clipping a hedge. He was 27 when he and his brother completed a working machine, which was pushed by two horses and ran on two wheels. They first took the machine out of the shed and into a nearby wheat field at 11pm, in order to conceal his experiment from prying eyes. Bell did not register a patent for his machine, his sole reason being that it was his contribution to agriculture and humankind and he therefore never made any financial gain from it. In 1831, a patent of a similar design as Bell's was issued to William Manning in the United States and another in 1833 to Obed Hussey, and the following year a vibrating cutter was patented by the McCormick brothers who mass-produced the machine.

Meanwhile after Bell completed his Divinity course, he travelled to Canada in 1833 and visited America, studying and discussing agriculture. He returned to Scotland from Canada in 1837, and six years later, he was ordained as a minister at Carmyllie Parish Church after the Disruption of Churches. Carmyllie was his only ministerial charge.

In Britain, farmers were not yet ready to use the reaping machine. In fact, Bell wrote in the Agricultural Journal in 1854 about his own machine 'like a child prematurely born, it came into the world before

Rev Patrick Bell's tombstone,
Carmyllie Churchyard

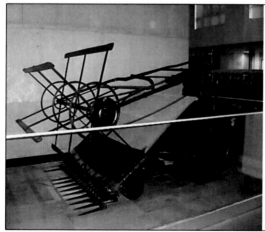

Patrick Bell's Reaper in the Science Museum, Kensington, London (Permission acknowledged)

the agricultural community were ready to welcome it'. After 1854 however, the reaping machine was in demand and was of great service to farmers for over a hundred years, although the scythe continued to have its use by harvesting an 'end rigg' round cereal fields to allow space for the reaper to manoeuvre.

In 1860, at the General meeting of the Highland and Agricultural Society, Rev Bell (now Dr Bell) was presented with a plate and £1000 in appreciation for his services as the inventor of the first successful reaping machine.

The Rev Bell died at Carmyllie in 1869 and was buried in Carmyllie Churchyard.

Reference: Melville, Lawrence, *Erroll Its Lands, Legends and People*

172

James Christie (b. c.1820 – d. unknown)

The Shepherdess

James Christie is known to be the stone carver responsible for much of the statuary and decorative carving at Hospitalfield. He is referred to in Hospitalfield records as being from Carmyllie. Details about him are vague but he is thought to be a son of a Carmyllie crofter and was born near the Slade quarries around 1820. It is thought that while working as a quarrier, his artistic talents were drawn to the attention of quarry owner, Lord Panmure. It is recorded that Lord Panmure provided funds for Christie to study at the Trustees Academy of Arts, Edinburgh with further support from Ouchterlony of the Guynd. He studied at the Academy from 1843. Patrick Allan-Fraser employed Christie at Hospitalfield in 1849 when he was starting his ambitious building programme at Hospitalfield.

Christie was also an artist as he painted Hospitalfield from the northeast but the painting is undated. He was responsible for at least three statues, The Piper, The Highlander and The Gentle Shepherdess (as above), the latter being the only one remaining in any condition. It is sited on the lawn in the garden of Hospitalfield but it is thought that there were originally several more statues judging from the remaining pedestals. Christie's most outstanding work is the carved marble fireplace in the Picture Gallery, which he completed in 1853. He probably also produced the faces on the arched gateway, windows and doors at the South Lodge. These have been defaced. Following his work at Hospitalfield, he worked in Edinburgh and died in Broughty Ferry, date unknown.

Picture Gallery, Hospitalfield

Carved marble fireplace, Picture Gallery

Reference: Conversation with Graham McNicol, local historian
Payne, William, *Hospitalfield House*, 2012

173

William Fyfe later **Fyffe (1847- 1917)**

'Ae Shoe'

John, William's grandfather, had been a shoemaker in Letham, Angus; nicknamed 'Ae Shoe' as he made only one shoe for his customer then asked payment for both, guaranteeing that he or she would return for the second shoe with no debt to retrieve on John's part. His second child and first son William, a yarn bleacher nicknamed "Coo Wullie" (he kept a cow) married Elizabeth Morton. Elizabeth died just four days after giving birth to William, junior, leaving grandfather John and his wife to raise the child. William Fyfe, Junior, in 1852 and at the age of 5, arrived at the Birns, Carmyllie, with his grandparents who had taken up an offer from Panmure Estate to reclaim 75 acres at the Birns, offering the first 10 years of his lease, rent free.

For nine years, young William walked over the moor to Monikie School where the headmaster Mr W.M. Alexander taught him. In the summer, he herded 'kye' and helped with the farm work. When he was 16 years old, he applied to an advertisement for a 'smart lad' in the counting house in Gourley's shipyard in Dundee. He was successful and received £10 per annum.

William became an asset to the Company, as he was willing to learn languages such as French and Spanish, which helped

The Birns, Carmyllie

Younger William

communication with foreign ships sailing into the docks. Before the Education Act of 1872, he realised that there were many labourers without reading and number skills, so with his assistants he held evening classes at the shipyard for over five years, teaching up to a hundred lads and men. At the same time he realised how men's lives were ruined through alcohol and became a keen member of the Temperance Society and became an active Temperance Reformer. In 1870, William was promoted to principal clerk at the shipyard and seven years later, he was transferred to the same position in the head office at the Foundry. He continued his linguistic studies, which was his mainstay in later years, teaching Spanish at the Morgan evening classes and also teaching privately.

A mature William Fyfe

In 1880, William published a volume of 'Holiday Sketches and Work-a-Day Essays'.

He died in 1917, age 70 and was buried in Easter Necropolis cemetery.

Reference: Maryfield Gazette, 10 June, 1915

Daniel Souter (1882-1937)

Daniel Gordon Souter was born at Slade Quarry Cottages to James Dick Souter and Annie Hardier and was the second eldest in a family of eleven.

Dan Soutar (PGA, Australia, 1991)

When he was 5 years old, he moved with his family to Carnoustie where he continued his schooling until he was twelve. He picked up the love of golf at an early age of 9 or 10 and began caddying every Saturday and after school hours in the summer, usually gaining one shilling after each game. He left school at 12 and in that same year he won a match between the caddies. When he was 14 he was apprenticed as a joiner and completed his apprenticeship five years later.

He joined Carnoustie Golf Club at 16 with a handicap of six. Remarkably, he won the Dalhousie Cup in the first year from over eighty entries.

In 1902, he took the decision to emigrate to Australia as working prospects were not good in Britain. In February the following year, he arrived in Australia and immediately joined the Marrickville Golf Club, playing as an amateur and winning the Commonwealth Championship at Adelaide and the Championship of New South Wales in 1904. After turning professional in 1905, he won the Australian Open by ten strokes and in that same year, receiving £20 as a reward.

For the next thirty years, he became a golf celebrity, not only in competitions but also as chairman of the PGA in 1911 and again in 1928 and 1929. His increasing knowledge of golf gave him the ability to design golf courses and along with his friend, Carnegie Clark, set up the course at Kingston Heath, his best-known creation. In addition, he went on to design courses in New South Wales and Christchurch, New Zealand.

Over and above all his achievements, he was known as an excellent tutor, spotting the talents of many young golfers. After his premature death in 1937, a newspaper reported a summary of his Genius '*His knowledge of the game and his administrative ability were recognised everywhere. He was a guiding hand of the PGA*'.

Reference: de Groot, Colin with Webster, Jim, *Pro Golf, Out of the Rough* (Australia: PGA, 1991)

175

TIME LINE

<u>**Date**</u>

800 BC	Iron Age
54BC	Roman Invasion under Julius Ceasar
AD50	Souterrain at West Grange of Conon Established
79AD	Agricola invades Scotland, Tacitus first refers to the Picts
AD80	Temporary Roman Marching Camps, nearest examples at Kirkbuddo and Kinnell
c250	W. Grange of Conon Souterrain abandoned
c400	Romans abandon Britain, Pictish period begins and Christianity arrives in Scotland Alleged 'old place of worship' at Grange of Conon Irish Saint, St Fechin, spread Christianity in the area – died c664
685AD	Anglican defeat at Nechtansmere recorded by the Venerable Bede of Jarrow (673-735)
843AD	Kenneth McAlpine crowned at Scone
c. 843 AD	New Kingdom of Alba formed Pictish language was giving way to Gaelic Conon referred as a tract of land
c900	Norse influence in North and east
1066	Norman Conquest – Battle of Hastings
1072	Malcolm Canmore becomes William the Conqueror's 'Man' at Abernethy – Norman period in Scotland begins
1124	David I, brings Norman knights to help administer Scotland Land granted to the Maules at Easter Fowlis then later Panmure
1165	William the Lion becomes King of Scotland
1178	Arbroath Abbey founded
1214	King Alexander ll gave the Abbots of Arbroath the right of free forestry over lands of Dumberachand (Dumbarrow) and Conon
1314	Battle of Bannockburn
1320	Declaration of Arbroath
1325	Strachans held lands in Carmyllie
1411	St Andrews University founded
1503	James IV marries Margaret Tudor – Henry VIII's sister

1513	Battle of Flodden Field
1560	Scottish Reformation causing Parishes to be formed in Scotland with a church and a school Carmyllie Parish shared the lands of Conon with St Vigeans
1561	Mary Queen of Scots returns to Scotland as Queen
1587	Execution of Mary Queen of Scots
1603	Union of the Crowns James VI of Scot becomes James 1 of England and moves to London
1609	'Lords Commissioners for the Plantation of Kirks' required the Carmyllie Laird, Strachan, to enlarge the Carmyllie Chapel to form a new Parish Church
1611	The history of the Maule family written by Commissary Maule a cleric at St Andrews, Printed in *Registrum de Panmure*
c. 1616	Ouchterlony family moved to Garden House, Guynd
1617	James VI visits Scotland. All parishes shared the provision of transport of the King from Kinnaird to Dundee, Carmyllie parish supplied 8 carts and 16 horses
1625	Marquis of Hamilton acquires superiorities of land belonging to Arbroath Abbey - including most of Carmyllie
1638	National Covenant signed in Scotland
1642	Superiority of the Lands of the Arbroath Abbey acquired by Panmure
1646	Sir Patrick Maule created Earl of Panmure
1649	Charles 1 executed – Cromwell Commonwealth begins
1653	No Church minister from 1654 – 1659 at Carmyllie Church
1660	Landlords now known as heritors - Four heritors in Carmyllie, Earl Panmure, Ochterlony of Guynd, Cononsyth and Carnegie Charles ll restored
1685	James Vll and ll crowned
1688	Glorious Revolution, William and Mary crowned
1689	Earliest known Carmyllie Kirk Session Records
1692	Massacre of Glencoe
1702	Queen Anne crowned
1707	Act of Union of Parliaments

1714	George I crowned – Stuart monarchy ended
1715	Jacobite Rising - The Old Pretender (James Vlll) leaves Panmure House with Earl James Maule - Earl Panmure flees to France.
1716	Panmure Estate and the superiority of the Guynd Estate forfeited
1727	George II crowned
1745	Jacobite Rising, Battle of Culloden Maules of Panmure refrained from involvement
1746	Cumberland's army billeted at Montrose after Culloden. Bonny Prince Charlie's followers lurked in the area.
1760	GeorgeIII crowned
1776	American Declaration of Independence
1804	Carmyllie Parochial School and Schoolhouse built
1810	Regency
1815	Cononsyth Mansion built
	Battle of Waterloo
1817	New Guynd Mansion House built
1820	Parish Church manse built
	Death of King George III Coronation of King George IV (1820-1830)
1830	Coronation of William IV (reigned 1830-1837)
1837	Coronation of Queen Victoria
1843	Disruption of Churches
1848	Free Church Manse built at Greystone
1850	Free Church built at Greystone
1853	War in Crimea begins
1855	Carmyllie Railway line, Elliot to Redford, opened
1860	Free Church School and Schoolhouse built
1873	Carmyllie Quarry production at its peak – Parish Population 1,300 Carmyllie Parish Church refurbished
1876	Carmyllie East School and Schoolhouse built

1884	Outbreak of Rinderpest amongst cattle stock in Angus
1897	Queen Victoria's Diamond Jubilee - Jubilee hall built at Carmyllie East School
1898	A firm, Duncan, Galloway & Co Ltd formed at Slade Quarries
	Arbroath Library opened
1908	Carmyllie Quarries closed
1910	Quarries re-opened
1912	Great Coal Strike
	Sinking of the Titanic
1913	Captain Scott and his team perished in Antarctic
	Drowning Accident, Canada, Guy Ouchterlony
	Duncan, Galloway & Co, Slade Quarries, in receivership on eve of war
1914	28 July Great War began
1915	Visit of German Zeppelin to the County
1916	Conscription, single men and childless widowers
	Battle of Jutland Battle of the Somme
	Regulation – darkening of Churches
1917	Conscription, men 18 to 51
	Col Ouchterlony's son (John) killed in France, near Ypres
1918	Outbreak of influenza
	Great War ended 11.11.11.
	Treaty of Versailles
1919	Supper for returned soldiers in East School, Carmyllie
	Twenty attended – Jas Falconer in the chair
1920	Carmyllie War Memorial unveiled by Col Ouchterlony
1921	Troubles in Ireland far from settled. Irish Free State established
1922	Sale of part of Dalhousie Estates north of the Elliot, including all Carmyllie lands
	Girl Guide Movement formed in Carmyllie
	Insulin discovered
1924	Telephone Exchange formerly opened at Redford by Mrs Morgan, Grange of Conon
1928	Alex Fleming discovered Penicillin
	First Motor Cars came to Carmyllie
1929	Wall Street Crash
	Carmyllie Passenger Railway closed

1936	Death George V
1937	Abdication Edward V111
	George V1 crowned King

1939   September, War declared on Germany

        Children evacuated from Dundee
        Petrol rationing began

1941   Churchill's speech 'We will never surrender'
        Japanese attacked Pearl Harbour and America joined the War

        Army personnel billeted in Carmyllie West and East Schools
        Tractors appear on farms

1942   Almost all foods rationed
1943   Union of Carmyllie East & West Church

        Italy joins Allies

1944   D-day offensive launched against German Forces

1945   First V1 & V2 rockets launched against London in January
        World War 11 ended in Europe in May and in Asia in August following atom
        bombing of Hiroshima and Nagasaki

1947   Coal Industry nationalised
        Severe prolonged snowstorm caused disruption to transport and closed schools.
        In Carmyllie supplies brought toMilton from Arbroath for collection

        India independent from Britain
        Marshal Plan (aid from America) until 1952

1948   National Health Service began
        Bread Rationing ended
        Berlin airlift began
        Passports to all Commonwealth Citizens

1949   NATO established

1950   First organ transplant operation

1951   Carmyllie Quarries finally closed
        Stone of Destiny found at Arbroath Abbey – stolen from Westminster Abbey by three
        students

1952   King George VI died
        Televisions more available
        Polio vaccination
        Seat belts in cars introduced

1953   Electricity brought to Parish of Carmyllie by North of Scotland Hydro-Electric Board
        Coronation of Queen Elizabeth
        2-Manual Pipe Organ installed in Carmyllie Parish Church

1955	School Milk Scheme stopped
1956	CarmyllieParish connected to County Water Supply New Police Station built adjacent to East School Austin A30 produced, priced at £507
1957	EEC established
1960	Carmyllie Hall built End of National Service Infamous Berlin Wall built 16 Trees planted at West School to commemorate the centenary Free Church School, later West School
1963	Severe weather between January and March John F. Kennedy assassinated in Dallas Playing fields at Carmyllie Hall opened
1964	Small wooden hall erected near Parish Church for Sunday School and Church meetings License granted to drill for oil inNorth Sea
1965	Carmyllie Railway finally closed. Station buildings were demolished and rails and sleepers uplifted Flying Scotsman made final run before going to private ownership, on view at the National Museum in York
1966	Nursery classes started at West School Stone of Destiny ceremonially returned to Scotland, in Edinburgh Castle
1967	First Heart Transplant by Dr Christian Barnard 11+ Qualifying Test abolished in Scottish Schools
1968	Televisions purchased for West & East Schools Martin Luther King, Civil Rights Leader assassinated. Robert Kennedy assassinated American Neil Armstrong, first man on the moon
1970	First oil pipeline from North Sea came into force Carmyllie West School closed 26 pupils transferred to East School at Redford Re-named Carmyllie Primary School
1976	Carmyllie Primary School extended and refurbished. East School Centenary Celebrations

THE ORIGIN OF CARMYLLIE FARM NAMES

It is difficult to be definite about the origin of place names, as they have evolved through landscape and language over approximately 1,500 years. Language alone in this area has changed from Pictish to Gaelic to Scots. Pictish up to around 900 AD, Gaelic to 1200 and Scots with input from the Norman French tongue from then onwards. However, it may have taken generations for language to change therefore names will be combined from Pictish, Gaelic and Scots origins. The name *Carmyllie* is an example of Pictish and Gaelic. – *cair* (Pictish) could mean 'Warrior's fort' but there is no obvious fort but *Kermill* (1240) meaning 'bare' is perhaps more apt. Later *Kermily* (1309) *Karmyle* (1511) and *Carmilie* (1561) are mentioned in the rental of Arbroath Abbey. In 1611 Commissary Maule brings in Norman/French with *Carmoulne Carmyly* and *Carmoulne*.[1]

The 'date' of the farm name means when the farm was first recorded for example, in 1611 the Commissary Maule, an historian, listed some farm names in Carmyllie as 'Mains, Auchlair, Quhythil, Westhilles, Midhilles, Backhilles, Paupertland, Newtowne, Miltone, Crospos Hil, Goit, Murheads, Newlandis and Corsden'.

The following is an attempt to find the origin of place names in Carmyllie:

<u>Origin</u>

Backboath	Both/Boch, Boath, a church marked on OS map (1865) as 'Site of St Lawrence's or Both Chapel', The farm called Backboath probably to distinguish it from Boath also with a chapel in Panbride. 1434	
Backmuir	Back of the moor	1729
Birns	Place associated with scorched stems of heather on dry heathy land 1794	
Burnhead	Head of the Black burn – reclaimed land	c. 1800
Carnegie	Carnegy (1541) Part of the barony of Panmure Site of Carnegie Castle on OS map 1856 Commissary Maule in 1611 writes that Carnegie contains the Gaelic name, *each,* which means 'horse', implying that the warden there (at Carnegie) kept the horses for Panmure, hence the reason that Carnegie got its name.	
Chamberlainknowe	'Chamberlain' - a person in charge of lands for his superior, probably appointed by Lord Panmure - 'knowe' round hillock	
Cockhill	'kok' – heap or lump	1601
Conon	Part of the Lands of Conon	1223
Cononsyth	*Connansytht* (1394*) Cononsyth* (1434) *Connansith* (1499) The *syth* part is probably a personal name Mathei filii Dusyth' of *Conan* recorded in 1219 Perhaps not part of Conon lands	
Crofts	A collection of crofts possibly within the Lands of Conon before the Reformation	

[1] Taylor, Simon, 2013, 'Place-names of Carmyllie' (unpublished), Glasgow University

Croftsmuir	A croft in a moor lying east of the Crofts, may have been in the Lands of Conon too.
Curleys	'Cur' or 'Coer' – justice, ferm touns, a track of land. 'leys' - land under grass. 'Thomas Maule gives to Duncan Lychtoun sadine of 'half landis of *Glaster* with half landis of *Cur'* 1482-1611 *(Panmure Reg.)*
Currend	*Cur* derived from 'pit, hollow' so Currend could mean 'end of hollow.'
Dilty Moss	*Dilto moss* (1611) 'ane gryt moss' Source of fuel*Diltown Moss* (1640) Gaelic translation could mean 'rainy, drizzly place' The source of the 'Glester' burn
Drummygar	*Drumnagar* ? 15th century. Long narrow ridge – one of the Marches of the Guynd
Dustydrum drum (1794)	*Hacwrangdrom*(1327) Duskiedrum *(1662) Duskie Drum* (1671) *Dusty-* '*drum'* may mean ridge 'Hacwrang' may mean field
East Skichen	*Scythyn*(1380) Skethyn (1533) E. Skichine (1794) 1509, ' annual rent of 20 s. which Thomas Maule receives from lands of Skichen in his barony of Panmure, granted by him to Friars Minor'within the town of Dundee' A suggested meaning for Skiechen - 'a shield like feature on the landscape.'
East Hills	The 'Hills' or 'Hilles' to the east of the high land 1600
East Ward	Formerly West Ward then Ward by 1794 Commissary Maule wrote that Carmyllie was the 'fourth part' of Panmure Estate and 'the ward' was a piece of land stretching as far as Wardneuk. The 'ward' or 'warden' had been in charge of 'the fourth part' for his superior(1750)
Forehills	Front of 'The Hills' 1680
Glentyrie	Certainly not lying in a glen but could mean 'glean', tyrie – Meaning gleaning a piece of land
Glester	*Glasletter (1254) Glaslectyr (1389) Glaster* (1482 see 'Curleys) Glas + leitir (Gaelic) means a slope with good pasture According to Commissary Maule it was formerly spelt *Glacelester*
Goats	*Goit* (1611) *Goat* (1794) 'gote' is a trench, ditch or watercourse There was a collection of pendicles - Big Goat, Little Goat and East Goat
Greystone	*Graystane (1509) Graystone* (1794) Largest cluster of buildings in the parish in 1509. Referred to as a tract of land and a stone (the local stone's colour is grey) perhaps was a march-stone
Greenfield, Clearbank	'Modern', (19th century) reclaimed land

Guynd	Gutheryn (1410) Guthyne (1497) Guthyn (1509) Guindy (1583)Gwynde (1611) Gunde (1611) In the earlier forms 'Guth' gaelic for 'voice' or 'music' which may refer to the sound of the water (Elliot Water) flowing through The Garden House built in 1664 is close by the Elliot	
Hayhillock	Grassy hill	1794
Hillhead	Reclamation and enclosures	1794
Lavrockhall	More 'modern' than West Lavrockhall. Again 'Lavrock' is the Scots name for a skylark and 'hall' was perhaps derived from 'hill'	
Loanmouth	A croft at the start of a track (demolished)	c. 1800
Lochlair	Achinlar(1382) Auchlair (1583) Part of the Lands of Carmyllie (1611) 'lair' – a myre - Farm on a myre – Reclaimed 1781	
Mains of Carmyllie	Home farm on Carmyllie lands (1485) Commissary Maule in 1611 mentions the Mains as the Mains – no change to the name	
Milton of Conon	Mill serving the Conon lands, later the mill was shared by the Guynd and Panmure	
Milton	*Milltowne* was an original setting for the Carmyllie Lands as Strachan, the Milltowne miller, between about 1309 and 1327, married Harry Maule of Panmure's daughter and the lands of Carmyllie were passed over to Strachan whereupon a manor was built 'up the hill' . *(Panmure Reg.)*	
Miltonhaugh	Level ground on banks of river	1740
Montquhir	*Moncur* as well as *Montquhir* and *Monquhyr* (1590-1611) Gaelic meaning could be *moine* 'moss or bog' and *curr* 'lying in a pit or hollow'	
Moss-end Mosside Mosston	Reclamation from Dilty Moss (c.1800) Mossy place – Mosstown, a cluster of dwellings 1722	
Muiredge	Edge of the Moor -reclaimed	1800
Muirheads	Head of the moor	1590
New Mains Guynd	Formed after enclosures	1800
Newton	Newtown – not a 'modern' town. Developed at the time of the 'run-rig' system, part of 'fermtoun' of Mains and Milton (1601)	
Parkneuk	Corner of the 'Park'	
Podge School Podge	Thick, wet clay soil	1848 1689
Redford	Reed ford, flowing water of upper reaches of the Black Burn suggesting reeds grew beside water at the burn crossing	

Saughmont	'Sauch' willow 'mont', moor – Moor with willow trees, 1794
Skichenmuir	Reclaimed from the moor bordering Skichen
Slade	Pauper's or Poper's lade. On the OS map as *Pauperslade*, 1622
Smallburn	Head of a tributary to the Glester burn Reclamation of land (1810)
Tillyhoit	*Tully Height* (1794) 'Tully' - Hillock or mound -'Hoit' – may be meaning high but a little obscure. One of the Marches for Conon Lands
Tuttiesneuk	*Tootiesnook*　One of the corners of Carmyllie lands where the herdsman tooted his horn to bring the 'kye' home.
Upper Greystone	Grey stone (1692) maybe a stone marker 1692
Villabank	House on banks of a burn　　　　　　　　　1794
Wardneuk	Corner of the Ward
West Lavrockhall	'Lavrock' is Scots name for skylark. 'Hall' may have changed from 'hill'
West Skiechen	See 'East Skichen'

Sources

Primary

Agricultural Returns, AF39/14/2, 1867-1910
Angus Census, Carmyllie, 1841-1901
Angus Valuation Roll, Carmyllie, 1876-1956
David Hume, Cashbook, 1871-1876, 1927-1938, 1942, 1950-1961
Forces War Records, (WW1), 9 Mar 2013
Free Church Cash Book, Carmyllie, CH3/492/1/18,
Free Church Kirk Session, Carmyllie (CH3/492) 24 June 1852
Heritors' Records,Carmyllie, HR/573, August 1842
Historic Scotland, Carmyllie Listed Buildings, Category B (1971)
James Kydd, Farm Cashbook, 1832-1865
Letter written by Ross Robertson, Lochlair to John Blair, Inverbervie, 30 May 1933
National Archives of Scotland (NAS) *Register of Sasines*,RS3/519/108, RS3/519/110, RS35/68/184, 1793, 1812
New Statistical Account (NSA) Vol X1, Carmyllie, RevWilliam Robertson, 1836 (Wm Blackwood & Son, Edinburgh, 1843)
Old Statistical Accounts (OSA) Carmyllie, Rev Patrick Bryce, 1790
Parish Kirk Session Records, Carmyllie (CH2/558) 1689, 1704, 1837, 1874
Presbytery of Arboath, Tiend Roll, Carmyllie Parish, 1927
School Board Minutes, Carmyllie, Aug 1875, 1886, 1893, 1894, 1897
School Log Book, Carmyllie East, 1873-1956
School Log Book, Carmyllie West, 1860-1970
School Register, Carmyllie East, 1905-1980
Third Statistical Account, ed. Illsley, William, Carmyllie, Rev James Thomson and Muriel Thomson (Arbroath: The Herald Press, 1977)
Stuart, John (ed), *The Registrum de Panmure,* (privately printed, 1874)

Maps and Plans

Ainslie Map, 1794
NAS, *Guynd Estate plans*, RHP 2600 and RHP 2618, 1868, 1880
Old Angus and Mearns by Timothy Pont, c. 1640
Parish Ordinance Survey, One inch (1:63,360) Sheet 49 (Arbroath) and Sheet 57, seamed, 1857-1863 (NLS, Ref 2622/13)

Personal Conversations
Alex Whitton
Anna Hair (nee Fyffe) 2012
Bert Souter
David Young, 2013
Gordon Law 2012
John Doward
Mac Hume
Muriel Thomson, 1985
Nettie Gibb, 1990s
Simon Taylor, 2013, 'Place-names of Carmyllie' (unpublished), Glasgow University
Violet Ritchie, 2013
Willie and Eileen Craig, 2012

Newspapers and Periodicals
Arbroath Herald

Arbroath Year Book, (Arbroath Herald) 1891-1955, 1922
Carmyllie UF Church Annual Reports, Rev John Thomson, 1908-1924
People's Journal, 1894

Other Sources
Brown, The Rev Thos Brown, *Annals of the Disruption* (Edinburgh: McNiven & Wallace, 1893) p.266
Gauldie, Enid, *Dundee Textile Industry,* introduction, xx
Jervise, Andrew, *Land of the Lindsays* (Edinburgh: Sutherland & Knox, 1853) p194
Law, Anne, ed, *Country School Diary,* (Neil Gray Bright Ideas Group,) 1985
Law, E Anne, 'Forfar and the Rise of the Coarse Linen Trade', *c* 1727-1830, Unpublished MPhil,
Machin, Ian, 'British Churches and Moral Change in the 1960s'; Offprint from Crown and Mitre: *Religion and Society since the Reformation* (Woodridge, The Boydell Press, 1993)
McBain, J.M., *Eminent Arbroathians*, 1179-1894, (Brodie & Salmon, Arbroath, 1897), p 348
Smout, T.C., *A Century of the Scottish People 1830-1950*, (Fontana Press. 1988) p 206
Warden, Alex, Vol.lll, p.101
Young, Mary, *Abernyte The Quiet Revolution'* (Perth & Kinross Libraries), 2008